W9-CMB-302

THE BAKITARA

PLATE I

Kabarega

THE BAKITARA
OR BANYORO

THE FIRST PART OF THE REPORT OF
THE MACKIE ETHNOLOGICAL EXPEDITION
TO CENTRAL AFRICA

BY

JOHN ROSCOE, M.A.
Hon. Canon of Norwich and Rector of Ovington, Norfolk
Formerly of the Church Missionary Society

CAMBRIDGE
AT THE UNIVERSITY PRESS
1923

S.B.N.-GB: 576.59253.6
Republished in 1968 by
Gregg Press Limited
1 Westmead
Farnborough Hants
England
Printed in Germany

12-11-78

PREFACE

MANY books on Africa have appeared during the past two or three years, and some of them are of great value to those interested in the opening up and development of that continent. In spite, however, of the light they have thrown upon difficult subjects, there still remains much that is of great importance to be investigated. From an ethnological standpoint, in fact, little has yet been learnt in comparison with what remains to be investigated; it is, however, encouraging to see so good a beginning made to the work, and those of us who have been privileged to take part in it cannot but rejoice as each new book appears.

The present book is the first volume of the Report of the Mackie Ethnological Expedition, which I undertook when the Royal Society honoured me with a request to do so. I trust that the Report will throw light upon many native customs which are as yet not fully understood, and, though it is by no means exhaustive, I venture to think that there is much in it that will be new even to those who have got into closest touch with the African peoples.

The expedition owes its inception to Sir James G. Frazer, who had for many years been anxious to have these African tribes more carefully investigated. He in turn aroused the interest of Sir Peter Mackie, who not only most generously financed the expedition, but took an unflagging and practical interest in all that was being done during the months I was absent from England.

The Royal Society very kindly undertook the oversight of the expedition and administered the fund granted for the undertaking. This alone would have been a great boon, but the Society went further, for the constant support and assistance of the Committee appointed to manage affairs relieved me of all anxiety, and ready help was always forthcoming when any emergency arose which called for action on the part of some person of influence at home.

Circumstances, arising chiefly out of the Great War, prevented me from obtaining any English companion. Such assistance would have been welcome and would have made the expedition more fruitful, but, as it was, I had to be satisfied with native helpers.

In this volume I have recorded the findings from a single tribe, the Banyoro, or, as I have called them, the Bakitara, which is their correct name. This tribe is given the first place in the Report because it is, on the whole, the most important of the tribes examined, though the other tribes, of which accounts will follow in due course, are no less interesting and by some people may be regarded as equally important. At any rate each contributes its quota of interesting ethnological information regarding the peoples of Africa.

I have made no attempt to write any grammatical notes or to make any remarks concerning the language beyond giving a short vocabulary for the use of students working at comparative philology. There are, indeed, many men now working as missionaries in the country and in constant touch with the speakers of those languages, who are far more competent to deal with this matter than I am. It will, however, be noticed that I have followed native usage where local names are concerned because, so far as I am aware, there is no standardised system, some people following the Kiswahili usage, others the Luganda, or that of any other language they happen to know.

The terms to be used to denote rulers of countries have also been a difficulty, for, though, in the cases of the local rulers who in the past were kings of their countries, the British officers have used native titles, such as *Kabaka* for the king of Buganda, *Mukama* for the king of Kitara, and *Mugabe* for the king of Ankole, yet if, in this book, local or tribal names and titles to correspond were used for other members of the ruling families, matters would become rather complicated.

To me it is always somewhat objectionable to find pages bespattered with native words, requiring constant reference to a glossary and of no value to any reader who is ignorant of the language; I have therefore avoided them as much as possible and retained our English titles of king, queen, prince, and princess, a procedure which makes the story more readily understood by English readers.

When speaking of the clans and the means by which clan is distinguished from clan, I have used the ordinary word totem rather than introduce the word *muziro* though some of the *miziro* do not fall in with the generally accepted totemic theory; for instance a cow that has drunk salt water is a *muziro* for a few hours. Again on p. 9 I say the aborigines are round-headed, this is in comparison with other Africans and would have been better expressed by saying rounder-headed.

The investigation was carried out without the use of an English interpreter, though at times it was necessary to appeal to some native who knew a language common to myself and the person under examination. Yet even in these cases all the information came to me through a native medium, uninfluenced by contact with the western mind. In almost every instance a man of the tribe with which I was dealing, who knew some other native dialect that I understood, became the interpreter, and to him I turned when I was in doubt or failed to understand the language of the tribe under examination. Thus, when the information was not actually first-hand, it was as near to it as possible, for there was no man attached to the expedition who, knowing English, could talk to me and give impressions influenced by western ideas.

I have thought it wise to write of the customs in the past tense because of the transition stage through which the country is passing and the changes now being wrought by the advance of education. It is not, however, intended to lead the reader to think that all these customs have passed away, for there are still many people who practise them as of old. Christian missions and a kindly Government have done much to enlighten and restrain, but there are still to be found natives who cling to their old superstitious practices and follow them whenever they can do so without arousing the anger of officers or missionaries.

In conclusion, I should like to express my thanks to the Committee of the Royal Society for their constant support and help; through them to the Royal Society for its patronage; and to Sir Peter Mackie for his very practical help in financing the expedition, for without his aid it could not have been undertaken. His sympathy, however, did not end with a gift of money, but during all the months I was away he constantly showed the kindest interest, helping and encouraging me in innumerable ways. To my friend, Sir James G. Frazer, I owe a debt of gratitude I cannot repay for his ever ready interest and the helpful advice which was always forthcoming. His letters of sympathy and encouragement were ever a comfort and cheered me during my journeyings. In addition to his other kindnesses, he has undertaken to read over the proofs of the Report, no light matter for a busy man to whom each extra task means an encroachment on hours of leisure already far too scanty.

I must also express my gratitude to the late Rev. W. A. Cox, Fellow of St John's College, Cambridge, who never wearied in reading over the manuscripts, and gave many valuable hints and suggestions which have been followed; to Miss Bisset, my indefatigable co-worker, who has done so much in getting the material into shape for the Press, and without whom it could not have appeared for some months to come; to the Governor of Uganda and his staff of officers; and, finally, to the missionaries whom I met, from all of whom I received continuous courtesy and help. I should like especially to mention Mr and Mrs Guy Eden, the Rev. H. M. Grace, the Rev. and Mrs H. Dillistone, and Miss Baker, who took me into their homes for weeks at a time and helped me in every possible way. I met also many other friends whom I cannot mention by name lest my list should assume unmanageable proportions. I remember, however, with gratitude the help they gave, and I treasure memories of visits to them and chats with them after long journeys in the company of natives alone.

The king of Bunyoro was most helpful and spent hours of his time in recounting what he remembered of the court as it was in his father's day. He also procured for me those men who had the most intimate knowledge of the customs of the country, and he arranged a week's pageant of the ceremonies of old, thus enabling me to secure photographs which I could not otherwise have obtained.

J. ROSCOE.

OVINGTON, NORFOLK.
January, 1923.

CONTENTS

CHAPTER V. THE KING (*cont.*)

(2) KINGS OF KITARA AND THEIR DUTIES

(3) THE KING'S COWS

(4) SICKNESS AND DEATH OF THE KING

(5) ACCESSION AND CORONATION CEREMONIES

CHAPTER VI. THE ROYAL FAMILY

(1) THE QUEEN

(2) THE KING'S MOTHER

CHAPTER VI. THE ROYAL FAMILY (*cont.*)

(3) THE KING'S WIVES

(4) THE KING'S CHILDREN

(5) PRINCES AND PRINCESSES

CHAPTER VII. PASTORAL LIFE AND THE TREATMENT OF COWS

CHAPTER VIII. AGRICULTURAL LIFE

CHAPTER IX. INDUSTRIES

CHAPTER X. CUSTOMS OF THE PEOPLE, Part I

(1) BIRTH

(2) CHILDHOOD

(3) MARRIAGE

CHAPTER XI. CUSTOMS OF THE PEOPLE, Part II

(1) ILLNESS

CHAPTER XI. CUSTOMS OF THE PEOPLE, Part II (*cont.*)

(2) DEATH

(3) INHERITANCE

CHAPTER XII. WARFARE

CHAPTER XIII. HUNTING

CHAPTER XIV. TRADITION AND FOLKLORE

LIST OF PLATES

MAP AND PLAN

CHAPTER I

INTRODUCTION

The country of Kitara—past importance—Kabarega and the British —*Kitara* and *Bunyoro*—physical features of the country—possible developments—the peoples—pastoral people—the king—agricultural people and artisans—freed-men—slaves

THE country of Kitara, which is now generally known as Bunyoro, was at one time the largest and most powerful of all the autocratic kingdoms in the lake region of Central Africa. In those days it stretched to the river Kagera in the south and into Buganda in the east, while on the west it was bounded by the Albert Lake and the Semliki River, and the Victoria Nile marked its northern border. The kingdom thus lay between long. 30° and 50° E. and lat. 1° S. and 2·50° N., and the influence of its kings extended far beyond their own land, for Busoga and the tribes of the Teso country paid allegiance to them and other countries acknowledged their power. Sir Samuel Baker in his book *Albert Nyanza* (edition 1913, p. 69) quotes Speke's impression of the importance of this country and its people: "Remember well that the Wahuma are most likely Gallas; this question is most interesting, and the more you can gather of their history, since they crossed the White Nile, the better. Formerly Unyoro, Uganda, and Uddhu were all united in one vast kingdom called Kittara, but this name is now only applied to certain portions of that kingdom." The people of Busoga called the country Buduli and the people Baduli.

It was not until some three or four generations ago that this country began to diminish in size and power. The great enemies of the Bakitara were the Baganda, who were a progressive agricultural nation, while the Bakitara were pastoral and to a large extent nomadic, valuing land only as pasturage for the cattle. The Baganda, therefore, encroached further and further into the land of Kitara, ever increasing their kingdom at the expense of their pastoral neighbours.

With the advent of the British in 1890, the power of the Bakitara decreased still further, for their king, Kabarega, the father of the present monarch, not only refused to permit the British to enter his country, but made much trouble by continual border-raids into Buganda. For several years he carried on a guerilla warfare until at length, when Mwanga, king of Buganda, had rebelled and joined him, a formidable expedition under British officers swept the country and king Kabarega was captured, after a brave resistance which only ended when his right arm was shattered and he could no longer hold his gun. Kabarega was exiled with Mwanga to the Seychelles, and his son was placed by the British on the throne of a much diminished kingdom.

In the Uganda Protectorate this kingdom of Kitara or Bunyoro now occupies only a secondary position and its dimensions have been reduced until at present it stretches from long. 30·50° to 32·50° E. and lat. 1° to 2·50° N. The population of the country is now, according to the Government Blue Book for 1919, 102,509, while that of Toro is 126,000. This, however, was at one time many times greater and it is not difficult to picture the kings of Kitara, in the day of their power, ruling over some two millions of people. The long years of warfare, with their dangers and uncertain means of livelihood, forced hundreds of the agricultural people to migrate into more settled countries. Many of the pastoral people who managed to keep some cattle sought refuge for themselves and their diminished herds among kindred tribes, who permitted them to settle on their land, while the large numbers who lost all their cattle had to seek employment as herdsmen among other nations. Many of the agricultural people are to be found in the districts granted to the Baganda at the close of the long warfare in 1890.

In the days of its power, the kingdom bore its rightful name, that is, *Kitara,* but of late years it has unfortunately been known by the name of Bunyoro, which was originally given to it by the Baganda in derision. The nickname arose from a peculiar custom obtaining in Kitara, where the king, when he wished to show favour to any member of the serfs or agricultural tribes, might make the man a free-man or *Munyoro* (pl. *Banyoro*), which meant that he was raised above his fellows and became a chief. When the Baganda got to know of the existence of this class of chiefs, they said, "You are only a nation of freed slaves; you are Banyoro, and your country is Bunyoro, the country of freed slaves." The name thus originally applied in derision has come to be commonly used and has unfortunately been allowed to be marked on the maps.

The physical features of the country are varied. If we include as I feel we ought, Toro, which has only recently become a separate kingdom and is ruled by a descendant of the kings of Kitara, the district contains some of the highest mountains in the lake region, and shows in parts the formations characteristic of volcanic country. Most of the land, however, is undulating plain, covered with somewhat coarse grass. On the whole it is a country specially suited for cattle-rearing, but the pasture-land has been neglected owing to the long years of cattle scarcity caused by the last king, Kabarega. For years this king, as already mentioned, carried on an active guerilla warfare against the British, during which the country was laid waste, the pasturage was neglected and not, as the custom was, regularly fired, and the agricultural people were prevented by the unsettled state of the kingdom from tilling their fields and were forced, by lack of grain, to leave Kitara and seek new homes in countries where they could live in peace and safety. When Kabarega was eventually driven into the Teso country to the north of the Victoria Nile, herds of cattle were carried off for the use of the king and his followers, and were never brought back, so that the country does not now possess the enormous herds of past years.

There are two large rivers, Kifumba and Kafu, of which the Kafu is the more important. It is not a swift river and is indeed in most parts swampy and held up by papyrus and pampas-grass. What current there is runs deep and the river, like most slow-flowing streams, is treacherous, because the depth cannot be judged except at the cleared ferries. In most places there are only a few feet of water, but this may extend in breadth for two or three miles. The ferries are usually at places where the stream is narrower and deeper and where a current can flow. There the stream is kept free from growths, and rafts, made of papyrus stems lashed together by strong creepers, are generally used for crossing, though there are also dug-out canoes. The ferry-men live on the banks at the ferries and people pay a small fee in kind to be taken over.

In various places there are belts of forest, some of them containing good timber which, since the British occupation, has been tested and found valuable for building and cabinet-work. In the past all that the natives wanted was a supply of small timbers for their bee-hive huts and wood for fuel. It will therefore be readily understood that much valuable timber was wasted by the agricultural people when virgin land was prepared for cultivation and timber was cut down and burned to clear sites for new fields, which as a rule covered each some three to four acres of ground.

In those parts of the country which are clearly of volcanic origin, and where there are many extinct craters, coffee is found to thrive and yield plentifully. In other places cotton is being grown with considerable success and rubber is being tried. The results from rubber have not yet proved good, but, as that and cocoa are still in the experimental stage, it is too early to give any reliable information: all that can be said is that the attempts are promising.

Past conditions cannot be said to give much evidence as to the possibilities of the country, for the agricultural community was satisfied with a few plantain-trees and their annual crops of millet for their staple food, though they grew, more as luxuries, a few kinds of vegetables, such as peas, marrows, beans, and sweet potatoes. The pastoral people were only interested in pasture-land, and all they did to ensure good grass-crops was to burn the grass off each year, which removed the coarse grass and fertilised the ground, encouraging the young tender grass to grow. This method also served to keep insects and reptiles in check, while the grass-tick, which is a carrier of disease as well as a cattle-pest, was removed.

Game abounds in most parts of the country, elephants and buffalo being very plentiful, while wild pigs, antelopes, and zebras roam about in numbers. Such plentiful supplies of food naturally attract numbers of carnivorous animals, among them lions and leopards as well as smaller beasts of prey. Lions are so common that they are even to be met with in the daytime, but smaller game is kept in check by the poor people, who hunt it for food.

The flora of the country is very rich and varied, though during the dry season there is nothing to be seen but a scorched and arid waste. When the rains come, however, they bring a sudden tropical growth, which changes a desert into a country of rich fertility, fascinating the eye with its beauty and the mind with its great possibilities.

This is still, too, largely a new land for the geologist, who has here a great work before him. Years ago the native, in some unknown way, became acquainted with the use of metals, and from this land went forth in early ages a knowledge of iron-working and smelting which revolutionised the world's methods of work. In still earlier ages stone, wood, and bone implements were used, and we find indications of stone-working in different places where there had been quarries, and knives, spears, axes, and spades had been made. When and how the people began to use iron we cannot discover and they themselves can give no satisfactory account of the growth of the industry, but they have gained a knowledge of the value of different ores, the hard and the soft, and they produce from the amalgamation of the two a metal of good quality. Few of the iron mines extend more than a few feet down or horizontally into the side of a hill, but the men know where and how to get the right kind of stone. They build furnaces for smelting and make and use bellows; they know what wood to use to get the best charcoal for their purpose, the amount of heat required, and the time needed for the smelting operation. We have advanced so far from the methods of these primitive workers that we are inclined to overlook the country and the people who revealed to the world the secret of iron-working; but here we find the smith, with his stone hammer and anvil and his charcoal fire, using the methods adopted by his ancestors who were the fore-runners of our iron industry. There is no doubt that this land is rich in iron, coal, talc, and possibly the precious metals, and the field offered to the investigator is a promising one.

The potters of the country use graphite for polishing the more valuable pots, and the stone has been mined for many generations. Petroleum springs are also known and their waters have long been used for magical rites, while in certain places salt is obtained from volcanic springs and used both for cooking and medicinal purposes.

The following pages deal more especially with one branch of the wonders of this land, the wonder of man himself. Other subjects are dealt with, but only in so far as they bear upon the great absorbing topic of man, the wonderful being who in his primitive state holds the key to many of the riddles of our day; and until we can apply that key by our knowledge of him, there are many doors which will remain locked to the scientific investigator.

The dominant people of the land of Kitara are not negroes but Negro-Hamites, who at some early date invaded the country, conquering and bringing under their own rule the clans of negro aborigines. They appear to have swept into the country from the north-east but the place from whence they came has not yet been decided. Their traditions point to their being an offshoot from the Galla stock, and there appears to be more reason for giving credence to this supposition than for accepting any other thus far put forward.

This Negro-Hamitic people, commonly known as *Bahuma*, were pastoral nomads, possessing immense herds of cattle and living practically entirely upon milk. They might eat beef, but for at least twelve hours thereafter, that is, until the beef was supposed to have passed from the stomach, they might drink no milk, for it must not come in contact with the beef. Vegetable food was taboo, but if, through force of circumstances, a man had to eat vegetables, he would refrain from milk for a lengthy period. After eating certain vegetables, which, however, only dire necessity would make him touch, he would, in addition to fasting, take a purgative before drinking milk. A woman was also forbidden to drink milk during her menstrual periods, though if it were possible to get milk from an old cow that was not likely to bear again, she might drink that. All these taboos connected with the drinking of milk had their origin in the idea that by sympathetic magic the cows would suffer from such contamination of their milk.

In the same way, for the sake of the cows, the pastoral people at first forbade intermarriage with the agricultural tribes on the land. The custom of allowing favoured peasants to marry into the ranks of the pastoral people arose after a certain amount of laxity had already crept into the observance of the milk-customs, and when intermarriage had become more common the old strict laws and taboos were rapidly forgotten. The effect of these mixed marriages was also apparent in the physical appearance of the race, though, owing to the fact that some pastoral clans have kept themselves apart, there are still to be found people who show little trace of negro blood, and whose purity of descent is traceable in the early Egyptian or Roman type of their features.

The clans were totemic, and most of their totems were connected with cows, some being cows with some peculiarity of colour or shape, while others were parts of cows or cows during some period or under special conditions; for example a cow might be the totem of a clan for a certain number of days after it had been with a bull, or after it had drunk salt water, or after it had borne a calf, and the members of such a clan might not drink that cow's milk until the special period was over nor eat its flesh if it died during that time, but afterwards it reverted to its ordinary condition and was no longer a totem. Most, indeed I believe all, clans had a secondary totem, but in many cases I have not been able to discover it. Clan exogamy was practised and members of clans having the same primary or secondary totem were forbidden to marry each other.

The king of Kitara, or *Mukama*, as his native title is, was an autocrat, holding absolute sway. He was on a level with the gods, in fact was almost a god himself, and, though he might appeal to the gods for advice and confirmation of his judgments, his word was final; he had power of life and death and no man might question his decisions.

The position of the king's residence and therefore of the capital was determined by a medicine-man by divination. A new enclosure was always built for a king on his accession, and during his reign he might move to another whenever he so desired, always consulting a medicine-man to find by augury whether the place was suitable. The deserted enclosure, and especially the throne-room, had to be burnt down as soon as the king had left it, for it would be desecration for others to enter or live there. Round the king's enclosure were built the enclosures of the members of the Sacred Guild and other important chiefs, who thus protected the king from danger of sudden and unexpected attack by any enemy. The chiefs of the Sacred Guild were a small body of special councillors, chosen, until quite recently, entirely from the Bahuma or pastoral people, who had to bind themselves to the king by a special and very stringent oath which was taken by drinking some milk from cows which were sacred to the king himself.

The king and the chiefs all possessed large herds of cows and the herdsmen in charge of these wandered about the country where they would, for cows might be pastured anywhere. The king's cattle were divided into herds according to their colour and were carefully kept apart from other herds, but the chiefs merely divided theirs into herds of about one hundred and put each herd under the charge of a herdsman, who with his assistants took them about the country as the conditions of pasturage demanded.

The aborigines of Kitara, whom these Negro-Hamitic people conquered and made their serfs or *Bahera*, were not quite of the prognathous type found along the west coast of Africa, for, though they were round-headed and thick-lipped, with broad, flat, bridgeless noses, they were more intelligent. They were, however, of a much lower type than the invaders and were not united as a nation, but formed a large number of independent tribes composed of loosely connected clans, chiefly agricultural, living by a rude cultivation of the earth which sufficed to grow food enough to keep them alive. The clans were totemic and the marriage system was exogamous, but marriage ties did little to form any kind of bond between clans or tribes. The pastoral people, sweeping through the country, united all these scattered tribes and formed one kingdom under a pastoral king, though, as these agricultural people were not nomadic and rarely moved out of their own districts, it is still possible to distinguish the tribes, which differ both in type and language.

The pastoral people looked on these agricultural people as their slaves or serfs, and a chief had many of these serfs who settled on his land and worked for him, building themselves houses more durable than those of the nomadic herdsmen, though not so large or so good as those of the chiefs. They were despised by the pastoral people, not because of their poverty, but because of their mode of life, for, in the eyes of a cow-man, anyone who ate vegetable food and cultivated the land, or worked at anything not connected with the cows, was low and mean. The serfs, however, were not slaves, for they were not bound to particular chiefs; they were free to move to other parts of the country and serve other chiefs without giving their former masters any indication of their intentions; nor indeed was a man bound to apply for permission to the chief in whose territory he meant to settle, though as a rule, he would present himself to his new chief and tell him of his desire to serve him. He was sure of a welcome from the chief, to whom each serf meant another labourer and an addition to his wealth, for besides doing building for him and perhaps herding his goats and sheep, each serf paid him a yearly tribute of grain and beer; this was not a compulsory tax but was regarded as a voluntary return to the chief for the land occupied. If a chief put a serf in charge of his goats and sheep, he paid him a proportion of the young for his work. A serf was not limited to a definite amount of land, he might cultivate as much as he wished, and there was no restraint upon him as regards the possession of wealth, for he might accumulate large herds of goats and sheep. For many generations, however, these serfs were not expected to keep cows, and were liable to be plundered if they did so; it was only in later years that this restriction was removed and they began to acquire cows, which they used chiefly for the payment of marriage fees.

These aborigines were not all agricultural, for it is in their clans that we find all the artisans of the country. It is a peculiar fact that the pastoral people, more intellectual and unquestionably more able than these serfs, have confined themselves so entirely to the care of their cows that, save in that one direction, no advance in culture can be attributed to them. The serfs, on the other hand, show in their methods considerable ingenuity and skill and, though they have failed to make improvements which seem to a more cultured eye self-evident, yet in other and often unexpected directions advance has been made. Iron-work, for example, is still very primitive, the anvil and big hammer are but blocks of stone, but the smelters pick out good ore and reject bad, and their methods of mixing the different kinds of ore to make good metal show evidence of careful testing and investigation. In wood-work, pottery, basketry, and the preparation of salt, also, there is, combined with the most primitive of methods, evidence of surprising improvement and advance.

Some generations ago a king introduced a new status among these agricultural people: any man who showed ability and rendered special service to the king was rewarded by being made a free-man, *Munyoro* (pl. *Banyoro*). This freedom entitled the men to marry any woman of the pastoral clans who was willing to form such an alliance; a wife was not difficult to find, for there were many daughters of herdsmen whose lot in life among their own people would always be hard, while if they married Banyoro it meant that they would become persons of wealth and ease, though they had to face the fact that they were marrying into the despised class. The man, however, left his former surroundings and was looked up to by his own people, even his parents kneeling before him to address him. Such marriages as these have in course of time brought about a lowering of the pastoral type, an ever-growing laxity in the observance of the milk-customs, and the introduction among the pastoral people of a vegetable diet. The children of these mixed marriages might marry even into the upper classes of the pastoral people, though there were some clans which kept their blood free from such admixture.

The serfs were looked upon as slaves by the pastoral people, but they were quite free to leave their masters and attach themselves to others when they liked. The possession of real slaves was, however, universal throughout the country, for even the poorest man might capture one or more during some raid or battle and afterwards be permitted by the leader to keep one. The wealthy people bought slaves when they needed them and a man's heir inherited his slaves along with the other property. Domestic slaves were regarded as superior to those who were used as labourers, and the domestic slaves whom a man inherited were regarded almost as members of his family and were not sold. A man might even marry a slave woman, and if she bore him a child she became free and was accepted by his clan, though her children might only inherit his property if he had no child by any other wife. The ordinary slaves, especially those who had been captured in battle, were bought and sold like cattle, and a man might kill a slave just as he might kill one of his cows and no one would question his action.

CHAPTER II

TOTEMISM AND RELATIONSHIPS

Two races in Kitara—three groups formed by intermarriage—marriage regulations—modifications in type and customs due to intermarriage—clans and their totems—the royal clan—secondary totems—list of clans and totems—relationships

THE people of Kitara belong to two distinct races, but by intermarriage an intermediate group was formed and the lines of demarcation between the three groups have become more and more vague and are rapidly disappearing. This was the result of a policy, adopted, it is said, by a king who ruled not many generations ago, by which certain restrictions on intermarriage were removed, and some of the more progressive men of the agricultural class or serfs were raised to the rank of free-men and permitted to marry women of the pastoral clans.

The two classes of which the nation was originally composed were (*a*) the *Bahuma*, or pastoral cow-men, who invaded the country and conquered (*c*) the *Bahera*, agricultural people and artisans, who were regarded as serfs. The third group, which came into being later, was composed of (*b*) the *Banyoro*, or free-men, the wealthy and important members of class (*c*) who had been raised from serfdom and might marry women from (*a*), the pastoral people, (*c*), the serfs, or (*b*) their own class, so long as they did not marry women of their own totemic clans. The poorer members of the pastoral class, the herdsmen, allowed their daughters to marry these free-men, though they avoided intermarriage with members of class (*c*), the serfs. Thus members of pastoral clans (*a*) might marry women of their own class, observing the rules of clan exogamy, or women from class (*b*), the free-men. Men of class (*c*), the serfs, had to marry women from their own class, but again of different clans, unless they had been raised to class (*b*), the free-men, by the king, when they might marry from classes (*a*), (*b*), or (*c*), as they wished.

The pastoral people forming class (*a*) were not negroes but of Negro-Hamitic stock, while class (*c*) was negro, and the result of the introduction of negro blood into (*a*) is evident, not only in its physical effect, but in the modifications introduced into their customs, which previously arose from and were solely concerned with the cows, while their food consisted of milk. The physical results have been to introduce a shorter and coarser type, possibly not less robust, but certainly less refined and, I imagine, less intelligent.

The Bakitara are a totemic nation, divided into clans numbering over one hundred. They can give no account of the origin of their totems though one or two men say that their fathers warned them to avoid some particular kind of food which became taboo and their totem. The greatest use of the totemic system seems to be for defining consanguinity in connexion with marriage regulations. This is by no means the only benefit of such a scheme of differentiation, for the system serves innumerable social and economic uses in daily life.

With the existence of the three classes, we get three distinct groups of totems, one belonging to class (*a*), the pastoral people, one to class (*b*), showing the mixture or union of classes (*a*) and (*c*), and one to class (*c*), the agricultural people. Some of the clans, doubtless those of the pure pastoral people (*a*), have totems which relate to cattle alone; the totems of others are connected with both cows and vegetables and are evidently those of men who have sprung from mixed marriages; while the agricultural class naturally have totems connected with the field. Some of the pastoral clans have totems which pertain to cows at certain times, after which time, when the conditions change, the animal is no longer a totem. For example, when a cow has drunk salt water, she is a totem to a certain clan during that day, and her milk may not be drunk by any member of that clan, but the next day the cow is no longer a totem and her milk may be drunk; again, for five days after a cow has mated, she is a totem to certain clans who may not drink milk from her nor eat the meat should she be killed, but after the five days that cow ceases to be a totem. Other clans have a part of a cow as their totem; some must avoid the tongue, others may not touch the heart, while others again refrain from eating the intestines. In each of these instances only this part of the animal is taboo; they eat freely from any other part and they may drink the milk.

The royal family have as their principal totem the bush-buck (*ngabi*), which is somewhat difficult to understand, for we should have expected a cow. It is possible that the present dynasty, which is said to have come over the Nile from Bukedi, was originally not of pure pastoral stock, or, at any rate, had not been so strict in adhering to pastoral customs. It is also rather peculiar that there are many other clans, not royal, which have the bush-buck as their totem. Possibly these were in existence in the country before the arrival of the present royal family. There are also many branches of the royal clan, but it is difficult to discover any reason for their splitting off.

Though most if not all clans have a second totem, few of them pay much attention to it; it is seldom named, and, so far as I can discover, is only mentioned when it is necessary to distinguish between persons who belong to different clans having the same primary totem. Owing to the slight importance of the secondary totem, which, in many cases, is not generally known, it has been impossible to secure as much information concerning the clans as is desirable.

Totems of Group (a), the pastoral people

Name of Clan	Totems
1. Babito (royal clan)	Ngabi, bush-buck. Maleghyo, rain water from the roof of a house.
2. Bachaki	Ngabi, bush-buck. Maleghyo, rain water from a house (subsection of Babito).
3. Abangamwoyo	Same totems, also a subsection of Babito.
4. Abachwa	Same totems, a division of Abangamwoyo.
5. Abagweri	Same totems.

Name of Clan	Totems
6. Abagumba	Same totems.
7. Ababambora	,, ,,
8. Abandikasa	,, ,,
9. Abahangwe	,, ,,
10. Abategwa	,, ,,
11. Abachwera	,, ,,
12. Abanyakwa	Ngabi, bush-buck.
	Ngobe, cow with short straight horns.
13. Abalebyeki	Ngabi, bush-buck.
14. Abanyuagi	,,
15. Ababoro	,,
16. Abakwonga	,,
17. Abadwalo	,,
18. Abajagara	,,
19. Abagomba	,,
	Koroko, hippopotamus.
20. Abamori	Ngabi, bush-buck.
21. Abagorongwa	,,
22. Abaziraija	,,
23. Abapasisa	,,
24. Abagaya	,,
25. Abatabi	,,
26. Abahemba	,,
27. Abatwairwe	,,
28. Abapina	,,
29. Abasita	Ente emira, cow which has drunk salt water.
	Maleghyo, rain water from the roof of a house.
30. Abasita	Busito, cow after mating.
	Muka, dew on grass.
31. Ababyasi	Busito, cow after mating.
32. Abacwezi	Ente emira, cow which has drunk salt water.
	Busito, cow after mating.
33. Abahemba	,,
34. Abaisanza	Etimba, cow marked red and black.
	Butweke, woman who enters a kraal, solicits the owner's son, and bears a child to him. She must never enter a kraal of the clan again nor may any member of the clan hold converse with her.
35. Abakurungo	Etimba, cow marked red and black.
	Butweke, woman who enters a kraal, solicits the owner's son and bears a child to him.

Name of Clan	Totems
36. Abagabu	Nkira, tail-less cow.
	Ezobe, cow of a particular colour.
37. Abasaigi	Nkira, tail-less cow.
38. Abasengya	Ngobe, cow with straight horns.
	Lulimi, tongue of animals.
39. Abasingo	Mulara, black cow with white stripes down face and back.
	Busito, cow after mating.
40. Abangoro	Mulara, black cow with white stripes. These split from the Abasingo because their companions had killed a man and they feared the consequences.
41. Abami	Mpulu, spotted cow.
42. Abayanja	Kitara, white cow.
43. Abazima	Mbogo, black cow.
44. Abasonda	Cow marked like a zebra.
45. Abatembe	Ngabi, bush-buck.
46. Ababyasi	Ekuluzi, cow with calf for the second time.
47. Abakwakwa	Ngobe, cow with short straight horns.
48. Abatwa	Milch cow.
	Nsugu, grass which has been put into the mouth.

Totems of Group (b), the free-men

Name of Clan	Totems
1. Abanyonza	Etimba, red and black cow.
	Ngobe, cow with short straight horns.
2. Abalanzi	Etimba and Ngobe.
3. Abalisa	Etimba, red and black cow.
	Maleghyo, rain water from the roofs of houses.
4. Abasumbi	Etimba, red and black cow.
	Ngobe, cow with short straight horns.
5. Abagahe	Etimba, red and black cow.
6. Abafunjo	Munyere, cow of some particular colour.
	Ngobe, cow with short straight horns.
7. Ababworo	Cow marked red and white.
	Maleghyo, rain water from houses.
8. Abalebeki	Cow marked red and white.
	Maleghyo, rain water from houses.
9. Abagimu	Cow marked red and white.
	Maleghyo, rain water from houses.

Mukama or king of Bunyoro

PLATE III

King in his ancient robes with chiefs of the Sacred Guild

Name of Clan	Totems
10. Abairuntu	Mulara, black cow with white stripes.
	Mjojo, elephant.
11. Abanyama	Mutima, heart of animals.
12. Abaitira	Eseleke, cow of a particular colour (? grey).
	Isereke, woman who is a stranger and is nursing a female child.
13. Abarega	Maleghyo, rain water from houses.
14. Abarigira	,,
15. Abangali or Abagabo	Nkira, tail-less cow.
16. Abakwonga	Ngabi bush-buck.
17. Abayangwe	Nkondo, grey monkey.
	Nkobe, large monkey.
18. Abagweju	A house burned down. The place is avoided and no vessel from such a house used.
19. Abatongo	Amara, the stomach of animals.
20. Abasengya	Ngabi, bush-buck.
	Maleghyo, rain water from houses.
21. Abakimbiri	Isereke, woman nursing a female child.
22. Abysima	Ngabi, bush-buck.
23. Abaraha	Akanyamasole, wagtail.
24. Abalageya	Nlegeya, bird.

Totems of Group (c), the serfs

Name of Clan	Totems
1. Abafumambogo	Abazaza nedongo, twins.
	Nsenene, grasshopper.
	Mbogo, black cow.
2. Abayaga	Kanyamukonge, bird.
	A fly.
	Millet.
3. Abahinda	Nkonde, monkey.
4. Abasambo	Obutweke, girl who has gone wrong.
	Kaibo-hasa, empty basket.
5. Aberi	Enyangi, bird.
6. Abasuli	Mbuzi, goat.
7. Abalaha	Akatengetenge?
8. Abasonga	Nsenene, grasshopper.
9. Abahango	,,
10. Abakami	Akamyu, hare.
11. Abasogo	Akaibo batera omutwe, basket put on the head.
12. Abagombi	Biweju, sugar-cane.

Name of Clan	Totems
13. Abachubo	Echu, kind of fish.
14. Ababopi	Ekigangoro, centipede.
15. Abazazi	Echu, kind of fish.
	Mamba, lung fish.
16. Abango	Akabaimbira, skin of leopards. These came from the Abasingo, and separated because of a quarrel over a skin.
17. Abaregeya	Njobi, monkey.
	Musokisoki, bird. These separated from the Abasengya.
18. Abaisanza	Epo, kind of antelope.
19. Ababiiro	Ndaha, guinea fowl.
20. Abanana	,,
21. Abaduka	The old skin of a drum.
22. Abahenga	Kagondo, small black water bird.
23. Abaho	Kalozi, fungus growing on trees.
24. Abanyampaka	Kagondo, small black water bird.
25. Abanyonza	Nyonza, bird.
	Kaibo-hasa, empty basket.
26. Abagimu	Mpulu, spotted cow.
	Maleghyo, rain water from houses.
27. Abahembo	Kaibo-hasa, empty basket.
28. Abasengya	Lugara, a wooden spoon.
29. Abagere	Njaza, an antelope.
30. Ababoro	Mutima, heart of animals.
	Kaibo-hasa, empty basket.
31. Abasanza	Maleghyo, rain water from houses.
32. Abakimbiri	Bumba, potters' clay.
	Grain left in the field all night at harvest.
33. Abasihiri	Yam.
34. Abagimu	
35. Abahamba.	
36. Abagangoro.	
37. Abagonza.	
38. Abadungu.	
39. Abaginga.	
40. Abakondwa.	
41. Abaseke.	
42. Ababaki.	
43. Abasindika.	

Relationships

Father, *ise* (generic), *tata* or *yaiya* (term of address).
Mother, *nyina* (generic), *Mawe* or *mama* (term of address).
Brother, *mugenzi* (son of the same mother), *mwene* (clan brother).

Sister, *munyanya*.
Husband, *iba*.
Wife, *mukazi*.
Son, *mwana mwojo* (to distinguish from daughter), *mutabani* (son of so-and-so).
Daughter, *mwana mwisiki* (distinguished from son), *muhala* (daughter, unmarried girl).
Father's father, *ise nkulu*.
Father's mother, *nyina nkulu*.
Mother's father, *ise nkulu*.
Mother's mother, *nyina nkulu*.
Father's brother, *ise nto* (spoken by a son).
Father's sister, *ise nkate*.
Mother's brother, *nyina lumi*.
Mother's sister, *nyina nto*.
Father's brother's wife, *muka ise nto*.
Father's sister's husband, *muko* (the father calls him *mulamu*). When a man dies and his son inherits, he rules his father's sister's husband, and can appropriate his property.
Mother's brother's wife, *muka nyina lumi*.
Mother's sister's husband, *iba nyina nto*. Some speak of him as father, *ise*; others disclaim him as a relative. A man may marry his mother's sister's daughters, though his wife may protest.
Father's brother's son, *mugenzi* or *mweni mwetu*.
Father's brother's daughter, *munyanya*. If the father be dead and his son be grown up, he can give this girl (his cousin) in marriage without consulting her father.
Father's sister's son, *mwiwha*. A son calls his father's sister's son or daughter, *mwana* (child).
Father's sister's daughter, *mwiwha* or *mwana* (child).
Mother's brother's son, *malumi*.
Mother's brother's daughter, *nyina nto*.
Mother's sister's son, *mwana wa nyina* or *mwana wa mawe*.
Mother's sister's daughter, *mwana wa nyina* or *mwana wa mawe*.
Son's son, *mujukulu*.
Son's daughter, *mujukulu*.
Daughter's son, *mujukulu*.
Daughter's daughter, *mujukulu*.
Brother's son, *mwana*.
Brother's daughter, *mwana*, or *muhala wange*, if unmarried.
Sister's son, *mwiwha*.
Sister's daughter, *mwiwha*.
Wife's father, *ise zala*.
Wife's mother, *nya zala*.
Wife's brother, *mulamu*.
Wife's sister, *mulamu*.
Wife's sister's husband, *muitwe*.

Husband's father, *sazala*.
Husband's mother, *nina ya zala, nya zala*.
Husband's brother, *mulamu*.
Husband's brother's wife, *mulamu*. If a man goes to his brother's wife there is no wrong; though the husband may call it impertinence or a liberty, he must not attempt to punish either party.
Elder brother, 1. *Mukulu*. 2. *Amkulata*. 3. *Omugate*. 4. *Machura*.
Younger brother, *muto*.

No distinction in terms is made between a father's elder or younger brother, both are little fathers, *ise nto*. The children of a brother live in the house as children, whereas the children of the sister only come to see her brother, whom they call *Mulamu*, and give him presents. The father's children call these children of their father's sister their children. Great-grand-children may marry each other.

CHAPTER III

RELIGION AND BELIEF

Ruhanga, the creator—the Bachwezi and their priests—consulting a priest—mediums—lightning—women-priests—two classes of medicine-men—rain-makers and their methods of work—punishment of rain-makers—amateur rain-making—the taking of auguries—ghosts and their powers—magic—sacred snakes and rivers—sacred hills—blood-brotherhood—fetishes and amulets—taboos and omens—superstitions

THOUGH the Bakitara had a great number of objects of worship, there was but one god, *Ruhanga*, the creator and the father of mankind. With him were associated the names *Enkya* and *Enkyaya Enkya*, whose identity it is not easy to separate from that of Ruhanga. One man asserted that they were a trinity and yet one god; but as he had been for some years a devout Christian, in constant attendance at the Roman Catholic Mission Station, his statement may have been coloured by Christian ideas. The general impression gathered, however, was that their belief was entirely monotheistic, and that, if the three were not one deity, then Enkya and Enkyaya Enkya were subordinate gods whose appearance in their theology was later than that of Ruhanga. There were no priesthoods or temples connected with any of these, but Ruhanga, and, more frequently, Enkya were called upon by the people in distress or need; prayers were made to them in the open, with hands and eyes raised skywards.

This evidently monotheistic belief was complicated by a misty and somewhat bewildering collection of beings, called the *Bachwezi* (sing. *Muchwezi*), who, though regarded as immortal and almost divine, were completely subordinate to Ruhanga, whose immediate descendants they were. After living as men in the country for many years, these Bachwezi suddenly departed, leaving behind them their priests, who could communicate with them and obtain blessing and favours from them. It was to these Bachwezi that the people generally turned for help and not to Ruhanga, who was regarded as having retired from active participation in the affairs of the world which he created.

There seem to have been nineteen of these Bachwezi, and their names were:

(1) Wamala
(2) Ndaula
(3) Kagoro
(4) Kyomya Luganda
(5) Mulindwa
(6) Mugenyi
(7) Ebona
(8) Luwangala
(9) Isumbwa
(10) Kyomya Mbuza
(11) Kauka wa Musinga
(12) Kalisa wa Hangi
(13) Mukulekubya
(14) Mugarana
(15) Kagaba wa Ruhanga
(16) Kazoba wa Ndaula
(17) Nkiro (or Nakiriro)
(18) Nabibungoda wa Ndaula
(19) Wangala

Each of the Bachwezi had one or more representatives who were the *Bandwa* (sing. *Mandwa*) or priests of the nation, and either claimed to be themselves mediums for the Bachwezi or were accompanied by mediums whose utterances they communicated to the people. A clan had always one particular Muchwezi to whom its members applied in difficulties through his priest. Though a shrine might be built to a Muchwezi in any part of the country where offerings were made to him, each had a principal shrine where his priest dwelt. The office of priest was always hereditary and its duties were quite distinct from those of the ordinary medicine-man, being confined to making offerings and prayers and receiving communications from the spirits, while the medicine-men took auguries and prescribed medicines.

The following information, taken from the *Northern Bantu*, was received from men in a different part of the country, and there is much of it that I was not able to find again. It was not contradicted and there is no reason to doubt its accuracy. As it was received fully ten years before the later information, such matters were no doubt fresher in the memories of the people, which would account for the greater detail. Some beings, whom I have there called "gods," are mentioned who are not included in my list above, and it is probable that these were peculiar to certain localities, and were not generally known.

Wamala, the god of plenty, gave increase of men and cattle and of crops. He had a temple near the king's residence, with priests and a medium. When the medium was about to give an oracle, he wore two bark-cloths, one tied over each shoulder; he also tied two white calf-skins round his waist, the skins having a row of small iron bells along the lower edge. On his ankles he wore small bells, and upon his head a special hat. It was customary for the king, and also for the chiefs, to consult this god, and cows with bull-calves were offered when they wished to consult him about their herds and to ask his blessing. Never less than two cows with their calves were sent to the temple at a time. These were taken in the evening about sunset and were milked by the door of the temple, and a pot of milk was taken into the temple from each cow. The priest placed the milk in a special place before the throne of the god and also scattered a little millet on the floor. After this the medium became possessed by the god and gave the oracle, telling what should be done if there was sickness among the people, or what remedies they should apply should there be some plague in a herd. Should sickness break out among the people or a plague among the cattle, it was said that the god Wamala needed an offering. The priest was then consulted and told the king what colour the bull should be which was to be offered. The bull was taken to the temple and killed by the door; the right shoulder of the animal was presented to the priest, and the heart and male organs were hung over the door. The priest now entered the temple with the meat, and cutting off some small pieces, threw them about before the god's throne, saying "Peace, Peace." The remainder of the shoulder the priests and medium ate by the door of the temple and the rest of the meat was eaten by the people who gathered for the ceremony. They lighted a fire and cooked the meat near the temple, and sang and danced during the night. From time to time the medium mixed with the crowd, bellowing like a bull and uttering the words "Peace, Peace" in deep tones. In the early morning the crowd dispersed to their homes. Sometimes a white ram was offered in addition to the bull. This animal, however, was kept alive at the temple roaming about at pleasure during the day and being taken into the temple for the night.

Ruhanga was said to be the creator of all things. He was held in esteem by all the people, but he had neither temple nor priest. People did not call upon him for assistance, because he had done his work and there was no need to ask further favours of him. Other gods could assist in multiplying men, cattle, and crops; they could also heal sickness and stay plagues. Hence the creator was not troubled about these matters, nor indeed was he thought of except when they desired to give him the honour that was due to him as the Maker of all things.

Muhingo was the god of war. His priest was never allowed to appear before the king. Each general sent an offering to him before starting on an expedition, and received his blessing; and again, when he returned, he sent an offering of cows and sheep. A priest accompanied the general on any punitive expedition, carrying a special drum which was beaten during the expedition to encourage the warriors and to make them realise that he was with them.

Ndaula, the god of small-pox, was one of the most powerful of the gods. He had a female medium who seldom left the temple precincts. The temple of Ndaula was built in the vicinity of the kings' tombs to the south-west of Bunyoro. The Baganda were accustomed to send offerings to the god to propitiate him and to stay a scourge of small-pox in Buganda.

Mugizi was the god of Lake Albert. His medium was a woman who wore a fringe of cowry-shells and small iron bells on her leather garment. The fringe was so made that it moved about like the waves of the lake when the medium walked. It was to this god the people went to make offerings when they wished to cross the lake by canoe.

Kauka was a cattle-god whose special duty it was to keep the herds free from foot-disease. The herdsmen resorted to him and sought his assistance when any animal fell lame.

Nyalwa was a cattle-god whose duty it was to keep cows in good health; occasional offerings were made to him.

Kagoro was the cattle-god who was able to make cattle prolific. He was frequently resorted to by herdsmen to assist them with particular animals, and to make them breed quickly. He was also the god of thunder. The people sent offerings to him when any one was struck by lightning and begged him to spare the people and not to be angry with them.

Kigare, the god interested in the welfare of cows, was one of the most powerful of the cattle-gods. His priest did not fear even the king and would order him to investigate any supposed carelessness on the part of the herdsmen. The priest of this god waked the herdsmen in the morning to go to milk the cows and to take them to their pastures.

Mulindwa and *Nyinawhira* were goddesses who cared for royalty. They had a temple within the royal enclosure. Their special duties were to watch over and care for the health of the royal family.

Kaihara was the goddess of harvest. Her medium was a woman. Before the harvest could be reaped, the people brought some cooked millet to the temple, when the medium, dressed with a special head-dress and a mantle of two cow-skins, took the food into the temple. She scattered a little of the food about in the temple and the people ate the remainder by the door, after which the harvest might be reaped.

Lubanga, the god of healing, was the god to whom the pastoral and agricultural people resorted for help in any sickness. His temple had a strong stockade of growing trees. When a suppliant went he took a pot of beer in which was a drinking-tube. The medium sucked a little of the beer from the tube and squirted it from his mouth on each side of the temple. He carried a stick decorated with pieces of bark-cloth, beads, brass ornaments, and other things worn by the people.

Munume was the god who had control over the weather. To him the king sent an offering of an ox and the people sent sheep and fowls which were sacrificed to the god, the blood being poured out by the temple and the people eating a sacred meal of meat with the priests at the temple-door. These offerings were sent when rain was wanted or when there was a continuous fall of rain and the people desired fair weather.

Gods of clans. There were many gods known to the various clans to whom members of the clan went to seek assistance. These gods, however, did not help the nation at large and could only be approached by members of the clan to which the god belonged.

The priests of the Bachwezi were consulted only by the pastoral people, generally with regard to the cows, and had nothing to do with the agricultural clans. When one was summoned, great preparations had to be made: a hut was prepared for him, often, indeed, a new one had to be built, a fat bull was killed to supply him with food during his residence in the kraal, and two new bark-cloths had to be given to him to wear while performing his duties. Each of the attendants who accompanied him had also to be provided with two bark-cloths to wear when at work.

The priest arrived at the kraal to which he had been summoned in the afternoon, and was at once presented with a goat and a sheep and sometimes also a cow. A shrine was built, and when the priest had examined and approved of the animals and the shrine, he retired to feast upon the meat of the goat. The sheep and cow, which were for use in his priestly duties, were tied up and carefully watched, for should one make droppings before it urinated, it had to be rejected and another brought and tied up. When it urinated first, the water was caught and the people sprinkled with it to bring them blessing.

That night the people of the kraal all passed before the priest who put two pieces of cooked meat into the mouth of each.

Next morning the priest decided which of the animals should be killed as a sacrifice, and the chosen animal was solemnly dedicated and killed ceremonially by having its throat cut. Its blood was sprinkled over the people and the kraal, and the meat was given to the priest.

In some cases the priest directed that a cow should be dedicated to the shrine. When this was done, the animal was thereafter sacred, and neither it nor its offspring could be killed or sold without reference to the priest, who could not give the necessary permission himself but had to discover the wishes of the god to whom it had been dedicated.

When the offering and the prayers of the priest had removed the cause of sickness, death or other misfortune from the kraal ordinary treatment might be applied to heal any disease, but without these preliminaries no medicine would have the desired effect.

The priest did not always visit the kraal when he was asked to help, for sometimes a man who was in any difficulty about his family or cattle would send a messenger with a present to the priest to ask for advice and a blessing. The messenger always spent the night with the priest and in the morning told him what was wanted, whereupon the priest took the messenger's hand, spat on it, rubbed it, and promised him his blessing. Spitting on the hands or person of a suppliant was a sign of favour, and a priest always spat upon a thing to give it a blessing before handing it to anyone.

If a message from the god was desired, the priest might either act as medium himself, or he might have an attendant who had that power. The medium, whether he was the priest or someone else, put on a bark-cloth and sat in his house waiting for the spirit to come upon him, while people outside sang and danced. When the spirit, as the people expressed it, seized him by the head, he gave the message as if it came direct from the spirit, speaking in the person of the Muchwezi under whose influence he claimed to be. If the priest was acting as medium himself, his listeners had to interpret the message as best they could, but if there was another medium, the priest was always present and interpreted the message to those who had asked for advice.

The priest of Kagoro, the Muchwezi who controlled thunder and lightning, had under him a company of medicine-men. If a man was struck by lightning and killed, his body might not be removed until the priest or his representative came and made an offering of a fowl, killing the bird and sprinkling the blood about to purify the place. He covered the man's body, which might then be taken away and cast down near an ant-hill, for it might not be buried. By the fact that the lightning had struck it the body was known to belong to Kagoro, and the people believed that, if they buried it, it would be dug up again.

When cattle had been struck by lightning, the priest of Kagoro himself had to come to the place. He brought with him a companion, Mwijwa, who consulted the augury, and then the two, sitting on the heads of the dead cattle, called upon Kagoro to spare them further calamity. An offering was made to Kagoro and all the meat of this, together with that of the animals killed by the lightning, was eaten on the spot before they left it. The priest then gave his blessing to the owner of the cattle so that he might soon recover from the effects of the disaster.

If a house was burned down, these two men came and gave their blessing before the owner could start to rebuild it. When the blessing had been pronounced, he might at once build again on the old site.

There were also women-priests who declared themselves to be mediums of the wives of the Bachwezi, whose names were:—Mugizi, Nabuzana, Kinyabwini, Nyabatimbu, and Kalega. They claimed to have special power to help women in child-birth, and men also applied to them to heal the illnesses of their wives and especially to make barren women bear.

In addition to these priests there were many medicine-men, who might be divided into two classes according to their duties. To the first and upper class belonged the rain-makers and a number of medicine-men who read auguries, using for the purpose the bodies of animals or fowls; these were consulted by the pastoral people in cases of illness either of themselves or their cows. They often employed as assistants medicine-men of the lower class who were satisfied with smaller fees than the more important ones. These also dealt in auguries, but made use of water, seeds, sticks, and other means which will be described later. Agricultural people generally applied direct to these inferior medicine-men, who were concerned more especially with them.

Rain-makers

The rain-makers were a body of men who claimed to be able to regulate the weather; they had pots, they said, for supplying rain, wind, hail, or any other type of weather.

Each district had its rain-makers whose duties were to look after the needs of the people in regard to weather, and the chief rain-maker of a district was responsible directly to the king. In recognition of their services they had the right to levy certain taxes. They could demand twenty-five cowry-shells from each household and when harvest came they took toll of two heads of maize from each field. This toll of maize was seldom collected by a rain-maker in person, but by a deputy whom he appointed and who was repaid by exemption from paying the tax himself. If the people refused to pay the rain-maker's tax, he would threaten to send heavy rain, wind, or hail to destroy the crops, and the people, who stood in great awe of him, were glad to pay and to do anything they could to keep in his favour. Should it happen that a rain-maker asked for tobacco when passing a house in the absence of its owner, and the wife, not recognising his office, refused him, the husband when he heard and realised who the applicant had been, sent with all possible haste a messenger, bearing tobacco and an offering, to express abject apologies for the mistake.

The rain-makers had to observe special food taboos and were never allowed to eat mutton, buffalo meat, or certain kinds of antelope.

When the people had tried in vain to get rain from their local subordinate rain-makers, and their crops were dying or the pasturage failing from drought, they appealed to the king, who sent to the chief rain-maker of the district a red and black bull, a female sheep, a black male goat, two white fowls, and two bark-cloths, the colours being chosen to represent the sky in different aspects, bright, dark, and variegated. The rain-maker told the king's messengers which of the animals he would require for the offering, then these were put in his hut and remained there with him all night.

Early next morning the rain-maker and his assistant, accompanied by several attendants who brought the offering, the medicines, the fetishes, and anything else required, set out for the sacred shrine. The rain-maker and his assistant each wore two black bark-cloths, those of the rain-maker being secured by a band round his waist to keep them from hampering his movements while at work. He wore a special head-dress decorated with cowry shells and beads and consisting of a band of leather round his head with a flap at the back a foot long by some eight inches wide.

I was allowed to visit one of these sacred places, which lay in the forest some distance from any path where people passed. A glade, some ten yards wide and four hundred yards long, lay between tall trees whose branches met above, making a sombre shade over the quiet place. No grass grew, but lemon grass was spread in the glade and a path led through it to the end where there were two pits, dug, so the people affirmed, not by the hand of man but by Ruhanga (God) himself. One was about four feet in diameter and four to five feet deep, and the other two feet in diameter and eighteen inches deep; both were lined with lemon grass, and when specially solemn and important offerings and prayers were to be made, shrines were built over them.

All the preparations were made by the priest and his attendants on their arrival. At the back of the larger pit an altar was erected consisting of three spears and a long cow's horn, which were stuck in the ground in a row. The horn was filled with herbs and decorated with cowry-shells, and the thick end, which was uppermost, was closed by an immense stopper or bung; by its side stood a short iron spear. In front of these, on a leopard-skin spread on the ground, was placed a stool covered with a second leopard-skin and on this lay the special rain fetish, a large buffalo-horn. Near the fetish were placed a bow and arrows which always accompanied it. On the other side of the skin which lay on the ground was a bag containing all kinds of things necessary for invoking the rain-god, and some of its contents were spread round the pit—small horns of goats and sheep (many of them decorated with strips of skin from goats, leopards, wild cats, or monkeys), bits of pots, roots, shells, and various kinds of herbs. Mingled with these were things of European origin, such as bits of tin and glass, which were calculated to add to the awe of any who approached. A few feet away, among the bushes, stood some twenty water-pots, most of them old, and round about them lay the fragments of many more which had been broken in use or by exposure to the weather. These pots were made use of during the ceremony to work the sympathetic magic which formed an important element in the rite.

The priest killed a fowl, or sometimes one of the animals, either the black goat or the sheep, and smeared some of the blood on the fetishes. The bottoms of both pits were smeared with fat, some of the blood was poured into each, and the body cast into one. The priest knelt while doing this and, after the animal had been sacrificed, he sprinkled millet, dwarf beans, and semsem into the pits.

A vessel of water was next brought from a spring near and the rain-maker raised his hands and prayed thus to Ruhanga: *Ruhanga, otukonyi. Omukama we nsi otuwulire. Abantu bafwa.* (Ruhanga, bless us. Thou king of all the earth, hear us. The people are dying from hunger.) With much ceremony the water was then poured into some of the pots and left exposed in order to draw down rain by sympathetic magic.

The meat of the offering was then taken from the pit, cooked, and eaten in the presence of the god. The bones were burned and the skin was used by the rain-maker for sacred purposes. The ceremony lasted in all some two hours or a little longer, and the procession then returned home.

On his arrival home the rain-maker went through further ceremonies at two or three shrines near his own hut, killing a black goat and smearing all the fetishes in these shrines with its blood.

On a hill on which was the sacred place of one of these rain-makers, there was a hole from which the man affirmed that the gusts of wind which frequently accompanied rain proceeded. After his incantations and offerings for rain, he took a red bark-cloth and covered the hole, carefully weighting the cloth, so that the wind might not rise too soon and blow the rain clouds away or come with too much strength and destroy the crops.

When the need for rain was not very pressing, these men did not go to their sacred places, but betook themselves to shrines near their own houses, where they made offerings and placed pots of water mixed with herbs near the shrines in the sun to attract the rain.

When the desired rain had not come, and the king was becoming anxious on behalf of the people, he might send a messenger again to one of the rain-makers with a black bull, a black goat, a black fowl, a pot of butter, a girl, and a cow and calf. The girl, cow and calf were gifts to the rain-maker and the sending of these things indicated the need for more vigorous efforts to bring the rain.

The rain-maker set off to his sacred place, taking with him the king's messenger, who was expected to take part in the ceremony so that on his return he might give a favourable report to his master. When the sacrifice had been made, the messenger was instructed to smear the fetishes with the butter as well as with blood from the offering, and one pot of water was poured over the fetishes, the other pots being left exposed among the bushes as before.

Sometimes, when the rain failed to come, one of the rain-makers sent to the king to tell him that it was necessary to make a special offering at an empty pit far away in the wilderness. A white bull was demanded as the offering and the rain-maker set off with his staff on the journey to the pit, which was some twenty miles from Hoima. The bull was offered to Ruhanga, the creator, and was then killed near the pit while prayer was made for rain. The party returned and it was asserted that rain invariably fell in a short time.

One rain-maker sometimes declared that, before going to his sacred place, it was necessary to go to a spot which he called "the lightning rock" to obtain water. This was a sacred spring near Kibero on Lake Albert[1]. The rain-maker took to the guardian of the spring two loads of grain, two bark-cloths, two copper bracelets, and two strings of beads, and in return received permission to draw a small pot of water, which he said was rain. The king permitted the man who did this to carry a special spear and wear a leopard-skin and beads while on the journey, and even sent them to him. He was also given a goat and a fowl which he took with him and killed among the trees near the spring.

Should the wife of the rain-maker be menstruating when the king sent to tell the man to make rain, he said to her "You are my blessing" and went to sleep alone in the forest somewhere near his house for two nights before he commenced his duties.

When he had completed his task he slept on the floor for two days before going near his wife. Should his wife bear a child while he was on duty, the child was heir to his office of rain-maker, even though there might be an older brother.

When the rain was excessive and was injuring the crops, the rain-maker was expected to stop it and people sent him presents of goats and fowls. His first procedure was to expose his fetishes to the fury of the storm for a time near his home, and call for sunshine, after which he put out empty pots mouth downwards and begged the rain to cease. Then, if the rain did not stop, he went to his sacred place where he

[1] This spring has been found to be a petroleum spring and has been taken away from the Banyoro by the British Government, who have excluded the priests from this sacred place.

King with members of his Council (modern)

PLATE V

King in Council (modern)

performed a more ceremonial exposure of the fetishes and placing out of empty pots with prayers.

The king sometimes sent a rain-maker a new red bark-cloth as a sign that the rain must cease. This he spread out before his house, placed his fetishes beside it, and told them that sunshine was wanted. This was often sufficient to stop the rain and cause the sun to shine brightly.

Should the rain-makers fail to bring rain when it was wanted, the king had a special punishment for them. Their chiefs had to come to the court, where the king ordered to be prepared for them a meal of liver, usually from a sheep or a goat, mixed with blood and fat and cooked with as much salt as possible. The men had to eat this and sit perspiring in the sun until they were tortured by thirst, but no man dared give them water. Sometimes they were kept like this for several days, fed at intervals with salted meat but allowed no water; and when they begged for a drink, they were told they must get it as rain or die. Their sufferings often caused them to faint and they have been known to die without any compassion being shown to them. Neither the king nor any of the people believed that the rain-makers were incapable of bringing rain and of controlling the elements; their failure was looked upon as stubbornness, which had to be dealt with sternly. Sometimes after a day of the terrible thirst the men would promise to go and bring the rain. They would then be allowed a respite of a day or two, and before this came to an end, the rain might fall.

In like manner, if there was an excessive downpour of rain, preventing the crops from ripening, and these men did not stop it in return for the offerings of the people or in answer to the king's command, the king sent for the chief rain-makers and put them in the rain in an open place near the throne-room, with great pots of rain water before them which they were compelled to drink. The amount they had to drink often made them ill, but "Work harder and stop the rain" was the only comfort they were offered.

People often tried to bring rain for themselves without

applying to the rain-makers. They made fires in their fields which emitted clouds of black smoke, and beat drums to imitate thunder, hoping thus to attract clouds and rain. These people were not genuine rain-makers and ran the risk of being accused of witchcraft and of being fined or even put to death.

When a man was starting on a journey and wanted to get through it without rain, he would get a few thorns from a kind of briar and throw them on either side as he started out. This would, it was said, ensure his getting through safely. He might use another kind of plant, *Kawungula*, which kept the rain from falling upon him though it might be raining behind him.

Medicine-men

Mulaguzi we Enkoko. This medicine-man was a royal servant of much importance, and not only possessed an estate in the country but had his house in the capital which he might never leave without special permission from the king and without putting a responsible representative in his place, for the king might summon him to the court at any time of the day or night, whenever circumstances might require his presence. If the king felt ill, or if any report reached him of sickness in the country, whether of people or of cattle, or of any invasion or calamity, or if he wished to send out an expedition for any purpose, he would first send for this man to come and find by augury what steps should be taken. A rumour that any chief was becoming too powerful or was showing signs of disloyalty was enough to make the king send for this medicine-man to come and by an augury reveal the true state of the case. Another of the duties of this medicine-man was to summon to the capital any medicine-man or rain-maker whom the king desired to see, and whenever he came before the king, he had to wear two bark-cloths, one knotted on each shoulder. On duty, he was always accompanied by a medicine-man of the lower order, who was a water-diviner.

When summoned by the king, the medicine-man and his subordinate came into his presence and were told the cause of his anxiety, whereupon the medicine-man asked for a fowl, which he took home with him. He kept the bird in his house all night and in the early morning he and his companion, who carried the fowl and the implements of his trade, came to the entrance of the royal enclosure. A bowl of fresh water was brought to them and they knelt on the ground two or three feet apart and set to work.

The fowl was put on its back and held whilst water was poured over it, and it was washed from its beak down. The medicine-man, holding its beak, rapidly cut its throat and watched the flow of blood: if it spurted out, or if the stream ran more freely from the left artery than from the right, it was a bad omen; but if the flow was steady and gentle and either ran evenly from both arteries or more freely from the right than from the left, the omen was good.

When he had learned what the bleeding had to tell him, he inserted his sharp knife, and, cutting the skin from the throat to the anus, proceeded to disembowel the bird, examining each part of the intestines and the liver and lungs, the markings and specks on which were counted and their position noted.

When he had collected what information he could from the fowl, he might direct that his augury be confirmed by the water-test, which was carried out by his companion, one of the lower order of medicine-men. This man came provided with a lump of clay and began his augury by digging nine holes in a line in the ground. In each hole he made a pot of clay like a native cooking-pot, eight inches in diameter and six inches deep. These were filled nearly to the top with water, and the man, having rubbed grease on his hands and arms, washed them in each pot until all the water was muddy, using as soap a piece of the clay with which he had made the pots.

He then took a small gourd-pot containing some liquid and dropped two or three drops into the water in each pot. The effect on the water was immediate and remarkable, for the muddiness cleared and there appeared either a star-shaped figure or clear broken patches. The star-shaped figure meant a good augury, while the blobs and patches were bad. The process was repeated in each of the nine pots and the augury given in accordance with the results.

If this confirmed the previous augury and the result was satisfactory, it might end the ceremony; but, otherwise, the chief medicine-man might say it was necessary to go still further and make the offering of a sheep and a cow or bull, consulting the augury shown by both. The king was asked to provide a cow or bull and a sheep of whatever colour the medicine-man named, and he sent for them to the flocks and herds kept for this purpose.

The animals had generally to swallow some of the king's saliva upon plantain-leaves and were then taken to the house of the medicine-man and kept there all night. At daybreak a number of herbs and tree branches of special kinds were laid down inside the main entrance to the royal enclosure. The king and the royal family assembled and the animals were marched round them four times. The sheep was then thrown on its back on the heap of branches and herbs and washed. Its throat was cut and the blood caught and set aside, the manner in which it flowed being carefully noted. The body was opened and the intestines examined for the markings and white specks by which these medicine-men read their auguries, and the cow or bull was treated in the same way. The medicine-man took some of the herbs from the heap on which the animals had been killed, dipped them in the pots of blood, and touched the king on his chest, his right cheek, his forehead, and under his knees. When, as was done in matters of less importance, goats or fowls were used, the king was touched with the blood on the back of each shoulder, on his left cheek, and under each great toe. Princes and princesses of tender age were washed from head to foot in the blood, but those who were grown up, together with the king's wives and all the servants who lived in the enclosure, had their chests touched with it, while some was smeared over the door of the throne-room and on the ivory tusk which lay across the doorway. Any blood that was left was sprinkled over the assembled people. The meat of the sacrifices belonged to the medicine-man, who thus not only made known the augury but by the offering averted further evil.

If the first augury had been unfavourable and the second was favourable, the first was ignored and the good result accepted.

If this medicine-man was taking auguries for a case of sickness and he saw in the house a man whom he presumed to be the heir to the sick man, he declared that the sick man would die unless he gave special offerings to ward off the evil.

The following account of ceremonies in which this chief medicine-man of the king took part is taken from *The Northern Bantu*:

Ceremony to avert famine. When famine appeared to be imminent and the cattle were also suffering from lack of food, the medicine-men looked for the house of a poor man who had neither wife nor child. The door was taken from the house, and they also provided themselves with an empty milk-pot, an empty butter-dish, a potato, a few beans and some millet. These were then placed in front of the chief medicine-man with a bunch of herbs. A procession was next formed, headed by the medicine-man, who carried the door, with the various articles and herbs laid upon it, to some adjacent country in order to banish from the country hunger, famine, and any cause that was bringing famine and want, and to cast them upon another nation.

Rite to prevent evil from happening during feasts. A ceremony was observed by the people when feasting and dancing took place, to prevent the gods from being angry or from sending evil, should any one incautiously offend them during the feast. The chief medicine-man would also visit the king and tell him that the year had been one of plenty and that the cattle and crops had been blessed, so that food would be abundant. After the visit the king would appoint a day for the people to come together and would present the medicine-man with two white sheep and two white fowls. The medicine-man would thereupon kill one fowl and one sheep and examine their entrails for a confirmation of his previous oracle. If the desired confirmation was obtained, he sprinkled the people with blood and offered the living sheep and fowl to the god *Wamala* to be kept alive at his temple. The people were then free to enter into the pleasures and joys of harvest. Sometimes, before the harvest festivities were celebrated, a barren cow, the fattest that could be found, was brought and killed. Its entrails were then examined by a priest and the blood of the animal was sprinkled upon the people. The priest also made a tour round the capital, saying "We must speak for the god. Let sickness, evil, war and famine grow fat at a distance and never come to us or ours." The priest took the meat of the animal and ate it in the temple.

Mutaka wa Manda of Bunyaga. This was another of the higher class of medicine-men, and to him the king applied for advice before undertaking raids and expeditions and before sending out an army to repel any invasion of which news or rumours had reached him. This man never took an augury and he had no special shrine, for the whole hill on which he lived was sacred and he made offerings on the top of it. The king sent him a cow which had to be white or white and red, and it was killed and eaten, the skin being kept by the medicine-man. When the sacrifice was over, he beat his drum and sent a messenger to the king to say that he might proceed with his plans, for things promised well. So great was the power and fame of this man that no one under any circumstances dared to rob him or plunder his fields. Even the hostile Baganda stood in awe of him, and when they raided the country left his property untouched.

When a man of a pastoral clan fell ill and the illness did not yield to treatment, one of the superior order of medicine-men would be called in to find out, by an augury taken over an animal, the cause of the illness, and also whether it could be cured or whether the sufferer would die. The taking of the augury completed the duty of this medicine-man, for he never demeaned himself by prescribing medicine or carrying out treatment. He told those who consulted him what member of the inferior order of medicine-men they should call in to deal with the illness, and then his work was done. The agricultural people dealt with the inferior order only and applied to them for the advice and assistance they required.

Of this inferior order of medicine-men there were many different kinds who were named according to the means by which they took their auguries.

Mulaguzi we Segeta. This man was appealed to in cases of sickness or calamity to tell whether the person affected would recover from his trouble. For his augury he had to be given a goat, which he killed, smearing the blood on a stick he carried with him. He put the stick between his great toe and the next, and, by rubbing his hand up and down it, was able to tell whether the person was going to recover or not. The stick was then placed in the doorway of the house to keep away evil.

Mulaguzi mulege etondo. Before this man would begin his work he had to receive a fee of a few cowry-shells. He took a forked stick and asked the applicant to spit either into the fork or upon a bit of rag, which he then put into the fork, fixing the stick in the ground upright. A small beetle, named *etondo*, was put on the stick. If it climbed up and ate the saliva, the man would recover: if, however, it turned down, an unfavourable augury was indicated, but this was never accepted until a second beetle had been tried: if it also turned down the stick, the man would certainly die.

Mulaguzi wa Mayembe. The method used by this man was not looked upon as a legitimate form of augury, and he was called a wizard. He worked in secret in his own garden where he cut off the top of a plantain, placed a few grains of millet on the growing stem where it was cut and watched it. If the pith or heart of the cut plantain shot out quickly, the omen was good; if it grew slowly, it was bad.

Mulaguzi we Nkaitu. This man had to be paid nine cowry-shells before he would begin his work. His apparatus consisted of nine small squares of leather, three by four inches in size, decorated with markings or shells, and a strip of cow-skin four feet long by a foot wide. He took three of the leather squares, held them one on top of the other, and threw them along the strip of cow-skin. By the positions they took up when sliding along the skin he read the augury.

Omogya. This was a medicine-man who gave people the power of growing rich. The person went to him by night and spent the night with him in his hut. In the morning early the medicine-man smeared the applicant with herbs and washed him in a pool of muddy water. From that he took him to a clean spring, washed him, and took him back to his house where he smeared him with butter and medicines from five gourd-pots. This ceremony gave the man favour in the sight of the king, which meant that he would be given cows and become rich.

Mulaguzi we Muchura. This man used the leaves of a plant known as *Muchura*. These he dried over a fire until they were crisp, then powdered them and took the augury by sprinkling the powder on water in a pot and watching the shapes it assumed.

Other medicine-men used nine small sticks about two inches long which they dropped into water, reading the augury from the positions they assumed.

Others again used seeds, usually of millet, which they put in a small gourd about the size of a tea-cup. This they held over a strip of goat-skin and shook it so that some of the seeds fell out. From the patterns formed by the fallen seeds they read their augury.

Kawonyawonya. One of these medicine-men, called Kawonyawonya, was a special servant of the king and claimed to be able to trace missing articles by scent. When he was asked to find something he would go to the place from which it had been taken, and after sniffing round like a dog, followed the scent until he came to the place where it was concealed, found it, and brought it back. He was always paid according to the success of his quest.

This man was also sent for by anyone who believed that a magical object had been hidden about his house to do him harm. He would then scrape and dig in the earth in various places and bring up all kinds of bits of things which he would not accept as magical objects; but at length he would discover a bone which had been hidden in the grass or in the thatch of the roof or somewhere in the house, and this he would declare to be the thing which contained the spell. He destroyed the object in a fire and thus removed the magic.

Fortune-telling. If the owner of a house wished to have his fortune told he sent to a man of another order of these medicine-men and asked him to come to his house, and on the day of his visit he prepared a feast and invited friends to come and dine with him. When it was evening and the food was ready they sat down to begin their meal, whereupon the medicine-man, who had concealed himself, slipped out from his place of hiding, snatched up the meat or a garment or anything he liked, and rushed off into the darkness. Next day he returned, took an augury, and told the result. For his services he was given a goat or anything else he cared to ask for.

GHOSTS

Though there were certain spirits which were feared, there was no knowledge of a spirit-world or of any spirits created apart from this world: the people stood in constant awe only of disembodied spirits of men, the ghosts. When a man who possessed property died, his heir had to build him a shrine in the house near his own bed, and generally dedicated to him certain cows whose milk was daily offered at the shrine, this being the place where the ghost came to visit his family and to take his meal of the essence of the milk. The rest of the milk was then drunk by the owner of the house and those of his children who were unmarried and living at home. No outside person might partake, and even the man's wife might not take any, for she was of a different clan. If the ghost was neglected or any member of the family did anything of which he did not approve, he would manifest his displeasure by causing illness or death among the people or the cattle. Powerful ghosts might also be persuaded by members of their families to cause illness to some person of another clan in revenge for some wrong. Sickness was always supposed to be caused either by ghosts or by magic; and a medicine-man had to be summoned to find out the cause by augury, for the treatment varied with the cause.

People who had no property and no power in this world were not generally feared when they became ghosts, for they were thought to have as little power then as before, and no steps were taken to keep their ghosts in good temper. The ghosts of some poor people, however, might be dangerous, owing to the circumstances of their death. For example, a sick man who came to beg for food and was refused might, should he die in the neighbourhood from want, cause some evil. If an epidemic broke out or someone fell ill shortly afterwards, the misfortune was attributed to this ghost and offerings were made to propitiate him.

The ghost of anyone who had been wrongfully accused and had committed suicide was very dangerous, even the ghost of a woman being feared under these circumstances. A woman who had been wrongfully accused of adultery would go and hang herself, and her ghost would then be a malignant influence. Her body was buried as near the place of her death as possible that the ghost might be destroyed or confined to that locality. If she hanged herself on a tree, the body was buried just clear of the roots, the tree was cut down and its roots were dug up; the whole was then burned to ashes and the relatives had to pay ample compensation to the chief on whose land the deed had been done.

Magic-working was also looked upon as a powerful means of causing trouble. By magic not only could people be detected when they had stolen anything, but anyone could be made ill, injured, or even killed, though they were at some distance from the magic-worker. An account of the methods of treating sickness caused by magic and by ghosts will be given in the chapter dealing with sickness.

Snake Worship

Two rivers, the Muzizi and the Kafu, were said to be the abode of sacred snakes. These rivers were subject to very rapid rises, which were often caused by storms high up in some part of the country which drained into them. There being no apparent reason for such risings, they were attributed to the sacred snakes.

At the Muzizi there was a medicine-man, *Kaumpinipini*,

who was in charge of the river and cared for the snake, to which he made offerings when people wished to cross. He affirmed that it was useless to attempt to build a bridge over the river for the snake would break it down, and the only means of crossing was by large papyrus rafts on which the people, after giving offerings to the medicine-man for the snake, had to be ferried over. The king sent periodical offerings of black cows to this snake and the medicine-man presented them to it with prayers that it would not kill men.

If anyone fell into this river, the only person who dared to rescue him was a medicine-man, *Muhinda*, who lived on the bank at the ford. A drowning man was said to be captured by the river snake, who would be annoyed if anyone but the medicine-man attempted to save his life and would avenge itself on the rescuer at some future time when he was crossing the river again. When a man was drowned, it was said that the river snake took him, kept the body for a time to remove the heart and tongue, and then returned it, for it was found floating after two days.

No man who had had sexual relations during the night would cross the river the next day unless obliged to do so, and then he would slyly drop seeds into the water, for he feared the snake would detect him and sink his raft. The owner of the ferry would refuse to take any man if he knew he had been with a woman the night before. No woman during her menses would be taken across, for the raft would sink. There was also a firm belief that circumcised persons, or any who had mutilations on the generative organs, would be drowned if they tried to cross; and any malformed persons had to buy their safety with special offerings before crossing.

Wells or springs of water were generally found in hollows on the sides of hills and as a rule there were trees near them in which tree-snakes were found, awaiting the birds and insects which came to the water. These snakes were from two to four feet long and bright green in colour with orange and gold tints on the lower parts. The people declared that they bit, but no person could be found who was ever bitten. They were thought to be the guardians of the water and were regarded as sacred, offerings being made to them.

Wells were also considered to have their special water-spirits, and when a path to a well was cleared annually, the owner made a feast with his workers. They killed a goat, allowing the blood to run down to the water, and then cooked and ate the animal on the spot as an offering to the spirit.

Pythons were held to be sacred, and in some places offerings were made regularly to them to preserve the people. A few men kept pythons in their houses, taming them and feeding them on milk with an occasional fowl or goat. It was said that these pythons did not kill children or animals in their own villages but went further afield for their prey. The king had a special temple at Ķisengwa in which a priest dwelt with a living python which he fed with milk.

No one would kill a python or drive it from his house should it enter, but if one became dangerous, the people besought the priest to allow them to destroy it, as it could be no sacred snake but only a dangerous reptile.

Sacred Hills

The hill Kahola was sacred because it was the home of a special earth-spirit, and offerings were made there for which the king sent regularly a black and a white sheep. On the hill was a crater which went very far down, the sides being covered with grass and shrubs and ending in a lake. A sheep was thrown alive into this lake and a fowl killed and thrown in. It was said that the sheep always came out alive for it followed a passage which led from the side of the crater through the hill to the outside and which was known only to the guardian of the hill, a freeholder (*Mutaka*) and medicine-man, who took possession of the animal. This hill was a favourite place for people who wished to make requests for prosperity, for children, or for rain.

On this hill were four holes from which it was said that the wind came. When there were violent gales which were doing damage to the crops, the king sent a sheep with the request that the guardian of the hill would cover the holes from which it was coming and save the land from famine.

On most hills there were places where offerings of fowls were made, those most favoured having steep craters or precipices down which the offerings were thrown. In one place only were offerings made to lions, to propitiate them and prevent them from killing human beings and cattle.

Blood-brotherhood

When two men formed so close a friendship that they desired to cement it in a manner that would bind them together for the rest of their lives, they went through a very solemn ceremony which constituted the taking of the oath of blood-brotherhood, a bond which nothing but death could dissolve.

The ceremony had to begin at dawn: so, if the two men lived some distance apart, one came and spent the night with the other that they might be ready to begin early. If rain fell during the night, or a cry of alarm was raised, or a child was born, or a dog had puppies, or a hen hatched chickens in either of their kraals, or if one of the men when going to the appointed place met a woman before meeting a man, the ceremony had to be postponed.

There were many onlookers and witnesses at the ceremony, the chief witness being the sister of the man at whose home it took place. The two friends sat down opposite each other and were given a razor of native make, with which first one and then the other, having pinched up a little flesh near the navel, made several slight incisions and caught a few drops of blood in his right hand. A coffee-berry was taken from its husk and each man took half the berry, rubbed it in the blood in his hand, and then held out his right hand with the berry in it to the other, who took it out with his lips and swallowed it. Each in turn next took a small bunch of leaves of *mituba* and *julwa* and brushed the other from the head down the arms, under the arms, and down the body to the feet. Each then promised to be true and faithful to the other and to his whole family, and they cemented their alliance with a sacred meal.

The two friends by this oath were obliged to help each other in all things and to shield each other from all injury and danger, even from the wrath of the king. To break the oath of blood-brotherhood meant certain death, for such a crime on the part of one man would be avenged by the ghosts acting on behalf of the other.

Fetishes and amulets

Fetishes were almost invariably horns of wild animals, buffalo-horns being the most venerated, though claws of large beasts of prey, such as lions, might also be used if the fetish was needed for wearing round the neck or under the arm, or for carrying on a shield. In the hollow of the horn or claw was put something prepared by the men who claimed to be the manufacturers of fetishes for the different gods. Thus two fetishes, outwardly the same, might be dedicated to quite different gods.

People carried fetishes about with them on certain occasions, using for this purpose small horns or claws, while each house possessed its large fetishes, some for guarding the whole household from dangers, while others belonged entirely to individuals. Though a fetish might fail its wearer in time of need, it was never admitted to be useless but the failure was explained by saying that some greater power, perhaps the fetish of a greater god, had been at work on that occasion.

Amulets took all kinds of forms, bits of roots of trees and herbs, sticks, or horns with powder in them, or shells, and so on. They were frequently ornamented and worn as decorations, though originally their purpose was medicinal. They were usually bits of things which had been found useful in time of sickness and were worn to ward off any return of the sickness they had cured.

Taboos and omens

Concerning fire.

Fire might not be taken from a house in which a woman with a newly born child was lying during the first four days after the birth. Infringement of this rule would cost the child its life.

When a house was built and the people entered it, no fire might be taken from it during the first day, because it would endanger the building, which would soon fall or somehow be destroyed.

When a woman was going to her field to dig a new plot, or when she intended to sow seed, she carried a little fire with her in the form of hot embers wrapped either in a roll of bark-cloth or in a bundle of grass. With this fire she lit her pipe when resting, but no man or woman might touch it, either to take any for starting a fire or to light another pipe. Should anyone attempt to do so, the woman would come and strike the fire from their hands and trample it down till it was extinguished, lest her ground should become barren or her seed fail.

Huntsmen carried fire-sticks with them when they went to hunt, for they were more portable and not so likely to attract the attention of animals as smouldering embers or fire-brands would be. The sticks were two in number, and were known as the *male* and the *female*. The female was of soft wood and was placed on the ground horizontally. The point of the male or hard wood stick was bored into the soft wood and turned rapidly by rubbing it between the palms of the hands until the friction of the point of hard wood caused a spark which ignited the dust rubbed off the soft wood. A little bark-cloth or some other inflammable substance was put over this and gently blown into a flame. These sticks were carried in the small goat-skin bag slung on the left shoulder, which also contained other necessary articles, such as tobacco and a pipe, a knife and a fetish.

When an owner entered a new kraal he took some fire from

the central fire (*nkomi*) of his old kraal to light the one in the new kraal, and during the first day no one might take a light from it.

When the death of the king was announced, all fires in the royal enclosure were extinguished and also the central fire, called *nkomi*, in each royal cow-kraal. Fresh fire was made from fire-sticks in the new royal enclosure, which was built for the new king, and other fires were lighted from it.

One of the duties of the heir of a dead man was to see that the fires in the kraal were extinguished, for the old life had passed away.

In the presence of the king no man might smoke or have fire with him, and no man would go to see the king if his house-fire had gone out during the night, for that was a warning that danger awaited him if he went on that day.

No work, such as building, and no journey could be begun if the house-fire had gone out during the night.

Concerning visits to the king.

A man might not visit the king if there had been a recent death in his family, or if his wife were menstruating. If he sneezed, if rain fell as he started, if the first person he met on his way was a woman, or if the fire went out in his kraal, he would postpone his visit for that day.

Concerning women.

A woman might not touch her husband's spear, or himself, when she was menstruating; though, among poor people of the agricultural clans, she might cook his food.

A woman might not drink milk during her menses except from an old cow which was past bearing. If such a cow were not procurable, she had to live on porridge and vegetable food, such as plantain.

When a man had a new pair of shoes, a new pipe, or a new spear, his daughters and grand-daughters might not touch them or bring them to him until the things had been one night in the house.

When a woman was sitting down, it was an offence

PLATE VI

Sacred cows of the Nkorogi herd being brought to be milked

Sacred cow standing on grass carpet to be milked

PLATE VII

Presenting the milk for the king to drink

Milking a sacred cow; milk-maids in attendance

amounting to immorality to step over her legs. If anyone wanted to pass into a house in the doorway of which a woman was sitting, she drew up at least one leg, putting the foot on the outstretched leg, and the man stepped over that.

If a man setting out to do any work met a woman before meeting a man, he had to return home and postpone his task for that day.

Concerning work.

Certain taboos and omens were almost invariably observed when a man set out to do any work, such as building or iron-mining, or any other of the ordinary occupations. If on the previous night rain had fallen, or his fire had gone out, or a child had been born in his kraal, or a dog had puppies, or a hen hatched chickens, or biting ants had entered his house, or a cry of alarm of fire or wild animals had been raised, or any of his relatives had died, he had to postpone his work for that day, for it would not succeed.

There were taboos and omens connected with every important event in a person's life, such as marriage, birth, building, travelling and so on; these will be noted in connexion with the events to which they belong and need not be repeated here.

SUPERSTITIONS

Dreams. When a sick man dreamed that his dead parents called him, he would die that day; and his belief in the significance of the dream was quite strong enough to make him certain to do so. Should he dream that he saw them when out walking and that they took a different path and left him to go on alone, he would get well.

Jackals. When jackals came into a garden near a house and barked night after night for a week, it was considered a bad omen. Some member of the family was sure to fall ill or some calamity to come upon them.

When a man wished to bewitch any person he trapped and killed a jackal, dismembered it and spread parts of it about near the hut of his enemy.

The nose of a jackal was believed to be of great value as an amulet to a blind man. If he could secure and wear one, he could always find his way home.

A warrior kept the nose of a jackal in his shield and was thus enabled to discover all kinds of loot.

Sneezing. Sneezing was regarded as a sign of refusal to do something; hence no person might sneeze in the presence of the king or of a superior, and no wife in the presence of her husband. In the same way, coughing, spitting, and blowing the nose were marks of disrespect.

Left-handed people were hated, and no one might hand anything to another with the left hand.

Hair, nails, and teeth. The hair and nail parings of a child were always given to its mother who put them in some special place, on the dung-heap if the child was of a pastoral family, and under a plantain tree if the family was agricultural. Those of royal children were preserved and buried with them when they died. A man also was always careful to put his hair and nail clippings in some place where they were not likely to be found and identified. If anyone walked over them it would cause the owner headache and, if found, they could be used to work magic against the owner. Cast teeth were treated in the same way.

A prince might never cut all his nails on the same day as long as his father was alive but had to leave the nail on his little finger for another day. Nails were always cut V-shaped and never broken.

CHAPTER IV

GOVERNMENT OF KITARA

1) THE CENTRE OF GOVERNMENT, DIVISIONS OF THE LAND, LOCAL GOVERNMENT, AND METHODS OF TAXATION

The king—the Sacred Guild—districts and district chiefs—duties of district chiefs—appointment of district chiefs—district chiefs as magistrates—right of appeal to the king—state labour—pastoral chiefs—*Batongole*—*Banyoro* or freed-men—*Bataka* or free-holders—*Bazairwa* or agricultural free-holders—chiefs holding hereditary offices—taxation of cows, labour, grain and salt

THE people of Kitara were a despotically ruled nation believing firmly in the supreme right of their king, who was regarded as something more than an ordinary man, as, indeed, approaching to the divine, for his power on earth was absolute and he had almost as great an influence over the heavenly powers. He was a completely autocratic ruler and all the wealth of the country, that is, the cattle, was regarded as belonging to him. Though each cow-man who had herds treated them as his own, yet the king had the right to take any cows from him, just as he had the right to take any man's daughter and make her his wife. It was therefore entirely to the king's advantage to do all in his power for the well-being and increase of the people and cattle in his realm and to take all possible action for the prevention and cure of sickness and the defeat of enemies, lest his cattle be lost and his people suffer.

Though the king's power was absolute he consulted in most matters a body of chiefs who were known as the Sacred Guild. These chiefs were his special advisers and protectors and were, to all intents and purposes, united as blood-brothers by a solemn ceremony of testing and admission to the Guild. This ceremony is described in the section on Inheritance, for the son of a chief of the Guild almost invariably inherited the right of admission, though he did not succeed directly to membership on his father's death but had to go through the ceremony of admission. Two chiefs, *Bamuroga*, who was a member of the Guild and had charge of the kings' tombs, and *Munyawa*, the head of the royal clan, were the most powerful of all the chiefs and during the interval between the death of one king and the accession of another, these two governed the country.

The existing chieftainships and divisions of the land of Kitara indicate how the government of the country grew and how the nation developed from its purely pastoral and nomadic condition.

The country was divided into some ten districts, like counties, each district having its overlord who was directly responsible to the king. There was no direct system of taxation of land though state labour, generally in the form of building for the king, had to be supplied when required. The original inhabitants of the land were the agricultural people who were called slaves and treated as such by the upper classes of the pastoral people, though they were free to leave one master and go to another if they wished. By the custom of generations they regarded themselves as belonging to the district in which they were born; and though they were at liberty to migrate, they rarely moved about except within that district, where they attached themselves to any chief with cows who settled near them, and regarded themselves as his serfs as long as he remained there. He would use them to build for him, to supply him with grain for food and beer, and often to look after his sheep, goats, and fowls. In this attachment to the land we see the remains of the original tribal system under which these agricultural people, who are now amalgamated under one king, dwelt in isolated and probably hostile groups. The differences in appearance and habits between these groups are still quite apparent to any observer.

The king at times appointed an intelligent member of one of these agricultural clans to govern a district, but the majority of district chiefs were pastoral people. The ten great district chiefs were:

1. Bikamba of Kikabya
2. Kanagwe of Munyabyala
3. Nyakamatura of Mubale
4. Rusongoza of Kikukya
5. Kikukule of Kibanja
6. Kadiabu of Kidoka
7. Mutengesa of Butengesa
8. Mwanga of Kyaka
9. Nyina Mukama of Mugarura
10. Lwigi and Budema of Kitagwenda

Each of these chiefs had his town residence in the capital as well as his place in his own district, for he was expected to live near the king. In addition to keeping the king informed of anything that was going on in his district, he had to be near to protect him from danger from rebellious princes or any other person who sought to do him harm. The king, in later years at any rate, was so engrossed in affairs within the enclosure in which he dwelt that he trusted to his chiefs to bring him all the news of the country. A chief always paid the king an official visit in the morning, when he would bring up any case in which he desired advice or a judgment; and if he had no special case of his own to discuss, he was expected to be present to listen to those of others. Later in the day he was expected to appear more informally to acquaint the king with what was going on, or with anything of interest that had happened. In the evening the chiefs almost invariably went to pay their respects and talk to the king, but these were quite informal visits and not for business, and a chief would not be considered to have failed in his duty if he did not appear. The morning visit was compulsory, and a chief fell under the king's displeasure and even ran the risk of being regarded as a rebel if he failed to attend without explaining the reason.

While a chief was thus resident in the capital, he had a representative in his district who acted for him, and who during his time of office was known and spoken of by his master's title. All that he did was attributed to the chief, who was entirely responsible for his actions. This representative sent daily reports to his master; and should any difficult case require litigation, he sent it to the capital to be dealt with by the chief in person.

When a chief wished to go to his district or to leave the capital for a rest, he had first to visit the king, present him with a cow and a calf, and ask his permission. He might have to wait a few days, and when permission was granted, the king sent him a gift of a woman slave or several cows and goats. To go without permission was rebellion and punishable by death. Before the chief left he had to present to the king the man who would represent him in the capital in his absence. This man, like the representative in the district, used his master's title while he was in office and the king always addressed him by it. He paid, like the chief, daily visits to the king to give him news from his master, to whom he had to send news of what was going on in the capital. A chief thus absent might be summoned back to the capital at any moment and had to obey such a summons without delay.

The king had the right to appoint men to these chieftainships, but once a man had been appointed, it was customary for his son to succeed him, unless for some reason he was not considered suitable, when a clan-brother would be elected in his place. The king had always to be notified and give his sanction before any man was officially announced as a chief; he might, if he wished, take the office into his own hands and appoint some one, even a man of another clan; this, however, was very seldom done.

The principal duty of a district chief was to see that peace was kept. Under him there were numbers of smaller chiefs appointed by the king, the man who was second in authority to the district chief being appointed by the king and chiefs in council and holding the title of *Ndibalaba*. Some of these secondary chiefs were pastoral people who only wanted grazing land, and the district chief had little to do with them except to settle any disturbances and disagreements between the herdsmen of different masters. The king had many herds in each district under his own herdsmen, who were not responsible to the district chief, so long as they kept the peace and were law-abiding, but only to the chief of the royal herdsmen. The district chief, however, had to keep a watch over them and see that the interests of the king were regarded and that nothing was done to harm his cattle. He had also to see that there was no trouble between them and the other herdsmen in the district; and if any herdsmen, whether belonging to the king or to others, were accused of causing disturbance, the district chief had the right to try them and fine them.

The chief was responsible for guarding the cattle in his district, both the king's herds and those of other owners, from human enemies, from lions, and from other dangers. If a lion or other wild beast was causing trouble, it was his duty to organise a hunt and kill it; and if any game pits dug in the district by huntsmen were dangerous to the cows, it was his duty to see that they were filled up. He was also expected to know the number of inhabitants in his district and how many cows there were in each kraal, in order to inform the king's messenger, who came periodically to gather the cow-tax.

Each district chief was also a magistrate, and anyone, whether a cow-man or a serf, might appeal to him from the judgment of the lesser chiefs. Agricultural people were usually satisfied with the jurisdiction of their own chiefs, but everyone had the right of appeal to a higher authority, and, in the last resort, to the king himself. No court-fees were paid, but the person judged to be in the wrong had to pay all expenses and compensate his opponent. Any man who failed to pay the fine imposed had his goods seized and sold. If an appeal was made to the king, the case was tried before him in the throne-room, but only a chief who was entitled to do so might pass the ivory tusk placed across the doorway; all others knelt outside. If the king was not satisfied with a given decision, he might reverse it, or he might permit a trial by ordeal.

Though state labour was one of the few methods of taxation in the country, a district chief might not call directly upon any agricultural people but his own to supply this. He had to demand it from the lesser chiefs, who in their turn summoned the agricultural people who were their serfs. No district chief could command food or beer from the agricultural people of his district, who were never regularly taxed for their land. After harvest the serfs took grain to their own chief, and, when he wanted more for food or brewing, he could ask for it as a favour, which they would grant as long as they had it, but he could not demand it as a right. From time to time a chief would send his people a bull for food in order that the meat might rouse them to new efforts.

In each district there were pastoral chiefs who were independent of any official in the district, but who had agricultural people under them; these men might be called upon by the district chief to supply workmen for the king or the state. There were also many *Batongole*, that is, chiefs who had been given estates by the king in the district and who used as serfs the agricultural people whom they found settled on these estates. These Batongole might be either cow-men or serfs who had been pages to the king or had done him some service for which he rewarded them with estates. They were responsible to the king alone and not to the district chief so long as they and their followers were law-abiding. The district chief could only interfere if there was trouble between them and others in the district.

There were also chiefs who had risen from the agricultural class and who were known as *Banyoro* or freed-men. These were men whom the king, in return for some service rendered, had freed from the restrictions of the lower class, giving them office and estates. Their parents and relatives then addressed these men with great respect and even knelt to them, so completely had they left their own class and entered a higher rank of society.

Each of these lesser chiefs had his agricultural serfs near his kraal. They were responsible to him alone and were under his command, though they might appeal from him to the king in any disputed case, and they might leave him and attach themselves to some other chief if they wished.

In addition to the many small chiefs there were what were known as *Bataka* (sing. *Mutaka*), or free-holders. These were men who had been given estates by the king for some service. The area of land granted to them was limited, so that when the family increased and more land was required, those who broke up fresh ground were regarded as ordinary tenants and not as possessors of the ground, which meant that they might be called upon directly by the chief of the district to supply state work, while the *Bataka* could not be approached directly for this form of taxation. In each district there was one special *Mutaka* who was head of his fellows, and the district chief had to apply to him and not to the individual *Bataka* when he needed men for state labour or for war. One of these *Bataka* was Tabalo Omukwesi of Nakwesi, who claimed descent from the man who ferried the first of the present line of kings over the Nile from Bukedi.

There were other free-holders, called *Buzairwa*, who were agricultural people and were the original holders of the land, so that the portions they held were theirs in their own right. From such holdings the king did not expel a man, nor did he give the estate to a man of another clan when the holder died, but, if he disapproved of the heir appointed by the clan, he would ask them to appoint another of whom he could approve.

All these holders of land could be called upon either directly or indirectly to provide state labour, which generally meant building for the king. The district chiefs were responsible for building and keeping in repair the larger buildings in the royal enclosure, and they called upon men in their own districts to supply the workers.

There were many important chiefs who held land under the district chiefs by virtue of some office, either within the royal enclosure or in the capital, which they held for the king. Their offices were hereditary in their clan though it was not necessarily the eldest or any son of the dead chief who succeeded. The following list gives an account of some of these:

1. Kabonerwa of Buligira. This man was the leader in all royal processions.

2. Oyo Bugome Rwalo, who imitated the actions of the king at feasts, beating his drum with reeds instead of drumsticks.

3. Mugema of Buchubya. By virtue of his office, this man took precedence of all chiefs who wore crowns, though he had no authority or judicial power over them and was not able to settle any lawsuit among them, for in such a case they had to appear before the king. This man belonged to the *Babopi* section of the *Ngabi* or royal clan, and the office went in rotation to each of the three divisions of that section, the *Mugema, Zigija,* and *Kisoja*. These men wore crowns even when not in office and were subordinate to the one who was in office.

4. Bamuroga of Kijagalazi. He was the principal chief and always acted as regent when the king was dead until the new king was appointed. He had also special charge of the royal tombs.

5. Kikato Lubaya of Kikomagazi. This man had to provide the special gate for the kraal of the sacred herd of cows and was in command of all the gate-keepers of the royal enclosure.

6. Kasumba of Bugachya. This man claimed to be a prince and to have come with the first king into the country. He also declared that he had the right to use an ivory door sill, like the tusk that lay before the doorway into the throne-room.

7. Kanagwa of Bugungu was keeper of an axe called *Kiriramiro*, which was used for killing people.

8. Muhaimi of Kihaimi in Bugangaizi was keeper of the drums.

9. Bwogi of Bugangaizi was keeper of *Njagu*, the royal clothing.

10. Kagoro of Ekibijo provided a girl who had to be in constant attendance on the king.

11. Muguta of Kyoka was said to have control over the lions of the country. Each year the king presented him with two cows, and he in return prevented lions from killing people and cattle. Women presented him with butter to smear on the lions in order to keep them from attacking people.

12. Batalimwa of Kichwera was responsible for two horns of medicated water which he brought daily and anointed therewith the king's head and chin.

13. Kyagwire of Kijingo was the priest of the Nile and the waters of the country.

14. Nyaika of Pakanya had charge of the royal bugle. He was said to have come with the first king as a slave and blew his bugle for him on any special occasion. He announced to the musicians when the royal band should start playing.

15. Manyuru ga Bungu of Kiyonga was a medicine-man who prevented lightning from striking the royal houses.

16. Kabagyo of Mukyotozi was the maker of a special crown.

17. Katongola of Bulwa was a royal medicine-man.

18. Kadoma, the chief herdsman of the sacred goats, once upon a time stole a goat from the king and ate it. This was a criminal offence; but instead of being put to death, he was made to wear a bell round his neck and ring it before the king at stated times. This came to be regarded as a sign of chieftainship, and his descendants have been chiefs ever since.

Taxation

Though there was no regular system of taxation, the king imposed other taxes than those of state labour, and these were collected in kind.

All the cows in the country belonged to the king, and he had the right to take any cows from any of his subjects, just as he could take any man's daughter and make her his wife. He might require cows for food or cows of a particular colour to add to his herds if their numbers were diminishing, and all he had to do was to send a special messenger to demand the animals from their owners. Each district chief was expected to know who was in his district and how many cows there were in each kraal, so that he could inform the king's messenger when he arrived.

The messenger wore his badge or insignia of office, consisting of the necklace on which were threaded the teeth which had been extracted from the king at initiation. His mission gave him special powers and he might act as judge and decide any cases which were brought before him on his way. For such services he would be paid a large fee.

The messenger took with him a retinue of boys and other followers, and when he and his company arrived at a kraal they were treated with great respect and liberally entertained, for the messenger was always open to bribery from a chief who wished to be relieved from paying part or the whole of his tax. The bribe would consist of goats, or sheep, or perhaps a bull or a heifer for the messenger himself, while his followers would also receive presents. The number of cows demanded for the tax were brought before the messenger in the evening, and he watched the milking then and next morning; if he did not approve of the amount of milk given by any cow, he might refuse it and another had to be brought to take its place.

A chief who was well known to be rich would sometimes try to deceive the messenger by professions of poverty. The messenger and his followers would then play a trick on the man. When the food was brought, one of the followers would insert in it a potato or the feather of a fowl. If it were night the messenger would call for a light to examine the food and would express the utmost horror and indignation at his food being contaminated by something he never ate; he would refuse to touch it, and no explanation would pacify him. The terrified chief, to avoid being accused to the king, would have to pay the messenger quite double the amount he would otherwise have been asked for.

When the messenger returned to court, he would keep all the cattle beyond the number demanded in his instructions and take the others to the king. The next day he appeared again in court to ask if all was well, bringing another cow from his surplus stock as a gift for the king, who would then commend him for his zeal.

At times some priest would announce to the king that he required a particular kind of wild animal for some sacred purpose, and the king would send a messenger to the part of the country in which this animal was to be found. The messenger wore the insignia of office and took up his residence in the district, where he had to be lavishly entertained, given presents and food, and treated with the utmost respect. The chiefs had to supply men to go out and hunt for him until the animal demanded was caught. If the hunters did not pursue their task with vigour, the messenger had power to fine them.

When the king required millet for brewing, he sent a gift of a cow, a goat, or a sheep to the chief of the district, who in return collected through the lesser chiefs a quantity of grain to send to the king.

When the king required salt for his herds, he sent an animal or perhaps two, to the salt-works. These were killed, cut into small pieces, and distributed among the workers, who in return sent liberal supplies of salt.

(2) LAW, CRIME, AND PUNISHMENT

The king as chief judge—the stocks—punishment of chiefs—freedmen, princes, and the king's wives—punishment for murder—homicide—suicide—fornication—adultery—trial by ordeal

Though the district chiefs had the powers of magistrates, everyone, even a peasant, had the right of appeal to the king and might bring his case to the king's court. After the morning milking the king sat on the throne and heard cases. Only a chief who had, by his rank, the right to do so, might pass the ivory tusk and enter the throne-room; the others concerned in the case knelt on the ground outside the doorway, and the onlookers squatted in the courtyard. Having heard the case, the king pronounced judgment and frequently gave his hands to be kissed by the man who won his case, an act which confirmed the decision.

Should there be talking when the king was in court and required silence, he took the sword *Busitama* which was always carried by a page in attendance on him. The page wore a lion-skin which hung over his right shoulder with the head hanging down in front and concealing the sword; to this skin the scabbard was attached by a loop of skin, and the two-edged sword was placed in it. When the king wanted it, he simply held out his hand and the page put the sword into it. Unless the chiefs succeeded in dissuading him, he would then strike down someone in the court. Often the offender would have to pacify him by paying a fine.

The king's power was absolute over all his subjects. When any man, chief or peasant, offended him, he might send a messenger to catch and kill the culprit and confiscate his property. If the man received warning in time, he fled to some friendly chief who hid him. The royal messenger did not spend much time searching for him, but seized as much of his property as he could lay hands on and returned to the king to report the escape. After a few weeks, the friendly chief would visit the king, tell him the man was alive and penitent, and plead his cause. If the king gave instructions that the man should be brought to him, he was sent for at once and came, bringing with him a cow. His advocate took the cow to the king, saying, "I have brought an animal for the king." If the king's reply indicated that he was favourably inclined, the culprit was hurried into his presence and knelt before him, hoping to be allowed to kiss his hands. If this was denied him he knew that the king was still angry and that he was not forgiven; he had to retire and try again after a time, until he was either forgiven or condemned to death. If the culprit was a chief of the Sacred Guild, that is, one of the body of the king's special councillors, his sentence was pronounced in the courtyard of the seventh sacred hut during the feast of the new moon.

When an offender of the lower orders was captured he might be put in the stocks, of which there were two kinds. One was composed of a log of the sacred *kirikiti* tree, four feet long and ten inches in diameter. Through this a hole was bored large enough to allow the foot to go through, and another smaller hole was made at right angles to it, so that, after the prisoner's foot had been put in, a peg could be inserted, narrowing the hole and preventing the withdrawal of the foot. The other kind was a stout branch, eight or ten feet long, with a forked end into which the man's neck was fastened by a peg inserted after the fork had been put in place round his neck. This forked stake was in all probability introduced by Swahili slave-traders, for it was in common use among them but was not an original form of detention in Central Africa. There was no state prison fare, and a prisoner had to be supplied with food by his relatives or he would be allowed to starve.

No chief or free-man might be so far dishonoured as to be put in the stocks. The king instead sent his messenger to tie a band round the right hand of such an offender and he had then to leave his stool, the seat of chieftainship, and sit on the floor. This was sufficient to mark him as a prisoner to be detained and guarded until the time came for his trial, when he was given an opportunity of pleading his case and, if he was able to clear himself, he was restored to office. If condemned, he was invariably put to death. No prince or princess might be put in the stocks but had to be guarded by special police until the king ordered their release or death, which for a prince or princess was usually by hanging. The sentence was carried out on a post which stood opposite the queen's throne in her reception-room.

Within the royal enclosure the king executed summary justice upon offenders. He was always accompanied by a page carrying the two-edged sword *Busitama*, and if anything displeased him, he held out his hand, the sword was placed in it, and he struck down the offender on the spot. When one of his wives offended, he might strike her down, or he might send her into banishment until he pronounced sentence. There were three places to which she might be sent, and the chief of the place selected had to look after her and give her vegetable food, but no milk. If she were sent to Buruli-Ekisaka-Ekyara or to Kibero, she might expect after a time to be pardoned and restored to her place, if some chief would plead her cause with the king. If, however, she was sent to Bugoma-Ekisaka-Ekiragula, though there was a chance of pardon, she would most probably be thrown into the Nile and drowned. Wives found guilty of adultery were sent to the last place.

Murder

To the primitive mind the only satisfactory method of avenging murder is to kill the murderer, but, should he escape, the death of some member of his family or clan would suffice to expiate the crime. In Bunyoro, accordingly, this was the only retribution which satisfied the people's sense of justice, for it was thought that only the death of the murderer or some member of his family or clan would pacify the ghost of the victim, which, if its relatives were dilatory or careless in thus avenging the death, would cause trouble in the clan. It was, thus, the idea that their own lives must pay for the lives they took which restrained men from murder.

There were, however, men who would run this risk to gratify their hatred or avenge some wrong. Such a man might lie in wait and take his enemy secretly, or he might go openly and kill him. He seldom sought to hide the body and would probably not take any steps for his own safety until he was found out, when he might seek refuge with a powerful chief or hide himself by fleeing to some other tribe.

If the relatives of the murdered man could catch the murderer red-handed, they would end the affair at once by killing him on the spot. Otherwise they took the matter to the head of the clan, and if there was any difficulty in tracing the murderer, a medicine-man was called in and the person and whereabouts of the wanted man ascertained by augury. When caught, if the accused man did not admit his guilt freely, he might be forced to confess. Sometimes it was found that the murderer belonged to a clan which was too powerful for the friends and relatives of the victim to take up the case unsupported, and, under such conditions, they applied to the king for assistance. If the case was clear, he sent to the clan of the accused man to demand the person of the murderer or of some relative, and the man given up was handed over to the injured clan, who killed him.

When the murderer was a member of a clan which held property of the king, such as cows, drums, or a spear, or was guarding a prince, his relatives had the right to refuse to give up a man to be killed without an appeal to the king. The relatives of the victim would then accuse the murderer before the king, who, having tried the case and found the evidence against the man sufficient, would give up to them either the actual culprit or, if he could not be found, some member of his clan.

At times a murderer escaped to another tribe and his clan disowned him, refusing to acknowledge him as one of their members. Then the case was tried by the chief of the district and might be sent to the king for his final decision. The only recompense which an injured clan would accept was the right to kill some member of the offender's clan, and a case of this

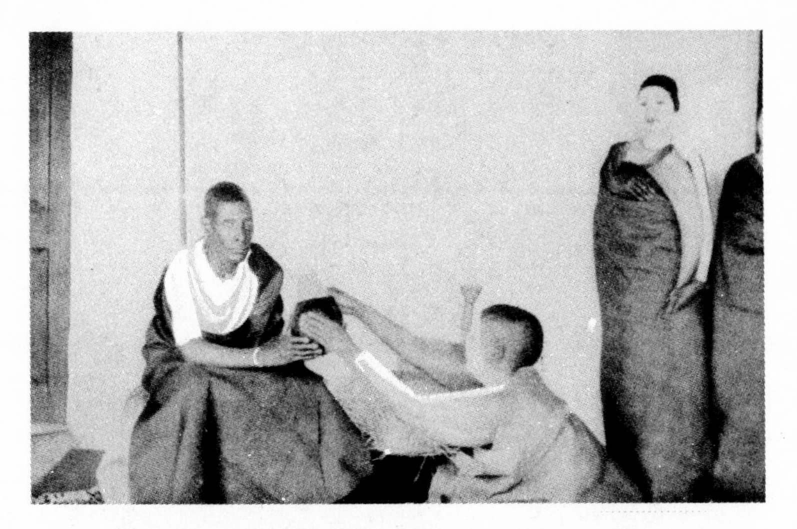

Presenting the milk to the king

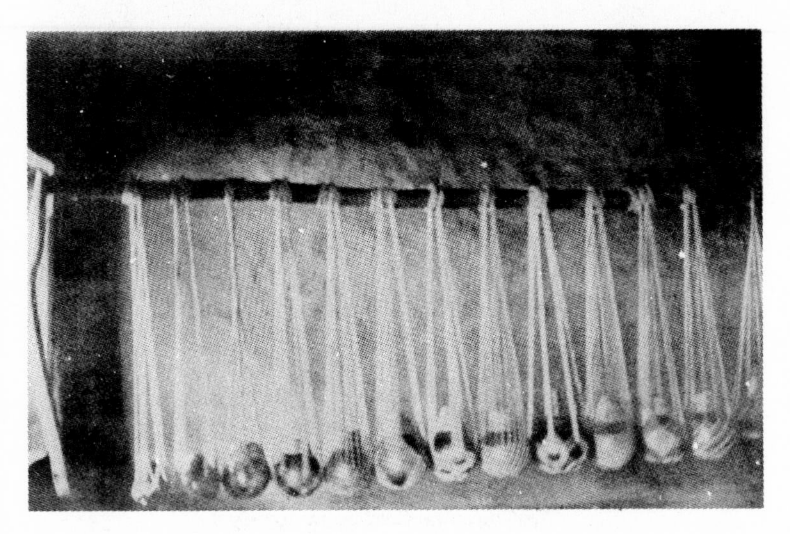

Milk-pots hanging in the dairy full of milk

Medicine-man taking an augury

kind would often run on for ten years or even more before a settlement was reached.

If a man wished to kill another but dared not attack him openly because of his power or superior rank, he would resort to magic, which might be used in various ways. He might kill a fowl on a path where his enemy was sure to step over the place. The blood was poured into a hole in which the fowl's head was also put, and the dust was swept over the place to hide it. Words of incantation were pronounced over the spot and the spell was complete. Another method was to push a bone into the thatch of an enemy's roof or to conceal it somewhere about his house. Any means would be effective, for if a man found that someone was working magic against him, he would certainly die of fear, unless he could be persuaded that the spell was removed by stronger magic, or that the man who was working against him had been reconciled and had consented to lift the spell.

Homicide

When a man accidentally killed another, for instance when he was out hunting, he had to tell the chief of the district, explaining the circumstances, and also to inform the dead man's relatives of the accident. If they accepted his statement no further steps were taken, but if they refused to do so and complained to the chief or appealed to the king, a special messenger was sent to investigate the circumstances and report to the king. If the latter was satisfied that there was no previous malice, he decided that the death was accidental, but the homicide had to make a feast for the dead man's relatives and give his family a cow.

Suicide

Suicide was common among both men and women. Among the pastoral tribes a man would hang himself or strangle himself because he had been discovered in some theft, or because he had by unfair means obtained a cow from another man and did not wish to return it, or because he had been forced to part with cattle as a fine. Any of these causes would be quite sufficient to induce him to strangle himself by tying his loin cloth or some other article round his neck. If he did the deed in the house, the house had to be destroyed and the main posts and the central rings, which formed the apex of the roof, burned. The rest of the materials might be used again for building. The body was buried quite near the house in which the deed had been committed. If he hanged himself on a tree, his relatives had to pay the chief of the district a sum of money, and had then to cut down the tree and dig up the roots. The body was buried near the tree, just far enough away to give the men room to dig up the roots. The tree and its roots were burned on the spot and no traces left, lest some other person might be influenced by them to destroy himself.

If a man burned himself to death in a house, his remains were buried beneath the ashes of the house. If he drowned himself and his body was found, it was not buried, but was taken out, weighted, and cast into the water again.

A woman would commit suicide if wrongfully accused of adultery or even if her husband complained of her for laziness or bad cooking. Another and common cause was that, having gone wrong in her husband's absence, she feared to meet him again. Women usually strangled themselves, and the same measures were taken with the tree or the house as in the case of a man.

Fornication

As girls married at an early age it was not often that they had either the desire or the opportunity to commit fornication, and a girl was usually handed over to her husband pure. Should a girl for some reason be kept with her mother after the usual age for marriage was past and be discovered to have gone wrong, the mother would tax her with the fault and would soon discover whether she had conceived. The signs of pregnancy were found not only in the absence of the menses, but also in the swelling of the breasts and the markings round the nipple. If a girl went with a man and escaped detection and no results followed, neither she nor any other woman would say she had done wrong. There was no idea of sexual union being wrong so long as there was no conception, and the only risk run by the girl lay in her being discovered to be with child. Then the parents questioned her and tried to find from her the name of the guilty man. When they had obtained this information, the father sought the man and charged him with the offence. He was generally one of the men of the kraal and usually acknowledged his fault and married the girl, paying a fine of one or two cows. If, however, the man denied the accusation, it was necessary to bring the case before the chief of the district, so that the affair might be investigated and his guilt proved or the real culprit found. If the girl refused to tell and the man could not be found, she was taken out of the kraal and sent away to friends, for her presence would bring ill-luck to her home: the children would die or the cows cast their calves.

When a girl named her seducer and the case had been proved, the man was asked to marry her. If he consented, the usual formalities were gone through and the woman went to her husband. If, however, he refused, she was sent to his house until the birth had taken place, and he had to supply a woman to care for her and administer the necessary medicines.

Among the pastoral people, when the child was a month or more old, the man brought the girl back. Her father took a white fowl and a white sheep or, if wealthy, a white cow. The fowl was killed and the blood allowed to run out by the door of the house; the girl stepped over the blood, bearing her child. The girl's mother brought a pot of water and sprinkled it on her daughter and the child with bunches of sacred herbs. The sheep or cow was killed and eaten and the girl, thus purified, returned to live in her own home.

In an agricultural family, the girl's father, when the child was a month or more old, took a white fowl and an egg and went to bring his daughter and her child home. When they arrived at the house the daughter stood outside while the father took the white fowl and cut off its head, letting the blood flow over the doorway. He handed the egg to his daughter who threw it down by the blood, breaking it. She then stepped over the blood and broken egg, thus removing evil from herself and preventing her from bringing any into her parents' house.

It was not unusual for a girl to go wrong while staying with an aunt during her confinement. If the parents discovered this, they learned from the aunt the name of the man and the girl was sent to him. When she was ready to return, the man had to bring her, and with her a bull and a sheep. The sheep was killed in the gate-way of the kraal and the girl and the cows went in over the blood. The bull was killed and eaten two days later. If the man was poor, he brought a fowl and a sheep instead of a sheep and a bull.

If the child was a boy, the father might redeem him from the mother's parents by paying six or seven cows; but should he refuse to do so, the child was regarded as a slave and had to bring his grandfather a goat from time to time. When he wished to marry and had collected the marriage fee, he had to give his grandparents a sheep before taking the marriage fee to his bride's parents. If the child was a girl, the grandparents kept her and were recompensed by receiving the marriage fee when she grew up.

Any man who sought to ravish a girl was put to death at once.

Adultery

The conception of adultery among primitive peoples often differs considerably from our western ideas of what is right and wrong in married life, and it is necessary, before attempting to judge of such matters, to know the point of view of the people concerned. In Kitara a man might marry a woman and she was then his by right and any children she might have were his. At the same time, the woman might allow any man who belonged to her husband's clan and thus called himself the brother of her husband to visit her couch, and her husband could find no fault with her for faithlessness, for this was not adultery; but if a wife consented to the visit of any man from a clan other than that of her husband, she was guilty of adultery.

It might happen that a husband was sent on some expedition by the king or went away on some journey, and during his absence his wife consented to the visits of some other man. Such risks were anticipated and a man leaving his wife for more than one night was usually careful to make her take a form of oath. She took a handful of grass from the floor and placed it with the fetishes, which was looked on as equivalent to saying upon oath that no man should cross the floor to her bed during her husband's absence. The husband then left with confidence in the protection of his god.

On his return home he would question his wife and might be satisfied that all had been well in his absence. Should he, however, have cut his foot by kicking a stone or stumbling over a tree-root, he was urgent in his demands to know whether his wife had been faithful or whether she had by unfaithfulness been the cause of his misfortune. He might resort to ordeal to extract confession.

If he discovered that his wife had had intercourse with some other man during his absence, he sought to discover who the person was and, if it turned out to be a member of his own clan, he took no further steps in the matter. If, however, the woman refused to tell the name of the person and the husband had reason to suspect that it was a man of another clan, he might flog his wife or tie her up to a post and inflict torture until she confessed. She was then taken to confront the man and he was charged with defrauding the husband. Should he deny the charge, the woman named the person he had sent to arrange their meetings, for a man generally used as go-between some person whose visits would not be noticed even by the woman's neighbours and friends. Sisters and sisters-in-law frequently assisted a wife to receive attentions and visits from some man friend whom they wished to help in the matter. If the man still denied the charge, the district chief referred it to the king who might administer the poison ordeal.

The husband had the right to divorce the guilty wife and demand the amount he paid in dowry for her. He might, however, consent to take her back and, should a child be born, the father, if it was a boy, had to redeem him with six or seven cows or the child became a slave. If it was a girl, the husband adopted her and took her marriage fee when she was grown up.

Trial by Ordeal

At one time a chief of any rank had the right to administer the ordeal by poison to persons in his own court. It was, however, found that too many people were being killed by this means and the king forbade his chiefs to use it, reserving to his own court the right of administering the ordeal to the persons concerned.

A chief who wished to try a case in this way had to use fowls, and when it was necessary to administer the ordeal, he called in a medicine-man. This man ordered each litigant to provide two fowls, and these he kept without food and guarded from any interference for a night. Next morning he took a fowl belonging to each person and made each spit into the throat of his own fowl. He then administered the potion to the fowls and tethered them in the sight of the spectators and the chief. The medicine-man wore his official robes and bells and strutted about, adjuring whichever fowl might belong to the guilty person to fall dead and thus prove his guilt. When one fell dead, its owner was accused, and, should he not accept this as final, the other fowls were put to the test to confirm the evidence of the first pair.

An appeal to the king was still permissible after this, and he had both parties brought before him. If they so wished, he ordered that they themselves should be given the potion. People were so convinced of the effect of their innocence that many would drink the poison without any fear. As in the treatment of the fowls, the two people were first guarded for a night to keep them from taking any drug that would hamper the action of the poison, which was administered on the next day. When they had drunk the potion, they were placed sitting near each other, and the medicine-man walked about calling on the draught to take effect on the guilty. Sometimes one person would vomit the medicine and thus escape its effects and be pronounced innocent. Otherwise they sat until they began to show signs of intoxication by aimlessly trying to scratch their heads or some part of their bodies, thus showing that the poison was taking effect. The medicine-man then put his tobacco bag or some other article down a short distance from them, and, standing a little way from it, told them to bring it to him. They could understand the request and would try to reach and pick up the article. One might after many efforts succeed, while the other would fall down, and, if he did not expire at once, would probably be speared to death. The goods of the guilty man were confiscated and possibly his clan was also fined or plundered. The person who reached the article laid down and was pronounced innocent in consequence, was rewarded, but he might suffer for a long time before he recovered from the effects of the poison.

The trial by poison ordeal was used especially in cases of adultery when a man denied the charge. The man and woman were each given the potion and if both fell they were equally guilty. The relatives of a guilty person had to pay a fine and they carried away the fallen, who could usually be restored to health by the use of an emetic.

Ordeal by fire. Sometimes a man would object to a chief's decision in a case of theft and appeal would be made to the ordeal. The medicine-man was called and informed of the charge against the accused and was asked to administer the fire-test. He brought a hoe and, having made it red-hot in the fire, rubbed it down the leg of the accused and of the accuser. The iron did not burn the leg of the innocent man and therefore the one who was burned was guilty either of theft or of bringing a false accusation. Before this ordeal could take place, the accuser had to pay a goat or a sheep, and, if the accusation was thus proved to be false, he had to pay the other an indemnity.

Akabindi. Another ordeal, called *akabindi*, was administered to extort confession. A small pot with a little fire in it was held with its mouth over the navel of the accused, where the flesh had been wetted so that air was excluded. As the fire consumed the air in the pot, the flesh of the navel, if the person was guilty, was sucked up into the pot. If the person was innocent, there was no effect. The excessive pain was said to make the person call out and confess, and when his guilt was thus proved he was fined.

Bead test. This was used to detect a thief who had taken refuge among a crowd of people. The medicine-man laid a bead on the eyebrow of each person tried and uttered magic words. If the man was guilty, the bead would fly into his eye, causing him considerable pain, but if the man was innocent, the bead would fall to the ground.

CHAPTER V

THE KING

(1) THE ROYAL ENCLOSURE

Position—building—the fence—the gates—the court-house—interior of the court-house—the queen's reception-room—the seven sacred huts—the royal spear—huts for king's wives—huts for visitors—the hut *Kasenda*—the hut of the king's mother's sister—the hut of serfdom—the king's servants

THE royal enclosure, called by the people *Kikali*, was always built in such a position that it commanded a view of a large expanse of country, the site chosen being either on the flat top of some suitable hill or on a stretch of land rising above the surrounding district. In choosing the site it was of the utmost importance to see that there was in the neighbourhood an adequate supply of water, not only for the use of the people but for the great herds of cattle.

The enclosure always faced south, and surrounding it were the enclosures of the principal chiefs, who formed its protection. Every chief's enclosure, even those in the country, however far away they might be, had to be built so that its entrance looked in the direction of the royal dwelling. A chief had to get his own people to build his private buildings for him; he could not call on lesser chiefs to provide men for these tasks, as he could when the work to be done was for the king or the state; and the size of his enclosure and the style of his houses depended upon the amount of labour he could command. There were no roads opening up the country, and no attempt had been made to connect the country residences of chiefs with the capital. The only tracks were those made by the cattle in their movements in search of pasturage, and by people passing from chief to chief and going to the capital.

Each king on his accession had to have a new enclosure, for he might not even begin his rule from the last king's throne-room. His first task when he became king was to bury the dead king's body, and while he was absent on this duty, a new enclosure of a temporary character was built on a site determined by an augury taken by the chief medicine-man. This was always in the vicinity of the old enclosure, which was then utterly destroyed by fire. The temporary enclosure served for the king's residence until he had completed all the death taboos and the ceremonies of his accession and had time to turn his attention to the building of his more permanent abode. This, again, had to be built on a site named by the chief medicine-man after taking an augury; and again the deserted enclosure was completely burned down, for when once the king had left no one might enter any of the houses in it. The same procedure had to be gone through whenever the king wearied of his site or when the priests advised him to move, and the whole state took part in the building of a new enclosure.

The enclosure covered a large area of ground, for the fence of elephant-grass some six feet high which surrounded it had a circumference of about two miles and enclosed a cluster of huts whose number ran into hundreds. The building of a new enclosure occupied a large number of people and the responsibility was divided among many chiefs. The whole country was responsible for the great court-house *Kaluzika*, the principal house in the enclosure, which was distinguished by a spear on its pinnacle. One man, *Nyakamatura*, was architect and overseer of the work, while the workmen were sent by different masters. Should *Nyakamatura* detect any man idling or working carelessly, he would accuse the man's master and levy a fine, and the actual offender was buried in a hole up to his knees, the earth being pressed in round his legs, and left there until the fine was paid. The rest of the enclosure was built by various district chiefs, each of whom was responsible for some definite part of the work and could call upon lesser chiefs from his district to come and help and to supply workmen.

The outer fence of the royal enclosure was a strong elephant-grass barrier and its up-keep was the duty of all the chiefs, each of whom had his special portion to look after. Should any man neglect his duty in this respect, he might be imprisoned, heavily fined, or deprived of his chieftainship. The main entrance in this fence faced south, and the gateway led directly into the courtyard in front of the throne-room. Outside, in front of this entrance, was the kraal of the sacred herd of cows, called *Nkorogi,* which supplied the king and his household with milk. There were several other entrances to the royal enclosure, and the most important of these were three gateways which did not lead directly into the enclosure but into a line of seven huts, the first of which was inside the enclosure, while the others extended beyond the boundary fence, each standing in its own courtyard. The outer walls of these courtyards were continuous; so that there was no break, except for the gateways, in the barrier. The first of the three entrances into this line of huts led through a passage into the first hut, which was just inside the actual enclosure. This hut was known as *Muchwa* and was the queen's reception-room, and the gate and passage leading into the hut formed her private entrance to it and through it to the royal enclosure. Another gateway led into the courtyard of this hut, and through it the sacred cows came twice daily and proceeded through the queen's reception-room to the courtyard in front of the throne-room to be milked; through it also came the king's cook when he brought the meat for a sacred meal of which the king partook in the afternoon. The third gateway led into the courtyard of the seventh hut and was the special entrance of the chiefs of the Sacred Guild. This row of huts extending beyond the actual royal enclosure had to be specially guarded and the guards would not hesitate to kill anyone who entered without permission.

The houses inside the royal enclosure varied in size from the king's throne-room, which was often forty yards in diameter and eighty feet high at the apex, down to the huts of slaves, six or seven feet high and eight feet in diameter. Each of the larger houses had its own compound enclosed by a fence, and the small houses for the servants and slaves were built inside these compounds. This plan and the regular arrangement which was invariably followed in laying out the enclosure made it very easy to refer, or to direct anyone, to any house among the many, for those which were not dignified by having names of their own stood in the court-yards of those of greater importance, each of which had its special name and recognised position. The principal house in the royal enclosure was the great court-house, *Kaluzika*, of which the main doorway faced the gate of the enclosure and therefore looked south and into the kraal of the sacred *Nkorogi* herd. There was no door, for no house in the enclosure, except the queen's reception-room, had doors; but in front of the doorway lay an ivory tusk over which the king alone might step. The chiefs of the Sacred Guild had the right to enter the throne-room, into which this doorway led, and each of them had a special place on which he might lay his mat and sit; this place was reserved for him, and for this right he had to make a payment in cattle. Neither the chiefs, however, nor any other persons who entered by special permission, might step over the tusk, which was so placed that room was left at either end for them to pass. This was the only barrier to the throne-room, but the stoutest heart would quail at the thought of passing it without permission.

The court-house was divided into four rooms, of which the front one, into which the main entrance led, was the throne-room, *Hamulyango*. This occupied about half the building, and in the centre of it, opposite the ivory tusk and the gate-way of the enclosure, stood the throne, *Nyamyalo*, on a platform of earth beaten hard. This platform, which was about two feet high, was covered with a leopard-skin and a lion-skin, and in the centre, over the other two, lay a white cow-skin on which the throne stood. The throne was cut from one solid block of wood, from which the centre was removed, leaving a solid top and bottom joined by eight curved bars or legs of wood, which were left while all the wood between them was cut away. This was ornamented with copper and iron wire, and over it was spread a lion-skin, then a leopard-skin, with, above these, a greyish white skin taken from a young cow. These were arranged by *Lukanka,* the man who attended to the throne and who had to set it in readiness for the king and then go away. The throne, however, might never be left alone, and two wives of the king slept at

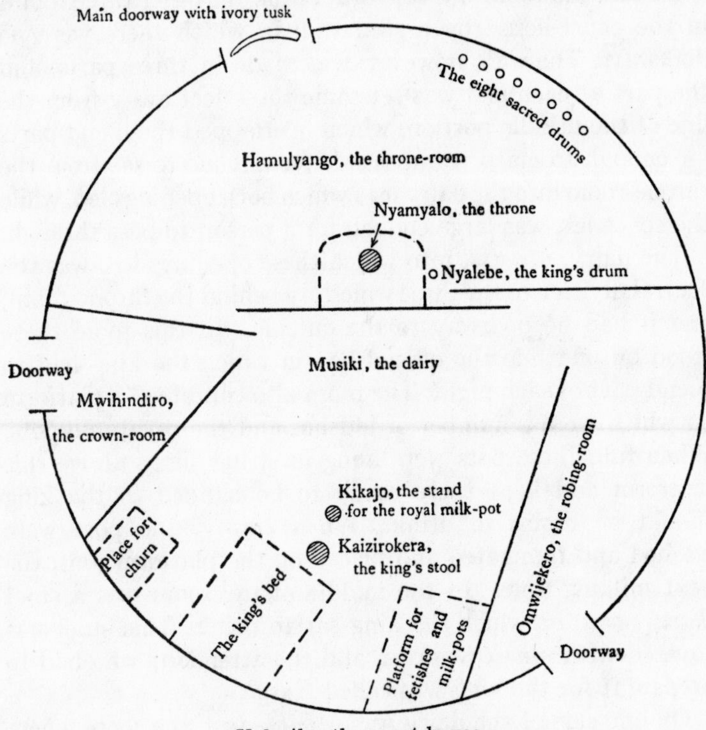

Kaluzika, the court-house.

night one on either side of it. These women were called *Abagarami*, and, though nominally wives of the king, had to be virgins; they were on duty for four days at a time, and should one be menstruating or should she have reason to consult a doctor, another had to take her place, for she might not go to the throne.

In addition to the throne there were in the throne-room nine drums, of which the ninth, *Nyalebe,* stood by the side of the throne. These were all sacred to the king and only he might beat them, but the ninth was especially his, for each king at his accession chose the special drum which was to stand near his throne, and which had to be a different drum from that of his predecessor[1].

The throne-room was separated from the other three rooms in the court-house by a reed wall in which there were no doorways. The wall, however, was made in three parts, and the part at each end was set some three feet away from the line of the middle portion, which overlapped these end parts far enough to make it impossible for anyone to see from the throne-room into the dairy into which both openings led, while the space left was large enough for a person to pass through.

The dairy, *Musiki*, into which these openings led, was the central division of the three which lay behind the throne-room, and it had no doorway to the outside. In this room there stood on one side the official bed in which the king had to spend part of each night. The room also contained a platform on which were a number of fetishes and the royal milkpots. When full, these pots were hung in string slings above this platform and kept there ready to be handed to the king should he desire to drink. When empty, the pots were washed and fumigated and placed on the platform until the next milking-time. In the middle of the room was a stool (*kaizirokera*) on which the king sat to drink. This stool was covered with nine cow-skins, and the attendant who had to prepare it for the king was called *Kasuli*.

On one side of the dairy was *Mwihindiro*, the room where the crowns were made and kept. This room had an opening to the outside, by which the king generally entered and left the court-house, using the front doorway, where the tusk lay, only on special occasions. On the other side of the dairy, also with a doorway to the outside, was the robing-room, *Omwijekero*, where the royal bark-cloths were kept and where the king went during the day to change his dress.

[1] The names of these drums were: Mugarara, Galisoigana, Mpugu, Musegewa, Lugonya, Tembalinda, Ramatanga, Munganjula, and Nyalebe.

In each of these rooms there was always a wife of the king on duty to guard the room and protect it from the intrusion of any unauthorised person, and also to carry out any instructions the king might give, the special duty of the wife who was dairy-maid being to supply the king with milk whenever he wished to drink. In all four rooms fires were kept burning in special stands of pottery during the night.

Next in importance in the royal enclosure was *Muchwa*, the queen's reception-room. This was the first hut in the line of seven huts of the Sacred Guild which stretched outside the royal enclosure and through which the king went in procession on ceremonial occasions. These huts had each two doors, one at the front and another opposite it at the back, facing through the courtyard to the door of the next hut, so that it was possible to pass and even to see straight through the huts from end to end of the row, and this was the path taken by the king when he went through. There were also gates in the fences which divided the courtyards of the huts, so that those who had not the right to enter the huts could make their way along the row by the courtyards without trespassing on forbidden ground.

The queen's reception-room, the first of these huts, was unlike any other house in the enclosure in that its doorways had doors which were closed at night. There were three doors, one in front opening into the royal enclosure, one at the back opening into the courtyard which separated it from the next hut, and a third leading by a short passage to a gate in the outer fence, which was the private entrance of the queen and princesses. Near this door was a platform with leopard and cow-skins, on which stood the queen's throne, a stool covered with a leopard-skin, a lion-skin, and a small cow-skin, which had to be white or nearly so, a few grey hairs being permitted but no other colour.

Opposite to the queen's throne was a pole, which was stained with blood and on which hung a rope. This was the place where offending princes and princesses, condemned to death by the king, were hanged.

Beyond the queen's reception-room stretched in a line the six other huts of the Sacred Guild each with its two openings, one in front and one behind, and its courtyard separating it from the next hut. Each hut belonged to a chief of the Sacred Guild who bore its name and had to be present in it when the king passed to perform the daily ceremony of herding the sacred cows. Fires were kept burning at night in all the huts, the floors were carpeted with lemon-grass, and in each was an earthen platform, two feet high, also covered with lemon-grass. In the courtyards of the second, third, and fourth of these huts the king might perform the ceremony of herding the sacred cows, if he did not wish to go all the way to the seventh hut, the courtyard of which was the special place of the sacred cows. The *Nkorogi* herd which supplied the milk for the king and his household entered the royal enclosure, when they came to be milked, through a gate in the courtyard of the first hut, and passed through the queen's reception-room to the court in front of the throne-room.

No child of the reigning king might enter any of these huts, the princes and princesses who went there being half-brothers and half-sisters of the king, and no woman might enter any of them beyond the queen's reception-room, into which princesses of the king's generation might go. A woman venturing to enter any of the others would be killed at once.

The second hut, *Kyamunuma*, was the hut of the princes, that is, the king's half-brothers, for his own brothers were excluded from the capital and his sons might not enter any of these huts. The reason for the exclusion of the king's full brothers from the capital is said to have been the jealousy of one king, for there was a time when the king's brothers visited him as his half-brothers did. One day, however, the king's mother visited him, wearing a bracelet which he coveted and asked for. She refused to give it to him, saying he could get one made for himself, and a few days later his brother visited him wearing the very bracelet. The king, seeing it, was jealous, declaring that it was evident his mother had a preference for this brother and that there would soon be

Royal fetish worn by king each morning when bathing

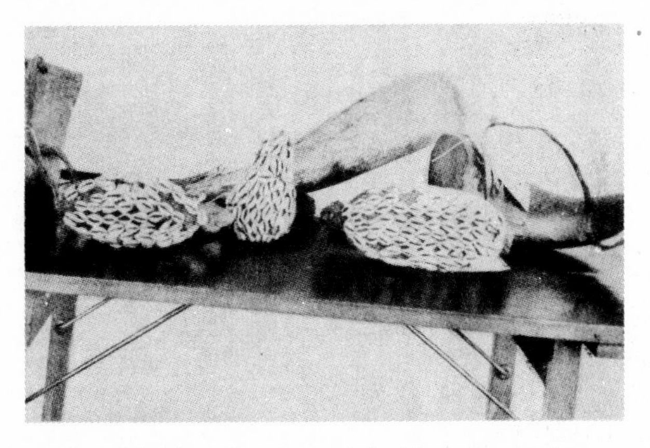

Royal fetishes placed round the king when bathing

Royal fetishes used in cases of sickness and to avert evil

Small drums and fetishes used at birth of twins

a revolt among the princes. He therefore sent a soldier to kill the brother, and from that time full brothers of the king went away into the country as soon as he came to the throne, and any message they wished to send to him was conveyed by a third party.

Princes might only enter their hut *Kyamunuma* when they had business to transact, and no prince might be there when the king passed through, so that it was empty except for the chief in charge.

In the courtyard of this hut was a stand for the royal spear, *Kaitantahi*, which remained here during the day and stood in the throne-room at night. The stand was only for emergencies, for the spear had to be held in an upright position while it was in this court; and if the man who held it had for any reason to leave the court, he was expected to summon someone to relieve him.

The third house was *Kyakato* and the fourth *Kitogo*, and into the courtyards of these no prince might go when the king was there. The fifth house was *Kamulweya* and the sixth *Kachumagosi*. This was known as the house which caused the brave to fear and tremble. Here it was that offending chiefs were brought before the king to be tried, and from it they were led to him in the seventh courtyard to have their sentence pronounced. No chief, however brave he had been up to that time, could find himself in *Kachumagosi* without trembling.

The seventh hut was *Lwemigo*, and the courtyard outside it was *Olugo*, which was even more sacred than the others. To it the king came on all special occasions, such as the new moon ceremonies and the coronation procession, and usually for the daily herding of the cows. Only the greatest of the land came here, and should any man have lost father or mother and be mourning, he might not enter. Attached to the fence of the courtyard was a canopy, *Omukaraiguru*, under which the king stood on rugs, and whenever he came here for any purpose the three cows which he daily herded had to be present.

There were a great number of houses in the royal enclosure for the king's wives, for most of them had their separate houses with huts for their attendants in the compounds. As the king had many wives, this meant a great number of houses.

When subjects of the king from distant parts came to visit him, he would assign to the most important of them a house in the enclosure in which to spend the night. These people came bringing gifts for the king: the Baganda brought bark-cloths and coffee, and the Bakedi ivory, cattle and beer, while the king in return gave presents of salt and hoes. Visitors from Buganda were housed in the hut called *Bamwenagaho* and those from Bukedi in *Banyoni*, while people of Kitara from a distance were sent to *Balwara*.

In one house, which was called *Kasenda*, there lived a woman with the title of *Mukaikuru*. The first holder of this title was said to have been a woman who was able to inform King Mpugu, the first of the present line of kings, when he came to the throne, of the necessary procedure in the accession ceremonies, the milk customs, and the new moon celebrations, for all the men who knew these matters had fled. In gratitude Mpugu created this office, the holder of which was always an old woman, and gave her the house *Kasenda* (v. Tradition and Folklore, p. 328). In the house there was a deep pit which was said to be there as a reminder to the king of the past, when his forefathers endured hardships on the east side of the Nile and had to live on grain which was stored in pits for safety. The floor of the house was smeared with cow-dung periodically, as was the custom in the better houses, and the work had to be done by princesses, for *Mukaikuru* was waited upon entirely by princesses. Only she and the princesses, her maids, might enter the house; and should any man or woman not of royal blood make their way in, he or she was killed at once and the body thrown into the pit. When the king left his enclosure to take up his residence in a new place, this pit was filled up before the house was burned.

Another house belonged to the sister of the king's mother, who was known as *Nyina Mukama Muto* (little mother of the king), and in it lived two women of the Mukwonga clan who fulfilled certain duties at feasts and at the ceremonies which took place after the birth of twins. Only one took part in these, but there had to be two on duty, in case one should be unable to officiate. They were regarded as wives of the king, but never bore children.

One house, called *Kapanapa*, was said to be specially built as a reminder of the condition of slavery in which the people once lived, and therefore only women of the serf class lived in it. The girl whose duty it was to sleep across the foot of the king's bed in the dairy lived in this house.

THE KING'S SERVANTS

There were in the country many small chiefs who were known as *Batongole* and were really superior servants of the king, whom he had rewarded for some special service by giving them estates and to whom he gave presents of slaves and cattle in lieu of pay. One of the duties of these chiefs was to supply the king with private servants for himself and his household. Not only could he call upon them for men to carry out the ordinary work of the daily routine, the gathering of fuel and drawing of water, the guarding of the gate, and so on, but they were also responsible for the building and up-keep of some of the smaller houses in the enclosure, and the king could demand from them men to undertake any special task, perhaps to act as messengers or even, it might be, to undertake some looting or plundering which the king wanted done quietly and expeditiously. Whatever the task was, they had to be ready to supply men to do it whenever the king wanted them.

The regular servants of the king who were supplied by the *Batongole* were:

(1) Drawers of water and guardians of the king's well. The king's water was drawn from his special well which was used to supply himself and his household only and had to be

guarded, for no water might be drawn from it except by these recognised servants. They had to keep both hot and cold water always in readiness night and day in case the king might call for it, and from this well they had also to supply the dairy-maid of the king with what she required for washing the royal milk-vessels, while the wives of the king were permitted to use the water for their personal needs.

(2) Fuel gatherers and keepers of the fires. These were members of the clan Bahemba, and six or eight of them had always to be ready for duty, for not only had they to gather all the firewood and other fuel necessary, but some of them were continually on guard over the fires in the royal enclosure to see that they were never allowed to die out. From this clan came also the two women who slept beside the throne at night, for the throne might never be left alone. A succession of women from this clan performed the duty in turn.

The gate-keeper of the royal enclosure was chosen from among the wood-gatherers and, while on duty, his official dress consisted of a skin robe knotted on the right shoulder and tied round the waist.

(3) Cooks. These might be chosen from any clan, but when one died his son succeeded to the office, which thus remained in the clan until there was some reason for a change. Each cook held office for a month, and was actually on duty for four consecutive days at a time, two of these being spent in purification and two in performing the duties of the office, the chief of which was to prepare and serve to the king his daily sacred meal of meat. The chief cook arranged the relays and each man might be called upon two or three times during his month of office, or he might, on the other hand, serve for only one period of four days. During the whole month the men had to live apart from their wives and all women and to avoid all abusive and obscene language and brawling. During the two days of service they had their faces, arms, hands, and chests smeared with white clay to show that they had been purified and were on duty.

The cooks also saw to the cooking for the people in the

royal enclosure, the king's wives, their maids, and other servants, but the king never had meat cooked for the chiefs, though he might present them with animals for food. The king did not see the food of his wives, which was sent direct to them, but, though in former years children were fed entirely on milk, it later became customary for him to send his children from time to time special meals prepared by his own cooks. This, however, was not a regular part of their work and was only done by his express command.

The beef used by the cooks for the king was from young bulls of the *Nkorogi* herd, yearlings, too young to have mated. The headman of each relay of cooks received a bull when he came on duty, and all the meat not required for immediate use was dried in the sun in order that it might last the month and even longer, for the next cook would use any that remained. Any cooked meat left over each day from the king's meal was eaten by the chief cook, who had to abstain from other meat for twenty-four hours thereafter.

As no cooking might be done in the royal enclosure, these men did their work outside in an adjoining enclosure and brought the food in. In later days the kings, instead of confining themselves to milk, began to eat vegetable and other foods, and it came to be a custom that cooked food of various kinds was kept ready for the king in a private house (*Ekyokya*) in the royal enclosure, to which he would come and call for what he wanted at any time of the day or night. Such meals were eaten in secret and no one was supposed to know anything about them. The food cooked and not eaten by the king was given to specially chosen wives.

(4) Brewers. The chief of these was *Bitagulwa*, who had a house in the royal enclosure. The king's beer was carefully prepared and kept in special storehouses in the royal enclosure, and *Bitagulwa* also kept a supply of beer which he dealt out to the king's wives.

Both millet and plantain beer were brewed for the king's use. There were no taboos or ceremonies connected with the plantain beer, but at every new moon and at the beginning of each new year the king had to drink millet beer to bring a blessing and increase the supply of grain. In old days the king was not supposed to drink any beer until evening, when he entertained his chiefs and might drink with them, but when he began to eat meals of vegetables and meat, beer formed part of them, a fact which was also kept secret.

(5) Keepers of goats, sheep, and fowls. The headman over all these was *Omukada*. The king himself was not supposed to eat any flesh except his sacred meal of beef, and no person who came into his presence might eat mutton. The sheep, goats and fowls were therefore kept for offerings, or for the use of the medicine-man when he wanted to take an augury. The headman, *Omukada*, had to be able to supply without delay an animal of whatever kind and colour the medicine-man demanded, and in order to have at hand a stock to meet all requirements, he went about the country carrying his staff of office, a large spear, and took possession of any sheep, goat, or fowl he needed. Should he find any person eating a fowl, he seized and fined the man, saying he was a thief who had eaten his goat, for, as people seldom ate fowls, he called the fowl a goat. He was also responsible for seeing that the animals were properly fed and kept in good condition for the use of the medicine-man. He might never enter the presence of the king unless accompanied by a servant with fowls.

The king also kept dogs for hunting, but these were looked after outside the royal enclosure by herdsmen or slaves, who brought them from time to time for the king to see.

(6) Herdsmen of the *Nkorogi* herd of sacred cows. These were men chosen from any clan and their chief was *Mukamisu*.

(7) King's Bodyguard. These were special police who attended the king and were taken from the agricultural clans.

(8) King's pages. Until quite recent times, only boys of pastoral clans might become pages to the king, but one of the later kings accepted the sons of serfs.

(2) KINGS OF KITARA AND THEIR DUTIES

Ancient dynasties—historical kings—severance of Toro from Kitara—Kabarega and the British—king Andereya—sacredness of the kings—milk diet of the kings—the king's day—rising—meeting the bulls—washing—greetings—milking the sacred cows—the milk-men—the herald—the milk-maids—the dairy-maid—the king's meal—the king in court—herding the sacred cows—visit of the queen—sacred meal of meat—the cooks—bringing home the cows—the king's milk—other meals—visits of princesses—entertaining cow-men—beer-drinking—inspecting the guard—bed—new moon procession and ceremonies—pronouncing judgment on chiefs—annual ceremony to bless the country—annual ceremony with the royal bow—beating the king's drums

It is impossible to get any reliable account of the early kings of Kitara, and though there are names given of kings who are said to have belonged to various shadowy and remote dynasties, yet no one can tell whether they really represent royal families of Hamitic stock who came into the country for a time and then left it or died out, or whether they are purely mythical personages. Some people say that the Bachwezi, who were divine beings and were represented by priests claiming to be descended from them, formed a dynasty of kings who reigned for a time and then departed from the country. Four other names are also given as being those of kings who formed one dynasty, but these are names only and nothing at all seems to be known of them: they are Hangi, Nyamenge, Ira, and Kabangera.

After these four shadowy personages, the information becomes a little more definite and it is possible to make a fairly continuous list of kings who seem to have had a real existence, though in some cases there is no information about them beyond their names. There are stories told about several of them, but these belong more to the realm of legend than of history and will be dealt with in my final chapter on Tradition and Folklore.

The following list gives the names of the kings, with, wherever known, the names and clans of their mothers:

1. Twale.
2. Baba.
3. Mukonko.
4. Ngonzaki.

5. Isaza, who disappeared leaving no sons and was succeeded by his Prime Minister.

6. Bukuku, Prime Minister to Isaza, who had no son, but whose daughter, Nyinamuiru, bore a son to Isimbwa, a man of the priestly clan of Bachwezi.

7. Ndahuru (Ndaula) Mucwezi, son of Nyinamuiru, who killed Bukuku in a quarrel about salt for the cows and became king.

8. Wamala (mother, Nyante of the Basengya clan). One version stated that Wamala, weary of the wickedness of his people, left the country taking all the princes with him. Another version named two kings who succeeded him, Kyomya and Kagoro, and states that it was Kagoro who left the country in disgust.

9. Mpugu Rukidi Nyabongo I (mother, Nyatworo of the Mukwonga clan) came over the Nile from Bukedi and became king. His clan was Babito, the present royal clan, and he was the head of the present dynasty.

10. Nyimba (mother, Nyagiro of the Banyagi clan).
11. Chwa I (mother, Nyaraki of the Banyagi clan).
12. Winyi Ruguruki (mother, Arapenyi of the Bananzi).
13. Oyo Kabambaiguru (mother, Nyagiro of the Bakwonga).
14. Olimi Ruhundwangeye (mother, Kindiki of the Bacwa).
15. Bikaju Kyebamba I (mother, Kindiki of the Basaigi).
16. Isaza Gabigogo (mother, Mpaija of the Babito).
17. Duhaga I, Mujuiga (mother, Kindiki of the Basaigi).
18. Nyamutukura Kyebamba II (mother, Kafunda of the Bacwa).
19. Mugenyi Jawe Nyabongo II (mother, Kajaja of the Bafunjo).
20. Kamrasi Kagoro Kyebamba III (mother, Kigiro of the Basito).
21. Kabarega Chwa II (mother, Kanyangi of the Bayagi).
22. Karukara Kitehimbwa (mother, Runyabwa of the Banyagi).
23. Andereya Bisereko Duhaga II (mother, Katabanga of the Basito).

In the reign of Nyamatukura a prince of Kitara, called *Kaboyo*, rebelled and fled from the country. He was taken into Buganda by a man Byakweyamba, who took him to Mutesa, then king of Buganda, and from there he returned to Toro and became a great chief. His son, Nyaika, continued to extend his power and left a son, Kasagama. When, in the year 1890, Captain Lugard (now Sir Frederick Lugard), the head of the Imperial British East Africa Company, made an expedition through Toro and along the eastern side of Lake Albert, to rescue the troops of Emin Pasha who had been left there leaderless, this Kasagama gave much help to the expedition, and in return was recognised as ruler of Toro, so that this portion of Kabarega's kingdom was lost to him.

In 1861, when Speke entered the country of Kitara, Kamrasi was at the height of his power. He ruled until 1870, and when he died his successor Kabarega spent several months fighting with his brothers for the throne. He was the last king to gain his throne by the old custom of fighting and killing all rivals. Emin Pasha spoke very highly of Kabarega, but this monarch had an inveterate dislike of white men and when, at the invitation of king Mwanga of Buganda, Captain Lugard and Mr Jackson, of the Imperial British East Africa Company, entered Buganda in 1890, Kabarega made much trouble by frequent raids on its borders. At length a strong body of British and native troops was sent against him; he was driven from his capital and for some years wandered about the country, constantly fleeing from the British forces. In 1897 Mwanga, having rebelled, was forced to flee from Buganda and joined Kabarega. Some months later both kings were captured and sent into exile. Kabarega fought bravely and was only taken prisoner when his right arm had been shattered and he could no longer fire his gun. His arm was amputated, much against his will, and he made a final attempt to follow the tradition of his ancestors and, when wounded, take his own life. The present king, Andereya, who was then a young man, had been taken prisoner with his father, and during the night after the operation, Kabarega compelled him to tear the bandages from his arm so that he might bleed to death. His plan almost succeeded, but the guard at the door, becoming suspicious, looked in and discovered what was going on. The doctor was summoned and the bleeding stopped. A soldier was placed in charge of Kabarega, and his son was removed to another room and placed under guard.

Another son of Kabarega, Karukara, was made king by the British but he proved to be an incapable person and after a few months was deposed and the present king Andereya, who has proved himself a satisfactory ruler, was set upon the throne. Before he came to the throne he had been under Christian instruction and had been baptized by the Protestant Mission of the Church of England, taking the name of Andereya, the native form of Andrew.

In the old days of the independence of Kitara, the king was an autocratic ruler; but he was more than that, he was the great high priest of the nation and was, in fact, regarded by the people as almost a deity himself. His person, his food, his clothing, his actions, everything connected with him was sacred, and he spent his life in daily intercession and ceremonies for the good of his people and the increase of the herds of cattle which constituted their wealth. Each day was filled for him with a succession of duties which had to be performed with the regularity of the sun, and there were guards who were responsible for seeing that each of these was performed at the stated time. So sacred was the person of the king that the very parts of his body were called by names which might not be used for ordinary persons; his weapons and other possessions, like those of the gods and heroes of ancient legend, had special names; his daily meals were ceremonies which were regarded as sacrifices for the good of his people, and when anyone handed anything to him, it had to be put in a kind of holder made of palm-leaf fronds, cleansed until they were perfectly white, and from this the king took it. There is no doubt that at one time vegetable food was absolutely taboo to the kings, who lived entirely upon milk and a very small quantity of beef. In later years they began to eat vegetable food, but this departure from established custom had, as previously noted, to be kept strictly hidden from the people, who regarded the meals of their king with reverence and awe. Until the introduction of Christianity, the kings did not dare to let their subjects in general know of these forbidden meals.

The king always dressed in bark-cloths and had a very large assortment of robes, which were almost all squares of bark-cloth some ten feet long by nine to ten feet wide. Some of these were white and some were dyed black, but the usual colour was brown, varying from a deep terracotta to a light yellowish shade. Many of them were decorated with geometrical patterns painted on them in black, but the most valued were those on which designs were painted with the blood of favourite wives and princesses, who did this work themselves, using their own blood and designing the patterns themselves. One bark-cloth often took many months to complete, for the amount of blood required was great. The king changed his robes frequently during the day and wore either one bark-cloth knotted on the right shoulder or two, one knotted on each shoulder. Round his wrists and ankles he wore single strings of beads and he also wore beads round his neck.

From the moment of his accession, the king was so occupied with his duties in the royal enclosure that, though he was free to leave it to go about the country and hunt, he was too busy to find time to do so. In his boyhood, like all princes, he had to learn the duties of a herdsman, and while he was thus engaged he acquired some knowledge of the country. After he came to the throne, he found that there was little or no time left for exercise and he soon became indolent and seldom, if ever, left the enclosure. His talks, however, with chiefs and the various people who came to see him enabled him to keep in touch with events all over the country, and his own herds of cattle were brought one at a time to the capital for him to examine them.

A description of a day in the life of the king will be the best method of showing the completeness of his absorption in the sacrificial ceremonies by which he brought prosperity to his people.

During the first part of every night the king slept where he liked, usually in the house of one of his wives, but about two in the morning he was awakened by a page, who led him to the court-house, for he had to spend the rest of the night in the official bed in the dairy, one of the divisions of the court-house. After he had entered this bed no one in the royal enclosure was expected to remain awake. As a rule the king slept here alone, but the queen came to this bed when she visited the king either at her own desire or upon his suggestion, and there was no rule forbidding him to take any of his wives with him if he so wished. Across the foot of the bed, in order that the royal feet might not be exposed or come in contact with the wood, slept a young woman, who was of the Abazazi clan and had to be a virgin. There were always two women of this clan who shared this office, for should one of them be menstruating she might not enter this room.

At cock-crow the maid arose from the foot of the bed and went round it to a place where a vessel stood ready. Into this she made water, and taking a small piece of bark-cloth, which was also placed in readiness, she dipped it into the urine. Coming back to the bed, she uncovered the king's feet, touched first one great toe and then the other on the underside with the bark-cloth, and covered them again, after which she retired to the house in the royal enclosure where she lived. This ceremony was called *kyonzire*[1] and was regarded as a purificatory rite, removing evil from the king in order that he might step forth without fear.

Two or three pages then announced to the court the fact that the king was awake by blowing on a kind of flute called *Nsiriba*, whereupon the royal and sacred spear, *Kaitantahi*, was removed from the throne-room, where it stood all night beside the throne, and was taken to a special courtyard where a man had to hold it upright, for it might never be laid down. The royal pages cried out "Hurra Mukama huraka bindo" which might be freely translated "Take heed, the king is awaking from sleep," and the king rose. He had to leave the bed at a particular place, for it was said that a king once hurt himself through getting out of bed on the wrong side. On the floor there slept a man of the clan Abasingo, and the king stepped over him as he left the bed. The chosen man was always very black, and the king when stepping over him was supposed to leave the darkness of night upon him.

[1] *Kyonzire* pl. *Byonzire* = anything offered in sacrifice alive and not for killing. Thus animals offered to gods or ghosts to be kept alive in temples or shrines were *byonzire*.

The king went first to the royal bath-room to which were brought various fetishes. On entering he seated himself on a stool and took from a page a special fetish; having touched his forehead and each shoulder with this, he spat upon it, and, rising from the stool, went to the doorway to meet two young bulls. These animals were brought to the bath-room each morning and soon got to know what was required of them, coming of their own accord as soon as they were set free from the cattle-pens. One of them, called *Ruhinda,* was black with a white forehead, the white being intended to drive away evil, while the other, *Lutimba,* was red and black. Each wore an iron bell round its neck as the sign of its office. The king took the black bull by the horns and, laying his head against its forehead, said: "Ruhinda nkyachi zireho ebibi" (Take away from me, O Ruhinda, all evil, magic, and enemies) or "Omunyamuomoso omugaiho" (Keep me from evil, magic, and enemies). Taking the second bull in the same way, he said: "Tenkatimbirwa ensi yange, bantu bange, amahanga" (Pour thy blessing upon my country and my people). He then released the bulls and they went away. If during this ceremony one of them made water, a page caught a little in his hand and touched the king's forehead with it, for it was said to bring blessing to him and to the land, and his prayer would be heard and answered.

These bulls were called the *Byonzire,* or living sacrifices, and were young animals, which had to be relieved of this office before they were old enough to serve cows. When they were considered full grown, they were replaced by two young bulls which were called their heirs. These new bulls were brought one morning together with the first pair, and should one of them drop dung before urinating while in the presence of the king, it was rejected and another had to be brought. When the king had inspected them he put his head first on that of the old bull and then on that of its successor, and the bell was removed from the neck of the one and put on the other. This was done with each pair and the old bulls were taken away to be killed; their mouths were tied, so that they could make no noise, and their throats were cut, a method of slaughter used only in the case of animals sacrificed to the gods. The men who were in charge of the bulls ate the meat during that day, but all they could not eat was burned with the skins and bones, for nothing might be left to another day, and no use might be made of the skins.

At the close of the ceremony with the bulls, the king returned to his seat in the bath-room and a fetish was placed on each shoulder, one between his feet, and one behind him, the last being a large cow-horn tipped with iron so that it could be stuck in the mud floor and stand upright. In the horn was water, and wives of the king and other women were always anxious to obtain this water after the bathing ceremony, for either drunk or rubbed on the body it was a most potent medicine which ensured pregnancy.

By this time two men-servants had brought hot and cold water, of which the hot was called the *male* and the cold the *female*, and one of the king's wives, having mixed them in a large gourd to what she considered the right temperature, poured some twice or four times over the king's hands and departed. Pages assisted the king to wash his hands and face.

The king's washing might never be done outside lest the gods should see him naked, and should any one ask for him during this time, the answer given was, "Halinaha mumabo" (he has duties).

When the washing was over the wife who had charge of the royal amulets and ornaments brought them and placed them on his neck, wrists, and legs, and the man in charge of the clothing brought a large number of bark-cloths from which the king selected one, donned it, and proceeded to the throne-room. On his way his pages and attendants greeted him, saying, "Balamya zonokali onogundu zonohokali" (Great king, you are better than all" or, more literally, "than hundreds," *onogundu* being herds of hundreds). His wives next came and either used the same greeting or said, "Arahizehota kurahikya" (Have you slept well?).

The people, gathered in the court before the throne-room, greeted the king with "Zonokali" or "Ngundu zona okali," which might be rendered by "The whole world is yours." This greeting was only used until noon, after which anyone who came into the king's presence did so without verbal salutation, merely inclining his head before sitting down, for officially the king did not receive visitors after the morning. When the king left the house, they said to him, "Hamulyango enzahire" (Go out safely); when he was going to sit down, they said, "Kahangiriza agutema" (Sit down in health); when he stood up, "Omubyemu agutama" (Rise in strength) and when walking, "Akyalo mbahira" (Go without fear, the land is yours).

When the king had seated himself on the throne, two cows were brought to be milked for his meal. He kept in the capital a special herd of eighty to one hundred cows for the use of the royal household. This was known as the *Nkorogi* herd and will be more fully described later (p. 113). Nine of the herd (eight cows and a bull) were specially sacred to the king. Of the nine, two, both cows with their first calves, one a cow calf and the other a bull, were brought before the doorway of the throne-room. The rest of the herd were allowed to wander about the royal enclosure while these were being milked.

The milking of these cows was a very sacred duty. It was performed by men who were prepared by purification and the observance of strict taboos. The milking of the cows was called *Kukorogi* and the man who did the actual milking was *Mukorogi*. This office of head milk-man was hereditary, and when a holder died, one of his sons was chosen to be his heir. If one of them died without a son but left a daughter, she would be called the heir, but in such a case she did not undertake the duties for the king, but went to be a servant to the queen.

Mukorogi's assistants were *Mugimbirwa*, *Mugurukizi*, and *Mbalabaisa*. They were taken from the Muhango clan, and a number of members of the clan held each office and performed the duties in relays. Several holders of each office, including that of *Mukorogi*, had to come to the capital for a month at a time and lived in special houses in the kraal of the *Nkorogi* herd which was opposite the main entrance to the royal enclosure. During the month they had to keep apart from women and be very careful in their language and conversation, which had to be most chaste; anything profane or abusive, or any offence against any of the regulations for their conduct was punishable by death. Each man was on actual duty for two days at a time, and he had to be purified and fast for the two previous days. They might not, while they were actually on duty, even see a woman and they had to be careful not to look at the king's wives who assisted in the milking ceremony. They might speak to no man outside their own company other than a near relative, and to him only if absolutely necessary. When they came on duty after the two days of special purification and fasting, they smeared their faces, chests, hands, and arms with white clay.

A boy herald (*Mutezi we ndulu*) drove the two cows to the place where they were to be milked. This boy had to be of the Batabi clan, though Kabarega broke through this rule and accepted boys of other clans. Two or three boys shared the office; each was purified for two days and came on duty for two days, for the taboos to be observed were so strict that they had to be relieved after this period. While on duty the herald wore the skin of a calf which had been killed at birth. The boy was too young to think of marriage or to have any sexual desires, but during his term of office he had to avoid playing with girls or even with other boys, lest he should be hurt, and he might use no profane language; he might lose no blood and therefore had to be careful not to walk where hidden thorns or sticks might prick or scratch him; his person was sacrosanct and no man might hurt him, for any harm done to him would affect the king. Should he fall sick whilst in office, he was sent away out of the capital to be cured, but should the sickness appear serious, he was killed by having the spinal cord severed by a blow at the

Rain-maker's sanctuary in forest. View of altar with spears in front

PLATE XIII

Rain-maker kneeling before altar in supplication

Side chapel in which water-pots are placed full of water or empty according to the need

base of the skull in the manner used for killing cows. His body was taken away by his relatives who were permitted to bury it.

Two cows, called *Nkorogi ya Muhango* (the cows for the king's meal), were brought to the throne-room doorway where some freshly cut grass was spread. Two wives of the king, both of whom were called *Bakurogesa,* now came forward. These were chosen wives, and were purified and whitened like the men. One of them carried a horn of water and a bunch of leaves or grass, while the other carried the milk-pots.

One cow was then brought to stand on the grass mat, and its calf, which had been tied up in the court, was loosed and allowed to go to its dam and suck. When the milk was flowing freely, the calf was pulled away and held in front of the cow. One of the men took the brush from the maid and cleaned the udder. The cow's hind legs were tied with a thong and its tail was held so that it could not whisk dust into the milk. The milk-maid with the water poured a little over the hands of *Mukorogi* who then held them aloft as if praying until all was ready for him to milk. He squatted at the right side of the cow and one of the men folded his garments under him so that they were out of his way and he need not touch them, for after his hands had been washed he had to be careful to touch nothing. The milk-maid placed a pot on his knees, bending over his shoulders to do so, for he might not see her. He milked as much milk as he thought fit into the pot, raised his hands again, and the milk-maid removed the pot by lifting it over his shoulders, and carried it to the dairy. The cow was then released and the calf allowed to complete its meal, while the second cow was brought and milked with the same ceremony. Should one of these make droppings during the milking-time, the milk was not used for the king for it was considered to be defiled; but if a cow urinated, it was hailed with expressions of praise, for that was said to bring blessing.

The milk-pots were handed over to the dairy-maid, another wife of the king, bearing the official title of *Omuwesengisa* or

Munyuwisa, who was purified and smeared with white clay in the same manner as the milk-maids, and had always to be a virgin. She had to be in constant attendance in the dairy to give the king milk whenever he desired to drink.

The holder of this office had complete charge of the milk-pots of the king, and no one but she might handle them. She had to wash and dry them before the morning milking; and after the morning milk had been drunk she had to wash them, dry them in the sun, and later fumigate them, a process which was called *Kuwitira* and was performed over a pottery furnace in which a particular kind of grass was burned. The fire was brought from the king's fire and the fetching and carrying of fire and water might be done by servants, but only the dairy-maid might touch the pots.

When she received the pots from the milk-maid, she put them on their special platform, and prepared everything for the king's meal. Then, coming into the throne-room, she knelt at the foot of the throne and said, "Luhango lutahiri" (The milk-pot has come). When she retired, the king rose and went to the dairy, and the door-keeper called "ahaha," and raising his arms added, "Araka kora Mukama atahiri" (Take heed and be silent, the king has gone to drink). During the milking there had been silence in the neighbourhood of the cows, and those who did not wish to stay had gone outside, but when the king went to drink there had to be absolute quietness within the enclosure. The people knelt down and covered their faces, and even to cough or clear the throat was forbidden on pain of instant death.

In the middle of the dairy there stood a stool (*Kaizirokera*) covered with nine white cow-skin rugs, which was under the care of a chief *Kasuli*, who had to put it ready and then leave, for only the dairy-maid might be present when the king drank. The king took his seat on this stool and the dairy-maid, purified and whitened like the others, knelt by him and handed him first a sponge, *Kikaraha*, on a handle, with which he wiped his hands, and then another sponge, *Kyahamingazi*, which was kept covered and with which he wiped his lips. The milk-pot was in a stand, *Kikajo*, which stood by the stool. The dairy-maid removed the cover of the pot, wiped its rim with a leaf sponge which lay on the lid, and handed the pot to the king. While he drank she held the cover before her eyes so that she could not see him and waved a fly-whisk, *Kihungyo*, to keep flies off him. As she might not look at him he had to let her know by making a sound with his lips, or by tapping on the side of the pot with his finger-nail, when he was finished. She took the pot from him and if he required a second, she wiped its rim as before and handed it to him. When he had finished, she handed him the mouth-sponge, with which he wiped his lips before rising to return to the throne-room. As he seated himself on the throne he made a noise in his throat and the door-keeper, hearing this, called "Mukama omusika orugirama" (The king has drunk and returned), whereupon the people might rise from their knees.

Two more cows of the special nine, called *Nkorogi ya Nyamutungo*, were then milked and the milk put aside to make butter for using on the king's person. The royal churn was called *Nyamutungo*, and the churning was done by women of the Balanga who were slave-women of the king. The other cows of the sacred nine were milked and the milk was put into special pots, some for the king's use during the day and some to be drunk by special wives of the king or otherwise used as he might direct. The nine cows then joined the rest of the *Nkorogi* herd, which were milked in their special kraal under the supervision of the head-man of the herd, *Mukamisu*, whose duty it was to see that the royal children, the king's wives, and the princes and princesses were all supplied with milk.

People might now come to greet the king and lay before him any cases for judgment. Important chiefs might enter the throne-room, where each had his special place reserved for him by payment of a cow. The king transacted business, heard appeals, and judged cases until about eleven o'clock, when the guard who acted as a sort of time-keeper told him it was time to herd the cows.

Before proceeding to this duty the king might change his bark-cloth, which he usually did several times during the day in the robing-room. Having done so he left the throne-room, and a strip of matting, eighteen inches wide, was spread out before him from the door of the throne-room to the door of the queen's reception-room. This mat was made of coarse grass stems and rolled up, so that when it was laid down and pushed, it unrolled itself and lay flat. No one but the king and one or two privileged attendants might walk upon it and it was rolled up again as soon as he had passed.

Whenever the king moved about the enclosure he was, as previously described, attended by a page who carried the royal sword, *Busitama*. Should anything offend the king he held out his hand, the boy silently placed the sword in it and the king cut down the cause of his displeasure. The page bore the sword, which was two edged, on his right shoulder and it was covered with a lion-skin. The head of the lion hung down in front of the page covering the sword which was attached to it by a piece of the skin cut like a thong and tied to the scabbard.

The royal band of flute players, the origin of which is described later, preceded the king from the throne-room to the queen's reception-room from which he went in procession through the seven sacred huts to the enclosure beyond the seventh where the three cows known as the *Amasajwa* awaited him. It was permissible for the king to have the cows brought to the courtyards of the second, third, or fourth huts, if he did not wish to go all the way to the seventh hut. While he passed through the huts his attendants went round them, and passing through the gates in the fences joined him in each courtyard. Mats, like that spread from the throne-room door, were unrolled across each court as the king went through and were rolled up again when he had passed. The queen was not obliged to be in her reception-room daily, though she had to be there on any special occasion, such as the new moon ceremonies; but the chief of each of the other huts, or his representative, had to be in his hut as the king passed.

In the court of the second house there stood, as the king passed, two men, one of whom carried the royal bow and arrows and the other the royal spear, *Kaitantahi*, which was brought here when the king rose in the morning and was taken back to the throne-room, preceded by a fire-pot (*ruswa*), after the cows were milked in the evening, and stood in a stand by the throne all night. When the king had passed these men and entered the third hut, the two men hurried round by the courtyards outside the huts to the place where the *Amasajwa* cows were to be herded. There they awaited the king and stood by him until he had accomplished his task, which was intended to bring blessing on the herdsmen of the nation.

The *Amasajwa* cows were three in number, a young bull, a heifer, and a fat cow. The name was taken from the young cow and means "not fully developed," and the animals had to be red or speckled reddish in colour, and were regarded as sacred. They must not be hurt or made to bleed, and if one of them fell ill it was killed at once. As soon as the bull or the heifer was old enough for breeding purposes or had mated, it was removed and another brought in its place (see Section (3), p. 115). The king stood and watched these, as if he were herding them, for a short time and then returned to the court-house which he entered by one of the smaller doors, passing through the dairy to the throne-room. He might turn aside in the dairy and refresh himself with milk but no notice was taken if he did so, for it was not an official meal and no one was supposed to know that he was taking food.

When the queen paid the king an official visit, which she did on all special occasions, she came to him on his return from herding the sacred cows, when she discussed with him questions relating to her estates and people and asked his advice with regard to any difficult cases.

The king was free from official duties for a short time after herding the cows and he might, if he so desired, leave the royal enclosure to hunt or walk; or he might rest or visit any of his wives, or attend to private affairs until nearly four o'clock, when he again made his appearance in the throne-room arrayed in fresh robes.

When he had taken his seat on the throne, the time-keeper informed him that the time had come for the royal meal, *Ruhango*. The king rose and, taking a drum stick, beat once on each of the nine drums which stood in the throne-room, ending with his special drum which stood against the throne. The beating of the drums was the signal by which the cook, who was already on his way, knew that the king was awaiting him; and the people in the royal enclosure were warned that there must be silence, for here again no person might even cough or clear his throat on pain of death.

As in the case of the milk-men, several persons shared the office of royal cook, *Mwokya*. Each dwelt in the capital for a month at a time, performing his duties for two successive days, after which he was relieved by a companion. For the performance of his duties the cook was purified; his face, chest, arms, and hands were covered with white clay, and he wore two bark-cloths, one knotted on each shoulder. The head-cook of each monthly relay, as he came into office, was given a young bull from the *Nkorogi* herd to be killed for the sacred meat. He had to dry some of the meat to ensure its keeping good during his time of office and even longer, for if there was any left the next man would use it. The skins of the bulls were appropriated by the men who killed them. They were always killed by having their throats cut, a mode of death reserved for animals intended for sacrificial purposes. The cook also might eat each day any meat left over from the sacred meal, but he had to refrain from other meat for twenty-four hours thereafter. The house in which the cooks dwelt was outside the royal enclosure, near the main gate, for no cooking might be done in the royal enclosure.

As the cook left his house to go to the king, he was accompanied by an assistant who carried a large basket, called *Kasingo*, containing meat and vegetable food covered with plantain-leaves. On the top of this stood a vessel covered with a bark-cloth in which was the boiled meat for the king. The cook walked in front slowly and solemnly, bearing the two-pronged fork with which he fed the king. They were not permitted to enter the royal enclosure by the main gate, but had to go round to the gate by which the sacred cows entered and proceed through the queen's reception-room to the throne-room. The cook entered without any greeting and knelt before the throne, while his assistant took the pot from the basket of food and, putting it down beside him, retired out of sight. The cook struck his fork down into the meat and, having secured a piece, put it into the king's mouth, for the king might not touch meat with his hands. Four times the cook repeated this, and if he should inadvertently touch the teeth of the king with the fork, his punishment was immediate death. When the king had eaten the four pieces, the cook covered the vessel and removed it.

The large basket was uncovered before the king who merely looked at it; the plantain-leaves with which the food had been covered were spread on the ground to form a cloth and the food was turned out on them. Either the king's pages or some young wives who had not yet been admitted to the king's bed were summoned by his orders, sat round this cloth and ate a meal before the throne-room in the sight of the king. The cook then returned as he came.

After this meal the queen, should she wish to do so, might come in her private capacity to visit the king before the sacred herd arrived for the evening milking. On this occasion she came without ceremony, accompanied by one or two attendants, and kneeling greeted the king, as all members of the royal family did, by touching him on the forehead with the finger-tips of her right hand, palm downwards, then under the chin, with the palm upwards. She sat down by the king's side until the cows came in to be milked, when she retired into the dairy until the first two had been milked and the king entered the dairy to drink. During the drinking of the milk she went outside and awaited the king's return to the throne-room, where she rejoined him and remained as long as she wished. If it was dark when she left, one or two of his torchbearers accompanied her to the gate, where she was met by her own attendants with torches.

The beating of the nine drums was the signal for the boy herald to leave the enclosure with several companions and go to meet the cows. The herdsmen brought the cows back from pasture to within a mile of the royal enclosure, and the boy met them at a point from which he could lead them to the enclosure without leaving the beaten track, so that there was no danger of his being hurt by hidden thorns or sticks in the grass. The two cows which were to be milked first for the king's meal were put in front of the boy, and the rest of the herd followed him. His companions led the way and some of the herdsmen followed the cows. As he went along the boy raised a shrill cry:

> Era akafwe efwe (if it dies, let it die).
> Era kahendeka ehendeke (if it breaks its leg, let it break it).
> Omwenzi wabyo aliho (the owner is present).

The people, hearing this cry, rushed from the path into side-roads or into the grass, for anyone who was found in the way as the cows were passing along was liable to severe usage at the hands of the herald's companions, who would not be punished even if they killed such a person.

The cows were driven up the hill and went in by the gate leading into the courtyard of the first oi the seven sacred huts, from which they proceeded through the queen s reception-room into the royal enclosure, the two in front being driven right up to the door of the throne-room where the grass mat was spread. The milk-men, who had remained in the kraal of the cows all day, awaited them with the calves, and the same procedure as at the morning milking was gone through. The milk was taken to the dairy-maid and the king retired to drink. After the milking the cows returned to their kraal by the way they had come.

Any of the king's milk which was left over at the end of the day was drunk by one of his wives who was specially appointed to the office, and who had to be careful how she lived and what she said. She was a virgin and when she was called to the king's bed she was replaced by another young wife. The mother of the present king Andereya held this office in her youth.

Though these were the only official meals of the kings they were expected to drink milk freely at other times and for many years they have been in the habit of eating vegetable and other food in secret. There was a special house, *Ekyokya*, in the royal enclosure where cooked food of various kinds was taken and kept hot so that the king might go there and eat when he felt so inclined. This meal was a secret one and no one knew of it but the man who looked after the food and one or two of the king's wives. One woman from the peasant class was in charge of the vegetable food while another brought the king beer from a house near that in which the food was eaten. The food was cooked outside the royal enclosure, for no cooking might be done inside; even the food for the king's wives and attendants was cooked elsewhere and brought in by a special entrance. The food, which might be millet-porridge or mashed plantain and beef, was served to the king, who ate standing, drank some beer and returned to his duties. These meals were never mentioned and no one was supposed to know about them.

After the evening milking the princesses, half-sisters of the king, might come to visit him privately. Should one of them be in the throne-room before the milking, she, like the queen, retired to the dairy and then went outside, returning after the king had drunk his meal. The king talked with any of his half-sisters in the throne-room and sometimes he would give one an estate or slaves, which always meant that he desired her to become one of his wives. Princesses whom he took to wife in this way did not necessarily come to live in the royal enclosure but were placed under special guards to prevent any of the princes from making love to them.

Sometimes the king entertained some of his cow-men in the evening. The men came before him and danced and sang their cow-songs, and for refreshment the king might order beer for them. This was brought in large pots by a wife, *Musengisa,* who was in charge of the beer. She might get some slave to carry the pot for her until near the king, but in his presence she had to carry it herself and had to be careful not to pass in front of him with it. This beer was drunk from the pot through tubes and not from any cup or vessel. One man drank at a time, while the others continued to entertain the king. Sometimes a chief would be present at these receptions, but they might not come except by invitation; princes often came, but they had to keep silence and were treated like ordinary cow-men. The king sometimes sat on a rug spread on grass to drink beer, while princes and cow-men had to kneel to drink. If any *Batongole* (small chiefs) of the agricultural clans were present, they might sit to drink.

Sometimes the king would present a man with cows on these occasions, and the man thus honoured had to kiss the king's hands as a confirmation of his ownership; if he did not do this, they might be taken from him.

Some of the more recent kings were in the habit of getting intoxicated in the evening at the beer-drinking and flew into violent tempers, so that it was necessary to soothe them. Their wives used every means to keep them calm, for at times they would injure or even kill a wife in their rage.

On other occasions some of the chiefs would visit the king to talk over matters of state, or he might go to see some of his wives until he was tired, when he would retire to a secret meal. During some part of the evening the king invariably wandered about the enclosure to see that all was well, and late at night he inspected the guards. The object of these parades was to see whether the guard was doing its duty, for, though it was permissible for the men on guard to lie down and even to sleep, they were expected to be sufficiently on the alert to challenge any passer-by. The king carried his spear and was accompanied by a page who bore the sword *Busitama* and his knife. When they passed one of the men on guard, the king stepped over him; if the man was asleep and did not hear him, the king usually pinned him to the ground by driving his spear through his ear and head. If, however, the man was not killed at the time in this manner, he would be warned next day that, if he was thus caught sleeping a second time, he would not escape. If the man was awake, he caught the king by the leg and refused to let go. The king would whisper "Loose me," but the man held on, saying, "Who are you who walk here by night?" and would not let go, until the king told him who he was. The next day the king would send for that man and reward him for his watchfulness with a cow.

Having finished his round the king retired to rest in one of his houses, probably with one of his wives, until the time came for him to go to the official bed in the dairy, when a page roused him. On his way to this bed he sometimes drank milk and the dairy-maid had to be in attendance to serve him. He then slept in the official bed until dawn, when the girl rose from the foot of the bed and anointed his toes.

Special Ceremonies of the King

New Moon Ceremonies

When the new moon was due, a watch was kept for it from the top of a mound in front of the gate of the royal enclosure. Here a priest stood with a drummer, and round them were the royal bandsmen with drums, flutes, and other wind instruments. Hundreds of people assembled round the mound.

When the moon appeared, *Bamuroga,* the principal chief and head of the Sacred Guild, went to the king and said, "You have outlived the moon and your people are a fighting people and rejoice with you. May you conquer." The king went to the door of the throne-room where he pronounced a blessing on the country, after which he sent word to the priest that the band should strike up and the festivities begin. For seven days the bands played, and dancing and rejoicing went on in the royal enclosure; then everyone adjourned to the enclosure of the king's mother for a day, and to that of the chief medicine-man for another day, making nine days in all. Inside the royal enclosure, in front of the king, any man might dance, but no woman who was not of royal blood; women of pastoral or agricultural families had to dance outside. The royal bands had to play continuously during this time except for a short rest between six and seven o'clock in the morning, when they snatched a little sleep. One or two at a time retired for food or rest, but the music might not cease.

When the appearance of the new moon had been proclaimed, a man was caught and taken away secretly. His throat was cut and the blood brought to smear the royal fetishes. These were brought out into the enclosure and shown to the king in front of the throne-room where the sacred cows were milked.

During the night on which the new moon appeared, the king might drink no milk, but only millet-beer, to bring prosperity to the land.

On one of the days of the ceremonies, the king, after he had drunk the morning milk, retired and changed his bark-cloth for the special robe and crown of the Sacred Guild. When he was ready he returned to the throne-room, left it by the main entrance where the ivory tusk lay, and walked on the royal mat to the queen's reception-room. At the door of the throne-room he was met by a number of attendants. One, *Enzini*, wore a crown decorated on the top with red feathers from the wing of a grey parrot; he might not enter the throne-room but waited outside until the king appeared, when he walked backwards before him on the royal mat, singing songs, for which he used what words he liked, to ask a blessing on the king. With him went another man, *Omugazi*, who carried the royal decorated staff. Accompanying these two were two or three drums, which had a special rhythm, and the royal band of flutes under the leadership of *Musegu*. This band consisted of about twenty players who served in relays; they were serfs but possessed estates in the country, where they lived when not on duty. When one of them received from the king a gift of a cow or a woman, he kissed the king's feet and not, as was usual, his hands.

Four other men also awaited the king here. Three of these carried the royal spears, called *Mahere*, *Kaizireijo*, and *Mutasimbulwa*, while the fourth carried a kind of two-toothed rake, *Olukandula*. To one tooth of this was hung a small bag, *Embibo*, containing seeds of small millet and semsem, while the other tooth had a tuft of *Ensaso*, a kind of tow or tinder for carrying smouldering fire. These emblems were to show that the people were once in bondage in Bukedi on the east of the Nile and had to cultivate the earth. These men walked backwards before the king as far as the queen's reception-room and then went round by the courtyards of the huts as the king went through the huts and met him again at the last courtyard. Here they stood with their emblems till the king set out on his return journey, when they went round the outside of the huts again and met him as he came out of the queen's reception-room.

As the king passed through the huts, the queen had to be present in her hut with her sisters. As she heard from the noise of the flutes that the king was approaching, she rose from her throne and took her place at the head of her sisters. Each princess, beginning with the queen, greeted the king by placing the tips of the fingers of her right hand on his shoulder with the thumb turned into the palm and then, turning her hand palm upwards and bending the fingers slightly, she touched him on the arm between the shoulder and the elbow. No words were used and the king passed on without any sign.

In the courtyard beyond the queen's reception-room was the man with the sacred spear, *Kaitantahi*, which was held upright here when the king was on duty during the day and stood in a special stand in the throne-room during the night. Here also was the man with the royal bow and quivers. Both these men left the courtyard after the king passed and hurried round to meet him in the seventh courtyard.

In the other huts there was no one present as the king passed through for the New Moon ceremonies, for the chiefs had all to await him, robed and crowned, in the seventh courtyard.

Against the fence of the seventh courtyard there was a canopy, *Omukaraiguru*, under which the king stood with his chiefs on either side. Ten to fifteen minutes were usually spent here, and the king might decide upon some expedition, or he might confirm the sentence in one or two cases which had been tried before but were awaiting the pronouncement of his final decision. The accused chief who was awaiting sentence was brought forward by *Omugazi*, the bearer of the king's staff, who supported him as he came. If the king permitted the man to kiss his hands it meant he was pardoned, but if his hands were withheld, the man knew that judgment had been given against him and he might expect death.

The king then returned to the throne-room and the queen came to visit him officially. Her sceptre was brought and placed before the throne and her rug spread by it. She discussed any official business she might have with the king until he rose to leave, when she followed him out of the throne-room, taking precedence of all the chiefs who were present, a sign of her superior rank.

At some time during the ceremonies which greeted each new moon the king offered a white bull, and a chief, *Kasalo Muluma of Kidume*, stood by him as his herald. As the king spoke a prayer and words of offering, Kasalo shouted them at the top of his voice to the people.

Annual Ceremony for blessing the country

Once every year the king performed a special ceremony to bring blessing upon the country. This lasted two days and, like all religious ceremonies, began in the evening. The chief priest with three assistant priests, three chiefs, of whom *Bamuroga* was the head, and the queen were the only persons permitted to be present during the whole of this ceremony, though another wife of the king had to be present at one point to carry a pot of beer.

After the king had drunk the evening milk and the *Nkorogi* herd had been milked, a white cow, a white sheep, and a white fowl were brought before him, and he looked at them to see that they were in perfect condition before he accepted them for the ceremony. The priest, who had already examined the animals, took them away and guarded them during the night, and in the morning, after the milk ceremonies had been attended to, he brought them again to the door of the throne-room. The cow, then the sheep, and lastly the fowl were killed by having their throats cut, and the blood was caught in a vessel. The right shoulders were cut from the cow and the sheep and the meat cut into small pieces and cooked.

Meanwhile the king stood at the door of the throne-room, holding the spear, *Kinegena*, and looking on in silence. When the meat was cooked some was put on the spear and he raised it up towards heaven with the following prayer:

Ai Nyarwa omulira hai igulu (god, hear me in heaven),
Amagufu ne gakuku (the ruler of living and dead),
Ompe kumera okuuhita ntunge (enable me to increase and surpass all),
Nzale mpangule amahanga (to have children and surpass the nations),
Nekali no kusinge (to remain the conqueror).

The priest next handed the king two bunches of sacred herbs. These he dipped into the vessel of blood and repeated a prayer, sprinkling the blood upwards.

A wife of the king, a woman of the Mukwonga clan, now came with a pot of beer, the priests carried the pot of blood and a basket with the cooked meat, and the king went to four places within the royal enclosure. At each place he put down a little meat, took some of the beer in his mouth and blew it over the meat, which he then sprinkled with blood.

The party returned to the throne-room and for the rest of the two days the king did not transact any business and saw no one except those who had taken part in the ceremony. Even the princes and princesses might not see him, and during these two days he drank no plantain-beer, only beer made from millet, and used only the wooden pot *kisahi* not the earthen pot *bubindi*. The priests and chiefs who accompanied him ate the meat of the cow and sheep during the two days of the ceremony, and the skin and bones and everything left were burned.

Annual ceremony of "shooting the nations"

About the beginning of each year the king took his royal bow, *Nyapogo*, with four arrows, and shot one arrow towards each of the four quarters of the globe, saying, "Ndasere amahanga kugasinga" (I shoot the nations to overcome them), and mentioning, as he shot each arrow, the names of the nations who dwelt in that direction. The arrows were sought for, brought back, and placed in the quiver for use on the next occasion.

Beating the king's drums

Once in every six months, at the appearance of a new moon, some special drums of the king were beaten. The chiefs were notified and had to be present at the ceremony, which took place about two in the afternoon, and great crowds of people gathered for this drumming. The king sat on his throne wearing two white bark-cloths, and the chiefs were expected to wear their best robes. Four drums were brought before the king, and he was asked which should be beaten, whereupon he took two drum sticks and beat on the first, second, third, and fourth, and then beat them again in the reverse order and named the one that should be beaten.

The rhythm of the drums was interpreted as beginning with "Enemiro" (be bewitched) and going on to say, "Nations, what do they want? We stand like men because the king is here."

When the cows came to be milked in the evening the drummers went away until the king had finished his meal, when they returned and one put his drum on his neck and went into the throne-room before the king, beating it. The king took the drum from him and beat it two, four, or six times, as he felt inclined.

that game-pits which might be dangerous to the herds were filled up. The king's men were directly responsible to their own head-man and the herds were brought to the capital in turn for the king and the head-man to inspect. They might have to remain in the capital sometimes as long as two months, but more often they left again after about a month.

Each herd had its chief herdsman with men under him and he made kraals in different parts of the country, wherever he considered that the cows flourished best. Each kraal contained as a rule about one hundred cows, though at times under exceptional circumstances as many as two hundred might be collected in it for a time. It was considered best for the health of the animals that there should not be more than one hundred in one kraal and one bull was considered sufficient to satisfy the needs of a hundred cows. It thus came about that the usual term to designate a hundred cows was, and still is, *onugundu*, a bull. The chief herdsman of a herd, though responsible to his head-man, looked upon the cattle over which he had charge as his own and his heir inherited them when he died.

There was always a herd of cows in the capital under the care of the herdsmen of the capital. These were either gifts, for chiefs were daily visiting the king and giving him cows, or the result of raids which had been made upon adjacent tribes. These remained in the capital until they had been separated out according to their colour and sent to their proper herds. From these, too, the king took animals to be given to chiefs or servants as presents or rewards, or to be used for food for his household. For his own sacred meals young bulls, yearlings from the *Nkorogi* herd, were used; but his wives had to be supplied with food, and daily presents were required for services rendered by men in different parts of the country.

Salt for the King's Cows

When the king's cows needed salt, the cow-men might rob any bearers of salt as they brought it for sale. Only the king's herdsmen were allowed to do this and no punishment was inflicted if it was proved that the salt had been used for the king's cows. The herdsmen of the *Nkorogi* herd might even make the cows of a chief leave the salt-water which was prepared for them in order that the *Nkorogi* cows might drink it.

More often the king, when short of salt, would choose a cow and send it to Kibero, the great salt-works, by special messenger. When they reached Kibero, the animal was killed at the chief's house, and the messenger feasted on some of the meat. The rest was cut up into small pieces and, with the bones, which were broken up, and the contents of the stomach, was made into little packets. These were thrown into the various houses of the salt-makers with the information that the king required salt. The men then brought their loads of salt and placed them at the house of the chief. The messenger sent it to the king who put it into his store for the use of his cows. The Bahuma who herded the king's cows had access to the king's store when they required salt for their herds.

(4) SICKNESS AND DEATH OF THE KING

Treatment of sickness—the royal spear represents the king—the nurses and guards of the sick-room—king's poison—death of the king kept secret—preparation of the body for burial—preparations for civil war—announcing the death—mourning—the fight for the throne—new king claims the dead king's body—burial of the king—care of the tomb—ceremonies of the tomb

The duties of the king were looked upon as of such importance that only an illness which made him absolutely unable to move about would warrant his leaving them undone, and he would attend the necessary functions even if he had to be supported. If, however, he were quite unable to do so, he would send to represent him the royal spear, *Kaitantahi*.

There was in constant attendance in the royal enclosure a medicine-man whose duty it was to give advice to the royal wives and their attendants. Within the royal enclosure no one except the king might lie ill; even if the malady was only catarrh, this medicine-man was summoned and had the patient removed at once, lest the king's health should be affected.

If the king showed any signs of illness, his chief wife, who was always ready to detect anything amiss, enquired into the cause, and, if it was a simple ailment such as a cold, she would summon the attendant medicine-man and take steps to put matters right at once. When, however, this medicine-man realised that the king's sickness was not yielding to his treatment, he called in others to assist him. Every medicine-man of the land had to obey the summons of the chief medicine-man if called upon to help with advice or drugs. Then auguries were resorted to and were taken daily over water, fowls, goats, sheep, or even cows, and every effort was made to discover the cause of the sickness and the proper treatment to adopt, for the medicine-men were aware that not only was their reputation in danger but their lives hung in the balance. A word from the king expressing doubt of their ability or zeal might cause them to be put to death and they were therefore indefatigable in their efforts to restore him to health.

One peculiar feature of the treatment was that, if the medicine-man resorted to cupping, all the wives in the royal enclosure were operated upon in the same manner and on the same part of the body. Another treatment in common use was blistering; and if the king was blistered, each wife had a blister made on the same place to show her sympathy with him and, by sympathetic magic, to help him. Then, when the king was convalescent, his wives visited him and were careful to show him the marks which proved that they had shared his sufferings.

The king was never said to be seriously ill, but to have a cold. His immediate attendants alone knew his real condition and they might not reveal the state of affairs to any outside person. His illness was called *Kusasa*, a slight ailment. At the time when the cows should be milked, or when they had to be herded, the king went to them and performed his duties, even though it was a pain to him to do so and he could with difficulty sit through the time of milking. If he was unable to get about at all and could not attend to these functions, he might not sleep in the court-house, but went to another house, either *Kabagaramu* or *Karuhonko*, for he might only be in the court-house when he was able to perform his official duties. When he ceased to do so, two drums (named *Ntimba* and *Nsego*) were carried with a royal spear, *Ruhango*, in procession, following the great royal spear, *Kaitantahi*, to the "herding" of the sacred cows, and thus the wives and people in the court knew that the king was ill and could not come out. Otherwise things went on as usual: the cows were milked and the milk carried in as though the king were there to drink it, but it was left in the pots until it was time to cleanse them, and then a special wife drank it. The meat was brought in the afternoon by the cook. The great royal spear *Kaitantahi* was placed in the throne-room to represent the king; it stood there when the sacred herd was milked and was then taken to see the sacred cows herded, after which it was brought back and placed in the throne-room until the king recovered and resumed his duties.

The chief medicine-man and the chief wife of the king were in control of the entire procedure and treatment of the patient, and the chief nurse was *Nyina Muto* (little mother), that is to say one of the sisters of the king's mother. His mother might not come, for she was regarded as a king herself. Other wives assisted in the work, and *Bamuroga* and other chiefs of the Sacred Guild kept watch. *Bamuroga* was head of the chiefs in all matters concerning the king and the country. Under the king he managed all the civil and political affairs of the nation. He and the head-man of the royal clan, *Munyawa*, shared the responsibility of government when the king was ill or when he died, and together they transacted the business of the nation. *Bamuroga* also had charge of the place of the tombs of the kings. The people who were in close attendance on the king were the only persons who were supposed to know anything of the real state of affairs. It was even concealed, as far as possible, from the wives who assisted in the nursing, and no information was allowed to spread outside the house of sickness.

In olden times it was unusual for the king to lie ill for any length of time: he would call his medicine-man and from him obtain a cup of poison which he drank and which ended his life in a few minutes. In more recent times a king only took that step when he was wounded, especially if it were in battle and if he were bleeding freely. For a long time now, indeed for several generations, the kings have ceased to lead the army and therefore have not resorted to the poison-cup, but have died natural deaths.

When the king died, it was not made known for some days and only those in attendance knew that death had taken place, that, as they said, "Kutuza," he "slept." The information was not allowed to pass beyond the house in which he lay. The daily milk was given by the dairy-maid to the young wives appointed by him to drink it while he was ill and they drank it without knowing the real state of affairs.

A young cow, called *Mugabuzi*, that had her first calf, was brought from the *Nkorogi* herd. She stood on the special carpet of spear-grass (*nsenke*) and the milk-man squatted on her left side instead of as usual on the right, and took a little milk from her, which was poured into the dead king's mouth, a ceremony called *Kugabula*. This cow was never milked again, but was reserved for the funeral rites, and her calf had all her milk until then. The cow was kept near the body each day when she came in from pasture, and she went with the funeral procession to the grave, where she was killed and eaten.

The king's head was shaved and his nails pared by a special wife of the Bakwonga clan. Old-fashioned beads, called *enta*, were put on his neck, wrists, and ankles, and his amulet for longevity was put upon him. His hands were placed under the right side of the head, his knees were bent up under his chin in the squatting posture, and his body was tightly wrapped in white bark-cloths. A young bull from the *Nkorogi* herd was killed and its skin wrapped round the body over the bark-cloths and stitched together to exclude the air. The meat of the animal was eaten by the servants who made these preparations, and they had to remain in the courtyard of the house in which the body lay and keep apart from other people. The body was placed on a bedstead and kept from two to six days until everything was ready for the announcement of the king's death. *Bamuroga*, with a chief *Nyakoka*, took charge of the body and set a guard, and it was their duty to prevent the news from getting abroad. The chief bull of the *Nkorogi* herd had its scrotum tied to prevent it from mating with the cows and it was kept thus until after the funeral when it was killed to end the mourning.

During the time before the public announcement of the death, the chiefs arranged as quickly as possible to have the young princes and princesses removed from the houses of their guardians in the capital to their country residences where they might be safe. This was done for the sake of national security in order that none of the princes who were fighting for the throne might capture a princess and perform any illegal purificatory rites. The king's herds were also taken to a distance for safety. When all these precautions were complete, the chiefs informed *Bamuroga*.

A fawn-coloured cow with its calf was then brought to the house where the body lay and a special milk-pot of wood, called the king's *kisahi*, was filled with its milk. An appointed servant took this pot and went to the top of the house. He stood on the pinnacle and called out, saying, "Amata gazaini" (the milk is spilt), and threw the pot to the ground. The guard of *Bamuroga's* men who were on duty there broke the pot, caught the man as he descended and killed him on the spot. The cow and calf were killed and the skin of the cow, with the broken pot and two white bark-cloths belonging to the dead king, were burned. The body of the servant who had announced the death was carried outside the capital and buried.

As soon as the cry, "the milk is spilt," was heard, all the women in the royal enclosure raised the death-wail. The widows put off their ornaments and good clothing and wore their oldest garments. The people in the enclosure did not wash, and allowed their nails and hair to grow untrimmed, paying no attention to their personal appearance but giving themselves up to wailing and mourning until the funeral took place. Only the royal family and the clans related to the king and the greatest chiefs took part in the mourning. The rest of the people in the country went about their business or assisted one or other of the princes in their fight for the throne.

The chief *Bamuroga* assumed authority and conducted all national business until the new king was proclaimed.

There was always at least a general understanding as to which prince a king wished to reign after his death, and that prince was ready to assume the place. Most of the chiefs would stand by this prince, by which the others knew he was the chosen of his father, for this was the only way in which he was distinguished from any other who might claim the throne. He had to prepare for trouble, for rarely did a prince ascend the throne without opposition from at least one brother, and he had to be prepared to meet any claimant in battle and prove his right to the throne as the stronger man, the victor in battle. A prince had always the assistance of the chief who had acted as his foster-father from his birth, and the smaller chiefs, the herdsmen, and the agricultural peasants took sides and joined the prince whom they favoured. There was a general rush to arms; fighting began at once and continued until one of the rivals was killed, when all his followers submitted to the victor and became his men. It seldom happened that more than two princes fought for the throne, the others would look on and accept the result of the combat. Sometimes, however, several would claim it, and whatever the number of rivals might be, the fighting would not end until only one of them was left alive. Had Kabarega died as king of his country under this regime instead of being deposed by the British, there would have been much fighting, for the princes who might have laid claim to the throne numbered about a hundred.

Before the fighting began the rival princes each sought out his mother from among the king's widows and carried her away to a place of hiding in the care of some chief. A mother who knew that her son would fight for the throne would herself at once try to escape from among the widows in the royal enclosure, for the mothers whose sons were rivals would seek each other's lives. The mother of a prince who fell was always killed by the order of the mother of the victorious prince before the new king was proclaimed. Fighting princes would often endeavour to steal some of their father's young widows for their own use. A successful prince would also often take some of his father's young widows who had never been called to his couch and make them his wives.

The fighting among the princes might last only a few days while sometimes it would go on for weeks and even months. Those peasants living at a distance who took no part in the conflict went on with their daily duties as though the country were at peace. The pastoral people, however, had to be ever on their guard lest their herds should be captured and used for food by one or other of the armies. As a rule the herds were driven away to some distance from the scene of strife and were fairly safe. Still, watchful care was necessary on the part of the herdsmen, for at any time a marauding party from one of the armies might come down upon the herds and carry them off for the army. As there was no king to rule the people, anyone with the power to do so would steal and plunder.

When Kamrasi, father of Kabarega, died, Kabarega fought fully a year. Kageya was the mother of Kabugumira, Kabarega's rival, while Namutengumira Kanyangi was Kabarega's mother. A chief Mbogo was with Namutengumira armed with guns, and he fought and drove away Kageya; she was then caught and killed by Kabarega, who himself later killed Kabugumira at Lukindo.

Bamuroga was kept informed of the progress of the conflict and was ready to give up the body to the right prince when he came for it. He and the members of the Sacred Guild, who took no part in the fighting, guarded the body from any usurper, for the successful prince had to come and claim the body and bury it before he could be proclaimed the rightful successor. There was little delay, for the victorious prince would come at once on the death of his rival, claim the body and take it to the place of the tombs of the kings which was in a certain part of the Bugangaizi district. All the kings were buried there save one, who was buried in Muruli. There were no sacred grave-yards except that of the royal tombs; other burial places were left and soon forgotten.

Before the funeral procession started, however, the king-elect called the chief medicine-man and told him to ascertain by augury the best site for the new royal enclosure. No new king could rule from the throne-room of his predecessor, but he had to select a new site and build afresh. The chiefs and their men set to work and built a new temporary enclosure during the absence of the king at the funeral, and the old one was burned down.

There was little sorrow for the late king after this lapse of time, though his successor and the people observed forms of mourning. Crowds of people accompanied the procession as though going to war, but they went in silence and slowly, taking four or five days on the way. Certain women went with the funeral, including the mother of the dead king, his queen, two chosen widows, and a number of other widows. A large number of chiefs, accompanied by their retainers, both pastoral and agricultural, also followed.

Bamuroga and his assistant, *Nyakoka,* with their men, had to set out before the procession, *Bamuroga* bearing his staff, for his was the duty of choosing the site for the grave, which was called *Gasani.* A large house had to be built and in it the pit for the grave was dug and prepared by the time the funeral procession arrived. Large numbers of men were set to work, for the house had to be built, the pit dug, and the earth carried away before they were permitted to rest.

When the procession reached the grave there was mourning

beside it for two or three days. The grave was lined with cow-skins, and upon these bark-cloths were laid, and in the middle a pile of bark-cloths formed a bed. The body was placed on the bed and covered with a bark-cloth, and the two widows who had been chosen went into the grave, raised the bark-cloth and lay down one on either side of the body, covering themselves as if in bed. One of the women chosen for this honour was from the Bakwonga clan and the other from the Balisa clan. They were covered with bark-cloths and died either from suffocation or starvation. Some people affirm that a chosen woman sat in the grave, the head of the king was laid in her lap, and she also was covered with the bark-cloths and remained there.

The grave was filled with bark-cloths and no earth was put on it. Round the edge a kind of border of beaten earth was made and this was all that kept people from walking into the pit. The floor over the grave was carpeted with grass and there were curtains of bark-cloth round the grave. One widow of the Bakunga, a branch of the Ngabi clan, was appointed to be in charge of the tomb. Ten or twelve other widows were sent to help her, and *Bamuroga* and his people were responsible for seeing that it was kept in repair. The ex-queen might not be one of the widows in charge of the tomb but was reduced to a rank little higher than that of the other princesses and retired to an estate in the country.

The dead king's spear and walking-stick were placed in the tomb with a basket which held his bead anklets and bracelets. His hair and nail-clippings, which were always kept, were buried with him.

Ceremonies of the Tomb

At or about the time of year when the king had been buried, the reigning king told *Bamuroga* to prepare a feast for the departed king. *Bamuroga* chose a poor man of the Babito clan to impersonate the dead king, and the man so chosen lived in regal state in the king's tomb and was called by the name of the monarch he represented, for he was said to be the old king revived. He lived in the tomb, was feasted and honoured, and had full use of the women of the tomb, the widows of the old king. The king sent him presents and he sent his blessing to the king, the country, and the cattle. He distributed gifts of cows belonging to the king as he pleased, and for eight days lived like a king. When the ninth day came he was taken away to the back of the tomb and strangled, and no one heard anything more about him. This was an annual ceremony.

Each year a number of cows were sent to the tomb of the last king and presented to him. These were sacred offerings and were killed at the grave by having their throats cut, a mode of death reserved for sacrificial animals. The ordinary method was to kill cows by a blow with an axe at the base of the skull. The blood of these animals was allowed to run over the grave while the flesh was given to the men and women caretakers.

(5) ACCESSION AND CORONATION CEREMONIES

Purification—the mock king—proclaiming the king—the crown—guardians of the crown—the king's dress—the prompter—the coronation procession—visiting the king's wives—the royal bow—overcoming the nations—bearers of the royal bow and spear—consulting medicine-men and priests—the "coming of the shield"

When a new king, having defeated and killed all his rivals, had buried his father's body and returned from the funeral, he could not at once take up his possessions and duties, for he had to go through certain purificatory ceremonies before he could be crowned. These took place in a temporary royal enclosure built during his absence at the grave, for the old one was destroyed by fire when the body was taken away.

The purificatory rite took place two or three days after the royal party returned from the grave and was performed by a princess chosen by *Bamuroga* and *Munyawa*. It was not an office gladly accepted and indeed the chosen princess usually undertook it weeping and begging that some other person might be selected, for she was afterwards sent away into the country and might never come back or see her brother the king again, but had to live away from the joys of the capital and the company of the other princesses. The ceremony of purification was called *Kutezi enoni* or *Kutukuza*, and the princess was called *Omutezi wenoni*.

A vessel of water was brought from the royal well by a youth who had to be in robust health and whose parents were alive and well. This boy went at dawn to draw the water and bring it to the gate of the royal enclosure. On his way from the well he had to be careful not to look behind him but keep his eyes fixed on the goal of his journey, where he found medicine-men and chiefs awaiting him. The chief medicine-man had white clay ready to mix with the water, and he handed the vessel with the mixture and two bunches of sacred herbs, made up of three native plants, *mwetango*, *nyawera*, and *musogola*, to *Bamuroga*.

The new king stood with his brothers and sisters in the court where the sacred cows were milked before the throne-room. Herds of cattle were brought and crowds of people came not only to see the ceremony but to be purified and receive a blessing. The chosen princess was given the two bunches of herbs which she dipped in the vessel, and, closing her eyes, she sprinkled the princes and then turned towards the cattle and people, sprinkling them also. To purify the land she waved the herbs and sprinkled the water towards the four quarters of the earth. When she had finished, she opened her eyes and said, "I see such-and-such a place," naming the place she had decided to ask for as her future home. Thus she sprinkled amid the darkness of death and opened her eyes to the new life, which for her was one of exclusion. The place she named became her freehold, and she was taken away to it and lived there during the reign of her brother or until her death, for she was never again permitted to come to the capital or to see her brother the king, though she might if necessary communicate with him by messenger. Should she outlive the king, she was strangled when his

Interior of Muchwa house (Queen's reception-room) showing post on which princes and princesses were hanged

Royal spear which personified the king.
It might never be laid down but always kept upright

Announcing the appearance of the new moon

People assembling in the Royal Enclosure for the New Moon festival

death was announced. Should she die first, another princess was chosen as her successor, but she might see the king and might outlive him without being put to death.

During this ceremony the king was present as a prince, for a young brother was persuaded by the chiefs that he was the chosen king and was placed on the throne. This boy was called *Mulagwa*, and during the ceremony he stood, robed as king, by the tusk at the door of the throne-room. He then returned to sit on the throne and a man came to make formal announcement of the death of the late king, using, however, words which indicated sleep and not death, which was never referred to directly. *Bamuroga* sent to the Bahanyusi clan, a branch of the royal clan, who chose one of their number to perform this duty, the man chosen being called the man to *kusemirana*, that is, to announce the death. When he had performed his task, he was given a present of cows and slaves, both male and female, and returned home in great pomp, escorted by crowds of people. From his clan the king might never take a wife, though other princes were not thus restricted.

The real king and the chiefs came to *Mulagwa* as he sat on the throne, offering him gifts and paying him honour. At the crowning of the present king's predecessor, Kabarega, the traditional ceremonies took place. On his return from the funeral his young brother Olumi was taken by *Bamuroga*, who told him that he was to be the *Mukama* or king, and all the chiefs agreed. The boy, however, knew what was intended, for he said, "Do not try to deceive me. I am not king and you only mean to kill me." Kabatongole, a princess, was brought to purify all and then the prince was placed on the throne and the chiefs brought presents. With them came Kabarega bringing a cow, and *Bamuroga* asked him, "Where is mine?" to which he replied, "I have brought it to the lawful person, the king." *Bamuroga*, pretending to be filled with anger at this slight, struck Kabarega with a cord on the arm, whereupon the latter went out in wrath, collected his warriors, and returned. *Bamuroga*, seeing them approach, said to the young prince, "Kabarega has come to fight," and, when the boy wanted to run away, he caught him, took him to the back of the throne-room, strangled him and buried him in the building. This boy-king was always chosen and killed during the ceremonies in order that death might be deceived and the real king secured from any evil that might attach itself to him during the rites or that might not be completely removed by the purification.

When the real king took his seat on the throne, crowds of the chiefs and better class people pressed forward, wishing him long life and congratulating him. The head of the royal clan, *Munyawa*, and the head of the people, *Bamuroga*, caused a herald, *Mudumi*, to announce to all the assembled crowds the fact that the new king, whose name he proclaimed, was the son of Mpugu and of the whole list of kings, whose names he mentioned, down to his father, the last king. Should this herald make any mistake in repeating the list, he paid the penalty with his life, for he was speared down on the spot. When he had completed his statement, the people raised the cry "Zonokali," which was a royal greeting and meant, "You are lord of all."

The crown of the king's father was handed to *Munyawa*, who stood by the king and placed it on his head four times, leaving it each time for a moment and then raising it. He paused and repeated the actions, placing the crown on the head of the new king eight times in all. This crown was then handed to a caretaker and a new crown, this time his own, was placed on the king's head.

Each king had his own crown, which was different from those of all his predecessors. These crowns were made by an expert who did his work in the room in the court-house where the crowns were kept. The outer part was made from the white fronds of palm-leaves and the fibre of the bark of a tree known as *Mukondwa*. This bark was wrapped in moist plantain fibre and buried where it would decay. When the pulpy part had rotted, the fibre was gently combed and brushed with wooden instruments. Princesses took these cleansed fibres and gently chewed them, a few at a time, to soften and clean them. They were then rubbed with another kind of fibre, called *mukomo*, until they were white, when they were either plaited into cord or twisted into fine thread and dyed different colours. The woven frame of the crown was made of this fibre and of palm-fronds, and was an open ring six inches wide, slightly narrower at the top, and lined with bark-cloth. On this frame beads and other decorations were stitched with the fibre thread, which was strong and white. The crown had a chin-strap covered with the long hair of the colobus monkey, which looked like a beard and hung to the waist. These skins were obtained from the eastern side of the Nile where the hair was longer than on the animals in this part of the country. Round the edge of the crown of the reigning king were eighteen eyeless needles of iron, brass, and copper, called the *Amasoke*. They were all six or seven inches long and two, made of iron, had twisted ends and were known as "the males." The needles were taken out each time the crown was put away by the caretaker. The crown itself was called *Muhundi*, and the man who made it *Omuhundi*. Some six crowns of past kings still exist but others were lost during the struggle against the British some twenty to thirty years ago.

On the coronation day, the king appointed two women from his mother's clan, who were called by him "little mothers," to take charge of the crown. They were also guardians of the king's nail and hair-clippings and had to cut his hair and nails whenever necessary. These were kept in a special bag or basket in which had also been put the stump of his umbilical cord, his first teeth when they came out, and the six teeth which were extracted at the initiation ceremony. Only one of the women was actually on duty at a time, the reason for there being two holders of the office being that one must always be able to be in the king's presence; should one of them be ill, owing to menstruation or any other cause, she might not approach the king. They were nominally wives of the king, but they might not bear children, and the king rarely called one of them to his bed; should one find herself with child, she had to procure abortion. They were also nominally in charge of the milk-pots, that is, they had to see that they were properly kept and new ones made when necessary, though the king himself generally gave the orders. The woman on duty wore an amulet to bring long life to the king.

After the crown had been placed upon the king's head, and the people had proclaimed him king in the presence of any princes who might still be alive and of all the princesses and the important chiefs, the company left the court and the chiefs made their way to the seventh court of the sacred huts. They had to go to their own homes first to robe and put on their crowns before going to meet the king in this court.

The princesses left the throne-room first and took their places in the queen's reception-room, into which only princesses of the king's own generation might enter, that is, only his father's daughters. There the princesses awaited the king as at the new moon ceremonies, though, as the queen had not yet been appointed, there was no one on the throne.

When the chiefs had left the throne-room the king retired, donned fresh bark-cloths, and had his crown put on his head and royal shoes, *Biganja*, on his feet. Round his ankles were strings of blue beads with fringes of beads, and round his neck a string of white cord, made of the same fibre as the crown, on which was hung a pair of lion's claws forming a crescent. In these claws was put a special medicine to protect him, and they formed a fetish which might be worn by royalty alone. On the first day of the coronation ceremonies he wore only one string of beads on his neck, but after that he wore a number of them.

Through all the ceremonies of the coronation there stood by the king a prompter, who was a woman chosen from the Bakwonga clan and was called *Mukaikuru*. This office was said to have been created by Mpugu, who was the first of the present line of kings. He came from the eastern side of the Nile and, being ignorant of the peculiar milk ceremonies, had to learn the whole of the cow-customs and all about the drums and other ceremonies, and only one woman was able to tell him. He was so pleased that he created this office (v. Tradition and Folklore, p. 328) and built her the house *Kasenda*.

When he was robed the king proceeded in procession, as at the new moon ceremonies, through the seven sacred huts to the courtyard of the seventh, where he stood under the canopy while the chiefs ranged themselves on either side and the three sacred cows stood near. The presence of the king here signified that he was accepted as king by the chiefs as he had been accepted by popular acclamation before.

After standing for a few minutes under the canopy, the king returned through the seven huts, resting in the third or fourth court, and sat in the throne-room until the time came for his daily ceremonies. All the chiefs crowded in, bringing presents of cows and calves, and swore fealty to him, and in return he bestowed presents and chieftainships.

On the next day he wore his crown and went a round of visits to all the houses in the royal enclosure and saw all his wives. Each wife gave him a present of a cow and a calf or a string of beads. When he reached the house *Kapanapa* he was given millet, beans, and semsem, which he threw in four directions. This house was supposed to be a reminder of Bukedi, from which country Mpugu, the founder of the present dynasty, came, and of their old state of serfdom there. On this day all the princes came to greet the king and he appointed the prince who was to be their chief.

A royal drum was beaten at stated times for nine days after the coronation.

The royal bow *Nyapogo*, the story of which is told elsewhere in this book, had to be restrung at the coronation. Whenever a new king came to the throne, the Bahinda clan gave a man to supply from his own body new sinews for this bow. For two days this man was purified, wore charms, and was dressed in two white bark-cloths. He kept apart from women and had special food. He himself directed the operation of having the sinews removed from his right side, but was said always to die soon after the operation. It was an honourable office which the victim never shrank from accepting. Along with the man's sinews were used those of a white yearling bull. The bow itself was decorated with brass and copper wire, and stood behind the throne.

When it had been restrung it was handed to the king with four arrows, and he shot these, one towards each of the four quarters of the globe, saying "Ndasere amahanga kugasinga" (I shoot the nations to overcome them), and mentioning as he shot each arrow the names of the nations in that direction. The arrows were sought for, brought back, and placed in the quiver for the next occasion, for this, which has been described before, was an annual ceremony, taking place about the beginning of the year.

With the bow there stood behind the throne two quivers called *Nda ya Mpuna* (the stomach of a pig), for they were made of the skin from a pig's stomach. These were produced with the bow at the coronation, and afterwards, whenever the king went in procession through the sacred huts, these weapons were carried to the door of the princes' house, *Kyamunuma*, where the king saw them. Their bearer stood there with the bearer of the royal spear, *Kaitantahi*, until the king had passed, and then both went quickly round the outside of the huts and stood again before the king as he entered the last courtyard. The bearer of the bow and quivers was a man specially sent for the purpose by an uncle of the king, officially known as *Mweganyuwa*. A number of men shared the office, for there were many taboos to be observed. The period of each man's duty was two days and during that time he must not see women, use foul words, or lose his temper. The bearer of the spear too, like the holders of many other offices connected with the king, was only on duty for two days at a time. No prince or member of the Babito or royal clan might touch the bow or quivers or the spear.

Three months after the coronation all the medicine-men were called to discover by auguries whether all was well with regard to the safety of the king. To each of the two great priests, *Kyagwire* and *Mihingo*, the king sent two calves, a bull, a cow, two beads, two bark-cloths, two hoes, and if he wished to do so, he added goats and sheep, two to each man. The cows sent to *Mihingo* had to be black, and those to *Kyagwire* red on one side and white on the other. The king sent his blessing with the gifts, which were given in order that prayers might be made to the gods for blessing on him.

After the rites of accession were thus finished, an army was sent out on an expedition which was called "the coming of the shield."

CHAPTER VI

THE ROYAL FAMILY

(1) THE QUEEN

Marriages of princes—queen a half-sister of the king—appointment of the queen—insignia of the office—confirmation of appointment—drinking the sacred milk—adultery of the queen—the queen's reception-room—attendance at ceremonies—visiting the king—the queen's enclosure and estates—the queen's messengers to the king—illness and death of the queen—appointment of a successor—informing the king of the death—a widowed queen

A PRINCE who became king was invariably married before he came to the throne, but he could not make his favourite wife queen, for that office might only be held by one who was a princess and therefore his half-sister. Union between a prince and his full sister was looked upon as incestuous; but princes often took their half-sisters (daughters of the same father and different mothers) to wife and, though such unions were not in any way punished and were even connived at by the king, there was no marriage ceremony and the princesses were regarded as paramours and not as wives. When a prince became king, however, one of his first duties was, with *Bamuroga*, the principal chief, and *Munyawa*, the head of the royal clan, to appoint one of his half-sisters to the office of queen, and the ceremony of her appointment was also a marriage ceremony, after which she was recognised as the king's wife.

The king's marriage to his queen was the only ceremony of marriage a prince ever went through, though any prince might, in addition to his half-sisters, take as many wives as he liked. When a prince took a wife, however, he did so without any ceremony beyond the payment of cattle whose value was equal to or even greater than the ordinary marriage-fee, and the girl went straightway into his harem. The children of such an alliance between a prince and one who was not his half-sister, that is, not a princess, were recognised as legitimate and were legal heirs to his property besides being entitled to any other benefits which might accrue from their parentage.

The king's first duty on coming to the throne was to bury the body of his predecessor, and he had then to go through a series of purificatory rites before he could choose his queen. When the day came for this, the half-sisters of the king gathered together in the queen's reception-room, the first of the seven sacred huts, to which the king proceeded from the throne-room. He was accompanied by many chiefs, most of whom waited outside, while he, with the two chiefs *Bamuroga* and *Munyawa*, entered the hut and announced in an audible voice the name of the princess chosen to be queen. The throne stood ready on the platform, and the queen-elect was assisted to it and took her seat on it in the presence of all her sisters. Two insignia of office were next brought to her. One of these was a long iron spear with two sharp points like a two-pronged fork, which was stuck in the ground, with the prongs upwards, near a pillar in front of the throne on the right-hand side; the points of the spear were protected by a neat roll of palm-leaf fronds, cleansed and bleached until they were perfectly white, and on one prong hung a little basket for coffee-berries. The other emblem was a knife of a particular pattern, named *Mukyo we kitobi*, which was laid on the platform near the queen, who was not yet permitted to hold it. She was also given a four-headed spear, which was intended for real use, for her new office carried with it estates and subjects and she had power of life and death over all her people.

When he had seen the queen placed on her throne, the king returned to the throne-room and sat on his throne. In a short time the queen was escorted to the throne-room by the chief who had brought her up (for both princes and princesses lived from birth with chiefs under whose charge they were) and also by *Bamuroga*, who bore before her the two-pronged spear and stuck it in the ground before the king. The knife was left in the queen's reception-room lying by her throne. A servant spread a cow-skin rug near the spear and upon this the queen took her seat. A cow and a calf, which the new queen had sent for from her old home, were brought to the door, and *Bamuroga*, pointing them out to the king, said, "The queen has come to ask for the hands," using the queen's new title, by which she was thenceforth known, *Mugole wa Muchwa* (the bride of the Muchwa house). Being permitted to kiss the king's hands was a symbol of confirmation in office, and the favour must be granted from the throne. The king, casting a glance at the cow and calf, extended both hands palm upwards, and the queen, kneeling, took them and kissed them. She was not expected to speak, but rose from her knees and walked backwards to the door of the throne-room, where she turned away and was escorted to her own new enclosure, which had been prepared in advance. This was always built on the open space in front of the royal enclosure to the west of the gate and was, like the royal enclosure itself, of a temporary character, for, after all the ceremonies and taboos of his accession were ended, the king would remove to a new royal enclosure of a more permanent character, and a new residence was built for the queen close to it.

Six months after her installation the queen had to perform the ceremony of drinking the sacred milk, a form of oath-taking which had to be gone through by every chief of the Sacred Guild. Until this time the queen, even though she had been confirmed in her office by kissing the king's hands, was, as it were, on trial. Should she prove herself unworthy in morals or in temper or by inability to manage her estates, she would be deposed and another half-sister of the king appointed in her place. The ceremony of drinking the sacred milk meant a special dedication of the person to the service of the king. It was like the oath of blood-brotherhood but even more comprehensive, for the person taking it became completely bound to the king for life and pledged his life for the king.

Before the ceremony the queen had to prepare a great number of presents for the king and the people who were in attendance on that occasion. On the appointed day the king ordered that a bowl of milk from the sacred cows should be set aside in a wooden bowl (*kisahi*) which was specially made for the purpose, for even the queen might not drink from the king's vessels, nor might she use the bowl which was kept for the chiefs on their admission to the Guild.

The king went in state to the queen's reception-room, where the queen was presented to him by one of his wives who had charge of the milk for the ceremony. This wife held the title of *Mulanga* and, though not a princess, was on this occasion present in the queen's reception-room. Outside the house stood a cow and a calf which the queen had brought as a present for the king, and *Mulanga*, pointing these out to the king, told him that the queen asked for milk to drink. The king ordered her to bring the milk, and she handed it to the queen, who drank nine sips from it, nine being the perfect number, paused for a few moments, and again took nine sips, making eighteen in all. She then approached the king, who presented his hands to her, and she knelt and kissed them, being thus fully confirmed in her office. On this occasion she was formally presented with the royal knife which till this time had remained beside her throne. As the king handed it to her, he solemnly informed her that, if she did wrong or made wrongful use of her rights and power as queen, it would be used against her to kill her. During the whole ceremony and until sunset of that day, the queen had to remain silent. She was attended by a maid who supported her and helped her along as if she were sick and faint, for the ceremony was supposed to be too impressive for her to stand unsupported.

From the king's presence the queen was conducted to her own enclosure, where she sat in state and was congratulated by her sisters and friends. As she left the royal enclosure every door was closed against her and triumphal arches, each of which was a barrier, were erected along her route, and her attendants had to deal out presents lavishly to the men who guarded the arches and to the keepers of the gates. In her own enclosure her own people likewise barred the way and had to receive presents. The reason for this was not merely the desire to extract gifts, but the necessity of impressing upon one and all the immensity of the boon which the king had been pleased to grant her and of exalting the office to which she had been raised.

The *Mulanga* followed the queen, carrying the milk-pot with the milk which had been left over. This had to be drunk by an elderly woman of the Bakwonga branch of the Babito clan, which was the royal clan. In the evening, as the cows returned from pasture, the queen called one of her maids and pointed out to her a good cow and calf. These became the property of this maid who from that time was considered to be specially devoted to the service of the queen and did not leave her throughout her life. The *Mulanga* stayed a few days with the queen and was then given a cow and a calf and returned to the king carrying the special wooden pot which had been used for the milk. She told the king what gift she had received from the queen and the king presented his hands for her to kiss, which was a token that she might retain the cow and calf which the queen had given her as her own property.

At the end of two or four days (it had to be an even number), the queen came to the king with a cow and a calf. When she came she had to observe certain taboos. There must have been a good fire in her hut all night; no baby might have been born in her enclosure; no alarm call might have been raised during the night; no chickens might have been hatched; no dog might have had pups; no person might have sneezed in her presence; and, when she set out, the first person she met on her way must be a woman or she must return and await a more propitious day. This bringing of the cow and calf ended the ceremonies.

Of old it was customary for the king to have his queen often to his bed, but for long it has been an accepted rule that the queen never bore children and that she was always at the king's disposal, as she could not be if she was with child or nursing a baby. There was no law forbidding her to have children by the king, but the custom was for her, should she find herself pregnant, to take drugs and bring on abortion. When the king wished her to come to his bed he sent a secret message to her and she came privately to him in the evening by her special entrance through her own reception-room, bringing with her one maid who awaited her in an adjoining chamber. In the early morning she would quit the royal enclosure as secretly as she entered it and only the gate-keepers at her private gate and the people in attendance on her and on the king knew that she had been there.

If the queen was discovered to have committed adultery with one of her brothers, she was deposed, deprived of all her wealth, and sent to live in some distant part of the country under the charge of a district chief.

The queen's official reception-room was the house, *Muchwa*, where she was present on any state occasion and where her sisters came to sit with her. Only princesses of her own generation might enter this house, the reigning king's daughters and the sisters of the last king were alike excluded. It was not necessary for the queen to be in attendance in her reception-room daily, though the king passed through it every day to herd the sacred cows, but on special state occasions, such as the new moon ceremonies, she had to be there with some of her sisters to greet the king. On such occasions she entered the hut by her private entrance at the side, which was guarded and opened only to her or her messengers. Her throne was placed in readiness for her and her sceptre was carried in front of her. She sat on her throne until the flutes announced that the king had left his throne-room, when she rose and stood by the door ready to greet him with the ceremonial royal salute on shoulder and arm which has already been described (New Moon Ceremonies, p. 109).

On ceremonial days, and regularly twice every month, the queen had to pay the king an official visit. She waited until he had returned to the throne-room after herding the sacred cows, and went to him there in state. Her sceptre was borne before her and stuck into the floor, and a royal rug was spread, on which she sat surrounded by attendants. When the king rose to go to other duties, the queen preceded all the chiefs and returned to her own enclosure. She came back to see the king in the afternoon, after he had eaten the sacred meat, but this time she came unofficially and accompanied only by two or three attendants. Entering, she greeted the king by touching him on the forehead and under the chin with the tips of her fingers. She sat on her rug by his side and talked to him until the cows came to be milked, when she retired to the dairy. When he came to drink she went outside until he had finished and then returned to the throne-room, where she might sit as long as she wished. If it were dark when she chose to leave, some royal attendants with torches accompanied her to the gate of the enclosure, where her own attendants, also bearing torches, met her.

In addition to her throne and reception-room in the royal enclosure, the queen had her own enclosure, which was always in front of the royal enclosure a little to the west of the main entrance. Here she managed her own establishment much in the style of the king's, though she had no sacred cows. When she became queen she inherited certain estates belonging to her office which she took over from her predecessor, who was her aunt. She inherited some cattle, but there was no sacred herd, so that those which became nominally hers were in fact the property of the men on her estates. From the pastoral people on her estates she could take each year a percentage of their cattle, though she could not take cattle from anyone in the country as the king could. Whenever she gathered this tax she had to give one cow to the king. At other times also she might send a demand for cattle for the use of her household to any of her people. On her estates there were also agricultural people who could be called upon for building and other work, but they were not tied to the land and were free to leave if they liked. She had power of life and death over the people on her estates and held her own court where she tried cases.

Though it was not necessary for the queen to visit the king

daily, she had two special messengers, a man and a maid, one of whom had to go every morning to greet the king from her. These messengers were allowed to enter by the queen's private entrance and were admitted directly to the king's presence. If the man was sent he went to the door of the throne-room and, kneeling before the ivory door-sill, he bowed his body twice, keeping his eyes fixed upon the king. The king looked upon him but made no reply. The man returned to the queen and reported that the king was well, that he had had a good night, and that he enquired how she was. Should the maid, who was called *Njijeza*, be sent, she entered the throne-room and, kneeling near the king, said, "Mugole wa Muchwa antumire nti orihizota?" (The queen has sent and asks how you spent the night). The king did not reply but looked down upon the maid, who, after a few moments, said, "Nagenda" (I wish to go). The king looked upon her again, and she retired to report to the queen that the king was well and sent greeting. Should the king be unwell and wish to communicate the fact to the queen, the messenger was not told this from the throne nor in the throne-room, but was led into another house to receive the message.

When the queen fell ill she was cared for by her own attendants, who sent for the royal medicine-man to see her in her own enclosure. Every remedy was tried and if she died she was treated in most respects like a prince: her head was shaved and her nails pared and the hair and nails afterwards buried with her; her legs were bent up into the squatting position and her hands placed together palm to palm under the left side of her head. In this she was treated differently from other princesses, whose hands, like those of men, were put under the right side of the head. The reason for this was that the queen was the only princess who was lawfully married. She was the wife of the king, while other princesses were never officially married, though they might be in every respect wives of the king or of their other half-brothers. The queen's mouth was opened and some milk from a cow chosen from her herds poured into it. This cow was kept and killed during the mourning. The ornaments of her office were taken from her and small bracelets and anklets of beads put on her. Her body was wrapped in bark-cloths and then in the skin of a young bull, the meat of which was given to the men who made the preparations. When the body was ready for burial it was placed for a few minutes on the queen's throne.

The news of the death was conveyed first privately to the king who was informed: "Mugole wa Muchwa atulise" (The queen sleeps), and he sent men to dig the grave in whatever place he appointed. No one was ever buried in the capital, though the body of a poor herdsman might be thrown into the grass for wild animals to devour. The queen was buried in the house of a man on one of her estates and the owner of the house was given a present to compensate him for the inconvenience and to show his position as guardian of the grave, for he continued to dwell in the house and had to keep the floor intact over the grave.

The king shaved his head for the death of the queen and for that of any near relative, but otherwise might show no sign of mourning. The mourning of friends and relatives for the queen went on for four months and at the end of that time the heads of the Babito clan chose several women of their clan, and the king, with *Bamuroga* and *Munyawa*, made the final choice of a successor to the dead queen. The new queen had to go through the same ceremonies as her predecessor, and when she had been formally installed she had to send to the king an official announcement of the death of the last queen, as every heir to property had to do. The ceremony was called *Kubika*, and was performed at the death of princes, wives of the king, and chiefs. In the early morning one or two messengers were chosen who were fleet of foot. These men took a bull and, starting about five o'clock, drove it towards the royal enclosure. When it had reached the entrance they shouted "So-and-so has left the king and gone to the king of the dead" (Afulire Mukama ayihongire Nyamiyonga). This cry was an insult to the king, showing that death had been too powerful for him and secured one of his people. When

Drums being carried for the New Moon ceremony

Drummers awaiting the signal to begin the dance
at the New Moon festival

cases and though she was at liberty to ask for the king's advice, she was also at liberty to put her subjects to death, merely informing the king of what she had done.

She often supplied the king with suitable girls for his harem, and the king placed some of his wives with her to be looked after. When one of these wives had been to live in the royal enclosure and found herself with child, the king's mother was responsible for her and sent her to one of her own chiefs. He had to care for her and then to take complete charge of the child as one of the king's chiefs had to do when the king put a wife in his charge.

Daily a servant of the king's mother went to the royal enclosure to ask for the king and to carry any messages. The woman, who was called *Njijeza* like the queen's messenger, asked, "Nyina Mukama orihizota" (The king's mother asks how you spent the night). The king did not reply. After a pause, the maid said, "Nagenda" (I wish to go), left the king, and, returning to her mistress, gave the reply, "He asks for you." Should anything be wrong, the messenger was sent to a special house and told in private as in the case of the queen's messenger. The king also sent a special messenger to ask for his mother daily, for it was not etiquette to ask the messenger who came from her.

When the mother of the king fell ill, she was treated very much as the king was, and had her own special medicine-men to attend to her and her maids to wait upon her. The king was frequently informed of the patient's condition, and of the treatment adopted, and, should she be seriously ill, he went to see her, but such a visit was generally understood to mean that her life was despaired of.

When she died the king gave orders for her burial, and appointed the place, which was in a house on one of her estates, in which the owners continued to live, so that she should not be left alone. Her funeral ceremonies were much like those of the king. A cow was killed for her and the skin buried with her, but not wrapped round her, for, being a woman, she was buried in bark-cloths. Her limbs were bent

daughter to someone who would pay the recognised marriage-fee, who would be a son to them and whose children would be of their own rank. Then, too, there were risks attached to the honour: if the girl offended the king or in some way incurred his displeasure, it meant that her parents fell into disfavour and would have their wealth taken from them. If the girl, on going to the king's bed, was found not to be a virgin, her parents, and often her near relatives, would be put to death with her. Cows and other bribes therefore were eagerly offered to *Mulanga*, and tears of entreaty shed.

However, if deception, bribes, and entreaties proved of no avail, the girl had to be produced and *Mulanga*, if she approved of her, would place a string of beads on her neck, which was the token of her betrothal to the king; the girl wore these for a few days, after which they were returned to *Mulanga* with a calf. The parents had to present *Mulanga* with a bull for her food during her visit, which might last two or three days, for she was a messenger of the king and had to be received with honour. When she had secured the number of girls she required, she returned to the royal enclosure.

If the girl was still too young for marriage, she had to be kept and guarded for the king until she reached a marriageable age. She had to be carefully prepared and fed, and her body daily rubbed with butter to make her appearance all the king might desire, and any carelessness in this respect called down the royal displeasure. The parents had also to prepare a trousseau suitable for the wife of a king: there had to be good bark-cloths to wear, a number of good ornaments, bracelets, necklets, and so on, a cow-skin rug to sit upon, a bed, and milk vessels. She must also have a maid to wait upon her and two cows with calves to supply her with milk. When all was ready the parents sent to *Mulanga* and told her they were ready to bring their daughter, who was now marriageable. *Mulanga* enquired from the king when he would receive the girl and informed the parents, who brought their daughter and all her belongings on the previous evening to some kraal near the royal enclosure so that they should be ready to go in the morning at the time appointed.

When the time came, *Mulanga* escorted the girl and her parents to the throne-room. The girl was veiled like a bride, covered from head to foot so that she could not see. The parents knelt by the ivory tusk at the door of the throne-room and *Mulanga* led the bride by the hand into the room before the king and said, "I have brought you a wife, and these are her parents." The father said, "I have brought my daughter to you." *Mulanga* opened out before the king the bundle containing the clothing and all the girl's goods, and the king inspected them. The cows which had been brought for the bride's food supply were driven before the throne-room for the king to see and judge them. When he had approved of them, he assigned a place for the bride; this was in the court-house, where a bark-cloth screen was hung to form a separate apartment at one end of the wall dividing the throne-room from the other rooms. For two days the girl remained there under the care of a wife appointed by the king. During the first day she might urinate, in fact the more she did so the better, for it was a good omen and blessing, but she might not otherwise seek to relieve nature. Should she do so it was a bad sign and she would be sent away in disgrace, or might even be put to death. The parents meanwhile retired to their place in the capital and awaited the king's permission to return home.

When the two days were ended, should all be well, the girl was sent to a house in the charge of one of the king's wives, and the king appointed a day when she had to be brought to him. During the interval she was prepared for his inspection by being fed with as much milk as possible and her body was daily rubbed with butter.

At the appointed time the same woman, *Mulanga*, brought her and presented her, veiled, to the king. The king ordered all except *Mulanga* to leave the throne-room and the girl was unveiled and all her clothing removed. She stood naked before the king, who had her turned round and round that he might see her. The king then appointed her a place with one of his wives in which to live, and she went there to await his summons to the consummation of the marriage, which might come in a day or two or might be delayed for weeks.

When the girl had been approved by the king, he sent for her parents and took leave of them, giving them a present of cows, after which they might return to their own home in the country. If the king was pleased with the appearance of the girl, the present might amount to twenty or more cows, but there was no fixed sum. The king also presented *Mulanga* with a cow for bringing him his wife.

Few wives of the king had more than one child and many had none, for it was not usual for a wife to be called to the king's couch more than once. Most of them had their own houses in the royal enclosure, though some were put under the charge of the king's mother, and one wife was appointed to be in charge of all the others in the enclosure. The wives might not leave the enclosure without permission and it was the duty of the gate-keeper to see that, if one went out for any reason, she had a suitable escort.

The wives kept cats and monkeys and made pets of them and put strings of beads on their necks. Should one of these bite or scratch a wife on the arm, she was sent away to her family, for such a mark was looked upon as a sign that she had a lover. It was usual for a man to bite the woman he loved on the upper arm so as to leave a lasting mark. The mark left by the animal, therefore, was taken as a sign of unfaithfulness. Women admired these marks of their lovers' affection, but a husband who saw one on his wife which was not of his own making knew something was wrong. An adulterer would therefore bite a woman on the under side of the arm where no one but herself would see it.

When a wife offended the king he would sometimes run his sword through her on the spot, but if he delayed execution and merely pronounced sentence, she might be sent, as described in an earlier chapter, to one of three places. At

Buruli-Ekisaka-Ekyara banished wives were guarded by the chief of the place, who might give them vegetable food but no milk. When they were sent there or to the second place, Kibero, they might be pardoned and restored to their positions at the request of some chief who would remind the king of them; but if they were sent to the third place, which was Bugoma-Ekisaka-Ekiragula on the Nile, one out of a number might be pardoned, and the others were thrown into the Nile and drowned. Wives who had been proved guilty of adultery were sent to the third place, for the punishment was death, but a guilty wife often strangled herself, in order to avoid this public shame.

In the royal enclosure the king's wives had their servants and attendants. Of these there were three grades. The first two classes were permanent servants who lived in the enclosure, one set being Bahuma maids whom the king and princes might take to wife, and the other daughters of peasants. The third class were servants, mostly from the agricultural class, who came in by the day and when they left the enclosure were free to do as they liked. It was this class that Emin Pasha came across and took to be prostitutes; many of them were indeed guilty of immorality, but it was pre-marriage, and they were later married to the man.

When a wife grew old, the king might superannuate her, providing her with cows to supply her with milk, and send her back to live with her people. She would be honoured by them and could visit the king from time to time whenever she was in need of clothes or any other thing, and the king often appointed one of these old wives to be midwife to a young wife nearing childbirth. Should a wife develop any disease, she was sent to her own people, but might come to see the king and get clothing from him.

When a wife of the king fell ill, she was taken outside the royal enclosure to some house prepared by a chief of her own clan, where she could be nursed and attended to by her relatives. The king sent his special medicine-man and some maids to look after her. If she recovered, she was restored to her position in the enclosure; but if she died, she was treated in the usual way. Her head was shaved and her nails pared, her legs were bent up until they came under her chin, and her hands were folded together and placed under the left side of her head. The body was wrapped in bark-cloths and buried in the house of some agricultural peasant. The king sent men to the chosen house to dig the grave in the middle of it, and the body was laid there. The people continued to live in the place and the owner was paid to look after the grave. The usual ceremony of informing the king of the death was performed, but a black bead was brought and buried instead of a bull.

The king was not permitted to show any signs of mourning for any person beyond having his head shaved for the queen or near relatives.

When a wife died who had a child, the king sent to her clan and ordered another girl to be sent to him. She became heir to the dead wife and took all her possessions. When, however, a wife who was the mother of a child by the king committed some offence and was put to death, no heir was appointed.

When a wife of the king who was the mother of a daughter outlived the king, her daughter might inherit her possessions when she died. The princess had to perform the same ceremony for her mother as the son of a prince did when his father died. A fine sheep was brought and killed. The heiress took the skin and placed it between the legs and over the stomach of her mother. This skin was called *Mbindisisi*, and was regarded with great veneration. An oath taken on it was peculiarly binding. A few beans or some millet were placed in the dead woman's hand and the heiress took them out of it with her lips, chewed them, and puffed them over tne body and round the room, thus proclaiming herself the legal heir to any property there might be.

(4) THE KING'S CHILDREN

Care of a pregnant wife—attendants appointed—taboos—birth—purification—bringing out and naming of child—child put to sit alone—child brought to the king—bringing up of children—birth of twins—bringing out of twins—cutting the first teeth—learning to walk—learning cow-keeping—initiation ceremony—treatment of princesses—initiation of twins—grandchildren of the king

The king had a great number of wives, but many of them never had any children and it was rare for any wife to have more than one child. It was one of the duties of the head of the wives in the royal enclosure to inform the king when any wife became pregnant, and immediate steps were taken to remove her from the enclosure, for no person might be ill there, illness being fraught with danger to the king. While arrangements were being made, the wife was put under the charge of *Kyalubanga*, the gate-keeper, whose duty it was to look after wives who were leaving the enclosure for any purpose. He sent a sick wife, or one waiting to be sent away for her confinement, to a special house of his own until other arrangements had been made for her. At such a time two gate-keepers were kept on duty so that one might always be on guard. Should a wife die in this special house, her body was taken by the gate-keeper to the hut of an agricultural peasant and buried there, and the peasant continued to live in the hut until he was sure the body had decomposed, after which he might destroy the hut and move away.

The king ordered one of his important chiefs, if possible one connected by clan relationship with the expectant mother, to prepare to receive her. This chief, who was called the *Mulezi* (Nurse), had to build a new house and provide the wife with everything she needed; her clothing, milk-vessels, and house furniture had all to be new and suitable for a woman thus honoured by the king. The king also appointed a woman to be nurse and midwife; she was called *Munyuwisa* and might be one of his elderly wives, or one of his mother's sisters, whom he called his "little mothers." Her duty was to give the wife daily medicine and drugs and see that she kept well. A maid also accompanied the wife from the royal enclosure, and she was supplied with other special attendants.

If a wife of the king who had come from the king's mother became pregnant after a visit to the royal enclosure, the king's mother sent her to one of her own chiefs who cared for her and her child as a chief of the king had to do when the king sent a wife to him.

Careful guard was kept over the woman lest any person of unprepossessing appearance should come near her, and various animals, such as monkeys, were never allowed to approach lest the sight of them should affect her and cause malformation of the child. Neither men nor women might touch her clothing nor might she touch theirs. She might only eat with young children or with the old woman who cared for her and who was past the age of menstruation, and any food that she left had to be eaten by a small child. No person might sit on her rug, she had to be careful not to sit on a bed or stool that had been used by any other person, and she might not turn over in bed without sitting up. She might not drink milk from a cow that had lost its calf, nor from an animal that had drunk salt water, nor from one that had been with the bull within four days. When she went to relieve nature, she had to take a gourd in which were certain herbs mixed with water. This had a long handle or spout and she placed it so that water streamed over the organs of excretion, thus preventing evil from entering her. She had to be careful to keep her breasts and stomach covered lest any person should see them and by magic cause some evil to enter her and injure her offspring.

When labour began, the woman in charge sought the assistance of one or two others. The expectant mother remained in the house, but not in bed; she was stripped of all clothing and stooped near a post of the house. A carpet of a special kind of grass was laid down for her to stand on, and one woman supported her at the back while the woman who was acting as midwife stood in front to see that all went well. If the woman cried out in bearing she was abused, or her head was covered with a bark-cloth to stifle her cry, and at times she was even nearly suffocated. If it was a case of head-presentation, all was well, but feet-presentation was disliked. It was called *Khabona* (an evil object) and portended death to the parents or to some of the clan. The midwife in such a case got a basket, cut out the bottom, and passed the child through it head foremost to rectify matters. In the case of cross-birth, they called in the king's medicine-man who was usually able to force back the limb which had been presented, and finding the other arm or leg as the case might be, to bring the two together and effect normal presentation; if he failed, he proceeded to dismember and remove the child and save the mother.

When the child was born it was laid on the floor while the midwife awaited the afterbirth before cutting the cord. The child's mouth, eyes, and ears were washed out and respiration was set up. The cord was tied with fine strong grass and cut with a strip of reed taken from the frame of the roof of the house. The placenta was buried in the house on the right side of the doorway by a man of the Bakwonga clan. The hole was lined with the leaves of the sacred tree *kirikiti* (*Erythrina tomentosa*) and the placenta, wrapped in a bark-cloth, was put in and covered with leaves and flowers. Among ordinary people, the placenta of a girl-child was buried on the left side of the door, but a princess was always considered and spoken of as a prince and treated as a boy.

This man of the Bakwonga also gave the child to the mother to nurse. He carried as an emblem two fronds of palm-leaf over his head and wore two cowry-shells on his neck in front and two at the back, while the mother had two on either wrist. These shells were kept for the child, and should it die in childhood they were buried in its grave.

The mother went to bed for four days whether the child was a girl or a boy, though the wives of ordinary men went to bed for four days if the child was a boy, and for three only if it was a girl. During this period the fire near the bed was kept burning and was carefully watched, for no one might take any of it away to another house or, what was still more strictly forbidden, use any embers from it for lighting a pipe. Nothing might be taken from the house, not even a pot in which to fetch water, unless it was for the use of the mother and child. Each day the midwife washed the patient and tightened her waist-belt, which was usually a leather thong used to tie the legs of cows which were restive during milking. From the hour of its birth the child had a daily bath; warm water was poured over it and it was well rubbed with the palm of the hand. There was no towel, but the child soon dried and butter was rubbed on it until no trace of grease could be seen. The stump of the umbilical cord of a prince or princess was kept when it fell from the child and was decorated as a neck-ornament which the child wore in infancy and which later was put in a small basket to be kept with the first teeth when they were shed and the hair and nail-parings, which were always preserved.

The birth was announced to the king as soon as it took place, and on the fourth day he sent a cow or a bull, of any colour except black, to the mother for her food. The skin of this animal was preserved and the mother wore it for a time and then gave it to the child, who used it until it was worn out.

At the end of four days the mother was escorted to the back of the hut and washed all over and purified. During her absence the hut was swept out and a carpet of fresh lemon-grass laid down. All the sweepings were thrown in some place where they would not be trodden upon or disturbed and where future sweepings from the house and all excrements from the child could also be thrown. Until this time no persons except those who lived in the house might see the mother or child, but after the purification relations might visit them.

The *Mulezi*, that is, the chief in charge, was responsible for seeing that the mother and nurse shaved the child's head, pared its nails, and gave it a name, which was always that of some noted ancestor. During a father's lifetime a prince might not cut all his nails at one time, the little finger being left till the next day. The hair and nail-parings of a prince were always made into packets and kept in a special basket to be buried with the body when he died.

When a baby was about four or five months old, it was considered old enough to sit upright, but until then it was carefully kept on its back. A small ring of bark-cloth, like a nest, was made by a man of the Bakwonga clan, a branch of the royal clan, who must be well and strong and of good repute. This man came to the house, and sitting with his legs extended in front of him laid the ring between them, or making a hollow in the ground, placed the ring in it. The child was then handed to him and he put it to sit on the bark-cloth ring, steadying it until it sat alone and unsupported. The man who did this was afterwards held in honour by the prince, who was taught to regard him with respect and to treat him with liberality when, in after days, he came to visit him and enquire after his health. When a child was thus put to sit alone, the king usually sent a present of a cow to the mother, and the relatives sent presents to the child. A feast was made at each special stage of the child's life, and the father was kept informed of the progress.

A prince or princess was nursed for two years but not more, and the king never saw the child until at the end of this time he asked for it to be brought to him. Should the mother wish to nurse it for a longer time, he said: "Do they wish to bring up my child as a peasant?" referring to the custom among the agricultural people of nursing children for three years.

When the child was brought to the king, the mother and nurse came with it, and the party was introduced by the chief in whose care the mother had been. The king had the child brought to him as he sat on his throne, and he took it and looked carefully at it. For about a month the nurse and the baby remained in the royal enclosure, and then the king told the nurse that she might take the child back again to the chief. The mother returned to her former place in the royal enclosure, being treated with considerable respect by her companions as being the mother of a royal child. It was not often that a wife of the king had a second child; there were

New Moon dancers

Preparing for a Royal procession, New Moon festival

Arrival of the sacred spears for New Moon procession

New Moon. Royal spears awaiting the king

a few instances of this when some special charm in the woman had made an impression on the king, but as a rule a wife was never called again to his bed.

In the general treatment of children no difference was made between princes and princesses: they were both called princes and received the same honour from the people. The chief to whom a child was committed was responsible for it and provided for it as if he were the father, in fact he spoke of the child as his and the child spoke of him as its father. A royal child hardly knew its mother except by name though she might take every opportunity she could get of seeing it, and the nurse was the person to whom it looked for sympathy and comfort in illness and trouble. The relations between a child and its nurse were very affectionate and a prince or princess would care for a nurse in old age as for a mother. A prince who became king would often listen to his nurse when the advice or persuasion of others failed to make any impression on him. In the case of princesses, the nurse, under the direction and with the assistance of the chief, was responsible for the moral conduct of the child until she grew to womanhood.

A prince who was born during the accession ceremonies of his father was called *Kija na ngoma* (he who came with the rejoicing), and might never reign.

The birth of twins was hailed with joy, for it was a fortunate event. They were said to be the children of the god of plenty, and special ceremonies were observed at their birth. If the twins, whether royal or of ordinary parents, were boy and girl, the joy of both the father's and the mother's clan was great. If, however, both were boys, it was thought that the god favoured the father's clan, and for some reason was ill-disposed towards that of the mother and would have to be pacified; if both were girls, the god was showing his displeasure with the father's clan and special offerings to avert calamity had to be made by the clan which was thus shown to be in disgrace.

When the midwife in charge of a royal wife saw that there were twins, she sent everyone out of the house except those actually needed, and by a sign commanded silence until the children were born. This silence was called *Kwase*, and was observed lest a word or ejaculation might cause the twins to die. If it was necessary to summon a medicine-man to help, the midwife might speak to give instructions, but she might not mention the word twins. When the children were born she raised a peculiar, shrill cry which made the fact known to those outside. Special twin drums were hung on a *kirikiti* tree (which had to be planted if there was not one in a convenient place) and sounded, and songs were sung. These drums were beaten whenever the mother nursed the children and also every day at sunset and sunrise as long as the mother and children remained in seclusion.

The king was at once informed of the birth of twins and sent his royal medicine-man. The children's mouths, eyes, and ears were washed and respiration started; but they might not be moved from the place of birth until the medicine-man came, nor might the cords be cut. When he came he severed the cords himself and gave permission to move the twins and wash them.

The afterbirths were put into lumps of clay which were the mounds of the black ant (*mpiki*). These were domes of clay eighteen inches high and about twelve inches in diameter, and were hollowed out and lined with leaves and flowers of the sacred tree *kirikiti* and flowers of the herbs *luweza*, *kasekera* and *ruira*; the placenta was put in and the hollow filled up with potter's clay. The lumps were then decorated with the wild creeper *bombo*, a species of gourd, and left by the fire to dry until the time came for the bringing out and naming of the twins.

The door of the house was closed by the medicine-man and another exit arranged at the back of the hut, leading into a small courtyard where the mother, who was called *Nalongo*, took exercise, for she might not be seen until the twins were brought out. The twins themselves might not be taken out of the house at all before a new moon appeared, and then only into the courtyard at the back of the hut, until the day when they were brought out to be seen by all. The king appointed a boy of the royal clan, who was known as *Salongo*, to represent him and to remain in the house with the mother.

Princes and princesses acted as their father's representatives and informed all his relatives of the event and of the time appointed for the bringing out ceremony. The mother's parents were informed of the event by a special messenger who carried two emblems, a knife for a girl and a needle for a boy, or two knives or two needles as the case might be. These he had to deposit in the house without being detected and he therefore went as a casual visitor. The parents had probably heard the news before the messenger arrived, but they were ignorant as to who he would be, and he sought, in the course of ordinary conversation, an opportunity of depositing the emblems secretly in some place before leaving. He did not mention his errand until he was at a safe distance from the house, when he shouted "Your daughter has twins," and fled. If caught, he might even be put to death, and he would certainly be roughly handled and might be fined.

When the twins were about four years old they were brought out with much ceremony from seclusion, for up to this time they were not allowed to be seen by any persons but their immediate attendants. The king took part in the ceremony, and the chief medicine-man, whose duty it was to make all the arrangements and inform the maternal grandparents of the time fixed for the ceremony, had to be present, wearing two black bark-cloths. The maternal grandparents arrived in the evening before the appointed day and were accompanied by large numbers of their clan-fellows. They sang and danced during the night, using magic to remove from themselves the evil that might be attached to the female twin and to place it upon the royal clan, while the royal medicine-man was engaged in protecting the king from any evil and in transferring any evil attached to the male twin to the maternal clan.

In the early morning after the king had performed his duties with the cows and milk, he came to take part in the ceremonies. Two sacred trees had been planted four to five yards apart and the twins, each of whom had two white fowls, cocks or hens according to the sex of the child, were placed, with the clay lumps containing the after-births, between the trees. The company danced round them for a time and then separated into two parties, the king at the head of one and the mother of the twins at the head of the other. A gourd containing medicated water was handed to the king and he sprinkled the maternal party four times, twice for each child, and scattered seeds of millet and semsem over them. He handed the vessel to the mother of the twins, who sprinkled him and the royal party and scattered grain. The gourd was then handed to *Salongo*, the king's representative, who sprinkled them both. Singing and dancing began again and continued through the whole day.

The mother, with the king's representative and those members of the royal clan who had represented the king in spreading the news and making arrangements, went, headed by the royal medicine-man, to carry the clay lumps to the forest, where they deposited them on the outskirts of the trees and danced round them.

On their return the king, the mother, and *Salongo*, the king's representative, had their heads shaved and their nails pared. Their heads were smeared with white clay and their hair and nail-parings were carried in procession to the forest to be placed with the clay lumps. This ended the purifying ceremony.

The king then made a present to the maternal clan and they made a similar present in return, after which he went to the throne-room and sat on the throne.

Salongo, the king's representative, came to the throne-room with the mother (*Nalongo*) and the twins. A rug was spread in front of the king and the mother sat on it. *Salongo* took hold of an arm of each child, one in his right and the other in his left hand, and lifting them placed them on the king's lap, raising and lowering them four times; he repeated this on the mother's lap, a performance which was intended to let everyone know that they were the king's children.

The party then left the throne-room, and the mother with her children and their nurses passed to the house *Kachwabemi*, which was inside the royal enclosure near the queen's reception-room. There they remained for a month. At the end of that time the mother went back to her duties in the royal enclosure, and for one night she went to the king's bed to end the taboos connected with the birth of the twins.

The twins returned to the chief who was responsible for them, and lived there. *Salongo* was given two cows and two women by the king and went back to his ordinary life. Henceforward he was regarded by the twins as a second father and was held in honour by them. The chief medicine-man also received two cows.

The mother of twins had to be careful never to have another child, as it was believed that the child born after twins would be unlucky.

Each month, as the new moon appeared, the nurse and the twins went to the sacred trees which were planted for them to lie between during the purificatory ceremonies. They marched round the trees four times, sprinkled a little millet and sang special twin-songs.

The king always showed an interest in all his children, and while they were still small they were brought to see him. As they grew older they learned to find their way to the royal court without the nurse.

The cutting of a child's first teeth was an event of importance; these were anxiously watched for, and should the first tooth appear in the lower jaw, all was well. If, however, it appeared in the upper jaw, it was regarded as an evil omen which would cause death in both the mother's and father's clans. It was called *Khabona* (an unlucky thing) and offerings were made to gods and ghosts to atone for the wrong which must have been the cause. The people danced round the child and purified it with medicines supplied by the medicine-man. Such a child received no presents at this time for, if possible, the fact was kept secret, and a medicine-man was sent for to extract the offending teeth. No matter what its rank might be, such a child might never come into the king's presence. When, however, the first teeth appeared in the lower jaw, all was well, there was rejoicing, presents were given to the child, and the king sent it a cow.

After the appearance of the first teeth, the child was encouraged to crawl and try to walk. Bells were fastened to its legs as it was thought the noise would tempt it to move them. One bell would not have the desired effect, because only one leg would be moved. At sunset the bells had to be taken off lest they should attract snakes, which were considered to be more dangerous at that time. A story is told which gives another reason why a child might not wear bells at night. One royal child went out and the people heard it toddling off. It was heard by those it had left and by those to whom it was going, but it never reached them. They said that the dead had carried it off, and now at times its bells are heard in the evening after dark, and people remove those on their children at nightfall lest the ghosts should be attracted and carry them off.

As soon as a prince was able to walk, he was given a boy companion to be with him wherever he went. He had also several other boys as servants, and slaves were given to him. Being so waited on, he grew up very autocratic, and during his childhood did much as he liked, for his nurse spoiled him and yielded to his wishes in everything. He was, however, taught to have a wholesome fear of the king, to obey the chief in whose charge he was, and to keep certain rules.

When a royal child shed his first teeth, they were given to his nurse, who kept them in a basket with the stump of the umbilical cord and other relics.

The king's desire was always that his children should be as well informed as any others with regard to the cow-customs, and princes had to learn them like the children of cow-men. About the age of six or eight a prince was taken away from the chief, his guardian, by order of the king, and sent to one of the royal herdsmen, who was for some years responsible for the boy. Here he had to learn each stage of cow-keeping, and there was little distinction made between him and the other youths of his age. He was, however, treated with deference and might not be injured in any way lest blood should be drawn, as this would be an infringement of one of the royal taboos according to which no royal blood might be spilt except by the special command of the king.

To begin with, he had to herd calves and when old enough to take his part in herding the cows and to accompany the herdsmen when they went out for the day. In his spare time he consorted with the other youths, learning various kinds of sport and games, hunting and taking his share in their youthful fights and quarrels. He had to learn to milk like the ordinary cow-men and also to understand the various illnesses of cows and their treatment. Thus he went through the usual course of training followed by the sons of pastoral families, learning also all their superstitions and their respect for the priests and medicine-men.

At about seventeen or eighteen the king would send for a prince to undergo the initiation ceremony which admitted him to manhood. This consisted in having the six front teeth in the lower jaw extracted, and was performed on all boys and on princesses as well as princes. There was no special instruction before the ceremony and the young people were not required to take any form of oath[1]. The king gave all the necessary instructions, appointed the time, and chose the spot, which was outside the royal enclosure. A cow-skin was spread on the ground and the medicine-man of the king was present with the expert operator, who did the work, and his assistant. The boys often cried bitterly and were much afraid when the time came. The assistant sat down on the rug and the boy sat between his legs and laid his head back on the man's chest, while the man put his legs over those of the boy and held his arms. The medicine-man ran the instrument, which was merely an iron spike some six inches long and a

[1] This custom is singular as the tribe have a pronounced dislike for mutilation of any other kind and avoid those who practise such customs. It is impossible to discover when or why this form of mutilation came into force.

quarter of an inch in diameter, along the gums of the teeth to be extracted, this being a magical means of ensuring success, and handed it to the operator. The latter sat on the patient's legs, forced the spike down into the gum below the first tooth on the right side, levered it out, and proceeded to do the same to each of the six. He pressed the bleeding gums together, gave the boy a little water to wash out his mouth, and went on to the next boy.

Princes were taken to a special house until their gums were healed. On their way there they had to expectorate only over the right shoulder, and in the house each had his special vessel into which he spat the blood until the bleeding ceased. This was taken away and emptied in some place where no one was likely to step over it, for if anyone did so the boy would die. For four days the boys might have no solid food but lived on milk. A prince's special boy-companion was operated on at the same time and remained with his master.

The teeth of the prince were handed to his nurse who had the other relics, such as the stump of the umbilical cord and the first teeth. She also kept his hair and nail-clippings, which had to be cut V-shaped and never broken. At death these were buried with the body. The six teeth extracted at puberty were later hung on a string to form a necklet, beads being added to make up the necessary length, and this in future was the special sign of the prince, which he gave to any messenger on special duty as a mark of office.

When the gums had healed the prince went to see the king, accompanied by the boy-companion, who carried the baskets containing the prince's teeth and his own. The king examined these, and, taking the first extracted from the prince's jaw, exchanged it for the last extracted from that of his companion. He then gave his son a wife and might also give him estates and cattle and a site in the capital. The chief with whom the prince had lived still took an interest in him and gave him presents of wives, cattle, and slaves, besides seeing that he had a house to live in and anything else he required.

Princesses were treated much as princes and were allowed

more liberty than women usually had, because they were spoken of and treated as boys rather than as girls. They were taught the usual work of churning and of caring for the milk-pots, but in addition they might learn much of the men's work. Though they were not allowed to milk, they had to herd the cows like princes, for they were regarded as unsexed by their rank, which forbade their marrying; the only princess who was married was the queen, for all other unions were irregular. The princesses took their places with the princes to have their teeth extracted and then returned to the chiefs who had brought them up from infancy and who were responsible for them.

Royal twins, as they grew up, had to be treated exactly alike; if one received a present the other had to get a similar gift; if one child offended, both were punished; if one pleased anyone, both benefited.

When twins arrived at the age of having their teeth extracted, the mother (*Nalongo*), the king's representative (*Salongo*), and the chief medicine-man (*Kibandwa Lubanga*), had to be present. The operation took place between the trees which were planted on the day when the children were brought before the king, and the twin-dances ended. Until this time the twins had to go each month, when the new moon appeared, to these sacred trees, but after the teeth had been extracted they could go or not as they pleased. Before commencing the operation, the dentist took first one and then the other on his knees; he was then given for each child eighteen cowry-shells, which he had to wear on his arms. The medicine-man placed the instrument against the gums of each child in turn and passed it on to the operator. During the time of the operation drums and fifes played.

When there were royal grandchildren they were never permitted to visit the king. They were not allowed to see him, but, as he took an interest in their welfare, it was usual to have a curtain of bark-cloth hung in the throne-room with a peep-hole cut in it. The children were then brought in and allowed to run about and play for a time, while the king stood behind the curtain and peeped through the hole at them. He might speak to them and give orders for them to run about, or turn round, or stand where he might get a good view of them, but they never saw him. When he had seen them, he would order some gift, usually of cattle, to be given to them.

(5) PRINCES AND PRINCESSES

Marriage of princes—princesses forbidden to marry—alliances between princes and princesses—*Mugurusi*, chief of the princes—the queen, chief of the princesses—punishment of princes and princesses—sickness and death of princes—inheritance—death of princesses

A prince might take into concubinage as many women as he chose. The king, his father, gave him the first when his teeth were extracted, and the chief with whom he lived, who was related to him through his mother and who had brought him up, supplied him both then and later with women. He would often, too, take possession of girls from pastoral families; when he heard of or saw some maid who attracted him, he sent for her, and few parents could refuse their daughters to a prince. It mattered little whether the girl he desired was already betrothed or not, he simply demanded her, and a gift to the man to whom she was betrothed, in addition to the regular marriage-fee to the parents, would remove all difficulty. A prince, unlike the king, always paid the regular marriage-fee, but, except on the most rare occasions, there was no ceremony and he took no vows. In spite of this there was seldom a case of a prince's putting away a woman whom he had taken.

If a girl's parents found that she had been seduced by a prince, they would scold her, and if she was found to be with child, the prince would try to obtain her. Her parents would, however, refuse to allow her to go until they had laid the case before the king, who settled it by permitting the prince to take the girl on the usual terms, which meant that he paid the common fine for seduction, probably two cows, and took the girl. He might, however, bring beer and three thousand cowry-shells or the equivalent in cattle, and marry the girl according to the customs of marriage among the pastoral people; but such a marriage would only take place if the prince were unusually devoted to the girl.

After monogamy ceased to be the general rule in Kitara, there was no limit to the number of pastoral women a prince might have as concubines, but there were a few clans from which, for one reason or another, members of the royal family might not take women. For example, a prince might not take a woman of the Abazazi clan, for the girl who slept at the foot of the king's official bed belonged to that clan; nor might he take a woman of the Ababyasi clan, because a woman of that clan once stumbled against the king in public. Princes were not allowed even to visit women of these clans.

In addition to their recognised wives, princes frequently contracted alliances with their half-sisters and would exchange visits with them, or rather the princesses would visit them from the house of the chief in whose charge they were. Though these alliances were condoned and even connived at by the king, no princess might bear a child. If one were discovered to be pregnant she fell immediately under the royal displeasure. She would therefore use means to cause abortion, and, if these failed, she would hide away in some distant part of the country until she had given birth to the child. Her absence from her recognised home would be explained as a visit to some friend, and the chief who acted as her guardian would be careful to give this explanation to the king if he enquired about her, and to allay any suspicions which might arise. When the child was born it was as a rule killed at once, but at times a foster mother might be provided and the princess would return to the capital and follow her normal life. Unions between princes and princesses who were full brothers and sisters were considered incestuous and avoided, but princesses were really encouraged to live promiscuously with their half-brothers; and only a princess who married the king, whether as queen or as one of his ordinary wives, was expected to confine herself to him.

If any man other than a prince was found to have made love to a princess, he was put to death. The princess had all her property confiscated, was reduced to abject poverty, and was never allowed to see the king again. The chief under whose charge the princess was and her nurse were also put to death. If a princess was discovered to have borne a child as the result of an alliance with a commoner, the princess, the child, the man, and his parents, if he had any alive, or, if not, some of his near relations, were put to death.

A prince who became king might still take any of the princesses of his own generation to wife, but those chosen by him were not permitted to have dealings with any other prince. They need not necessarily live in the royal enclosure, indeed they seldom did so, but the king put special guards over them at their own homes to prevent any of the princes from making love to them. When the princesses came to visit the king after the evening milking, he would show his preference for any of them by giving her a gift of cattle or an estate, which was a sign that he wished her to come to his bed.

When a prince came to the throne, he chose one of his half-brothers to be head of the princes. The election took place at an assembly of the members of the royal clan which was summoned by the king, the prince chosen taking the titles of *Kasunsu Nkwanza* and *Mugurusi*, and being distinguished by a tuft of hair which was left unshaved on his head and on which beads were strung. With the office went an estate at Miere in the district of Mwenge, and in affairs of the clan this man took precedence of the king, but he might never become king. Kaboyo, the grandfather of king Kasagama of Toro, held this office at the time he revolted against his half-brother, the king of Bunyoro, and left the country. This prince had the right to hear any complaints and difficulties of the princes and their people, and he could either settle them, when they were not serious matters, or, if necessary, lay them before the king. If some matter concerning the royal clan had to be discussed this prince appeared before the king in state, dressed as a chief, and, presenting a cow to the king, said, "Sir, I want you to give me the person whom you have in the court, that we may talk and settle a certain matter." The king fixed the day and time when he would meet his half-brothers, the princes, in the second of the seven sacred huts, *Kyamunuma*, where princes transacted all their business. He went not as a king but as a prince to the council of princes, and the matter was discussed and quietly settled.

Should this *Mugurusi* die before the king, his son took the office without any form of election and was accepted by the king as a chief. After the king's death *Mugurusi* was treated as an old man and retired to the country to live among his cattle.

The head over the princesses was *Mugole wa Muchwa*, the queen. She judged their cases and took matters to the king if necessary.

No prince or princess might ever be punished by being put in the stocks. The king alone could order their punishment and, if it were death, they were hanged in the queen's reception-room where the rope always hung on a post in front of her throne.

No prince or princess who was not of the same generation as the king might enter any of the seven sacred huts, and no prince who was a full brother of the king might come to the capital.

When a prince fell sick, he was treated in the same way as other men, and the method will be described in detail later. If he had his own house and estate he would be nursed by some of his wives, but the old nurse of his childhood, if still alive, would, by virtue of her peculiar position as practically mother to the prince, take a special charge and act as head-nurse.

When a prince died his wives set up a funeral wail. The raising of this peculiar cry was especially the duty of the women while they and the men who were present prepared the body for burial. The women shaved the head, pared the nails, bent the legs into the squatting posture with the hands folded together under the right side of the head, and put special bead-ornaments on wrists and ankles. The men went to the dead man's herd, brought in a young cow with her first calf, and milked her. Some milk was poured into the mouth of the dead man, and this cow was not milked again for human food.

When a prince died leaving a son, the son was the heir and had to be present at the funeral ceremonies. The men brought a fine sheep from the dead man's flock and killed it. They gave the skin to the son who reverently placed it between the legs and over the stomach of the dead man. This skin was only used when there was a son. It was called *Mbindisisi* and was regarded with great veneration, an oath made upon it being so sacred as to be absolutely final and binding, and the rite was a very solemn one. A few beans, like dwarf beans, or some millet, were placed in the dead man's right hand and the son took them out of it with his lips and, after munching them up, puffed them over the body and round the room, thus proclaiming himself to be the legal heir to any property there might be.

In most things the inheritance ceremonies of a prince were similar to those of a chief, which will be described in detail later, but a few details were peculiar to a prince. After four days a responsible member of the clan made a stool of *kirikiti* wood, and putting the heir to sit on it, announced him as heir and gave him two sticks as spears. Then any who had claims came and put them forward. The dead man's property, children, wives, and cattle, were brought out and purified, as in the case of a chief, by a sister of the heir, who, shutting her eyes, sprinkled them with a bunch of herbs dipped in water and white clay, and finished by throwing her bunch of herbs at a cow, which became her property. No prince was ever given a crown, he had a stool only and he might only spread a cow-skin on it, never a leopard or lion-skin.

The body of a dead prince was buried in the house in which he died, and with him were buried all his hair and nail-parings, which had been kept by his nurse. The grave was lined with cow-skins and bark-cloths, and the body was laid upon bark-cloths. Numbers of bark-cloths were thrown into the grave, but earth was laid on the top and the floor beaten hard and smooth. The first earth put in the pit was pushed in with the elbow.

Mourning went on for at least four days and often for much longer.

After the funeral the house was never restored or rebuilt, but was allowed to decay and fall upon the grave. One of the widows lived in it until it fell down and the site was not used again, though the new owner might build quite near.

Unmarried princes were buried in the house of some agricultural peasant, and a near relation, usually a "little mother" (a sister of the mother) came to live there while the owner built another house near.

Princesses were treated like princes, that is, as if they were men; and when they died, their hands were placed under the right side of the head. The queen alone among princesses was, as the wife of the king, treated in this respect as a woman, and had her hands placed under the left side of her head. Princesses were buried in the house of an agricultural peasant, and the "little mother" or sometimes the mother herself came to live in the tomb. A princess's sister might inherit her property.

When any child of the king died, the drums named *Nerabanabayo* and *Yabago* were beaten at four o'clock in the morning, and this was the only sign of mourning permitted to the king on such an occasion.

CHAPTER VII

PASTORAL LIFE AND THE TREATMENT OF COWS

The cattle-owners and their serfs—the herdsmen—barter—food—clothing—ornaments—salutations—building a kraal—entering a new kraal—the huts—watering the cows—routine of pastoral life—milking the cows—cleaning the kraal—herding the cows—the milk-vessels—the children—care of the cows—salt—bleeding cows—cattle-breeding—the bull of the herd—birth of calves—twin-calves—taboo on milk from a cow after calving—taboo on milk for women—cattle diseases and treatment—sheep and goats—fowls

THOUGH for some years now the pastoral people of Kitara, who were the ruling class, have abandoned the strict milk-diet on which they used to live, and vegetables, plantains, and millet have become regular articles of food among them, they were until recently purely pastoral, and their lives were wholly devoted to the cows. If a man did not possess cows of his own, he made his living by looking after those of some chief.

The district chiefs possessed large herds, which were not necessarily confined to their own districts, for pasture-land was common to all and anyone might pasture his cows where he chose. The wealthy pastoral people or *Bahuma*, who were not in charge of districts but were themselves responsible only to the king and not to district-chiefs, had also large herds of cows, and their herdsmen were responsible for their behaviour to the chief of the district in which they happened to be. These wealthy Bahuma often wandered about the country with their herds, though they generally had settled habitations in some place where they built more durable kraals. They moved the sites of these kraals at times for sanitary reasons and because the daily scraping up of the mire caused by the cows left in time a hard rough surface unsuited for the animals; as a rule, however, they did not move far, for each pastoral chief, whether he ruled land or not, would have a following of agricultural people who were not nomadic but

Royal carpet for the New Moon procession

New Moon ceremony. King standing under the canopy in the seventh sacred court awaiting a prisoner for sentence. Sacred cattle in the foreground

New Moon ceremonies. King presenting his hands for prisoner to kiss to confirm his pardon

New Moon ceremonies. King resting on his return procession through the seven huts

built themselves more permanent dwellings than the cow-men near the fields which they cultivated. These would probably remain behind if the chief moved far away, for, though he regarded them as his slaves or serfs, they were not bound to him, but attached themselves to the land and were free to join any chief. As these peasants were the chief's workmen and did his building, cultivated grain and plantains for him, herded his sheep and goats, and did other tasks which were looked on as derogatory to a member of the pastoral tribes, the chief found it to his advantage to make a new home only a short distance from his original dwelling. These kraals were usually somewhere near the capital, but the cows moved about in any part of the country under the care of herdsmen. Many of the *Banyoro*, the free-men, also owned cows and often wandered about the country with their herds.

The herdsmen who were employed by owners of cattle were always of the pastoral class. They might possess a few cows of their own but not enough to live upon in comfort, and would take charge of some chief's cattle, whose milk supplemented their own supply and enabled them to keep a wife and family. Two cows, yielding an average supply of milk, were considered sufficient for a man to live upon, and, if he had a wife and one child, he required at least three.

The owner generally divided his cattle into herds of one hundred, each herd under the care of one man, sometimes his own son. A hundred was the number of cows usually found in one kraal, and one bull was considered sufficient to satisfy the needs of that number; in fact this was so commonly accepted that the term used for one hundred cows was *onugundu*, a bull. The herdsman in charge of a kraal would employ six to a dozen men and youths.

In the old days the cows furnished the pastoral people with the essentials of existence and the means of purchasing anything else they desired. Spears, knives, milk-pots, water-pots, and other articles were obtained in exchange for meat, butter, or skins, or by selling sheep and goats, of which the pastoral people possessed flocks and herds, kept for them as a rule by some of the agricultural serfs. Salt, which they considered necessary for the health of the cows, was obtained by bartering meat, butter, or goats.

The food of the pastoral people was milk, though if a man had not sufficient cows for his family to live entirely upon milk, they took it in turn, some taking milk in the morning and the others eating porridge and drinking beer or water, while in the evening the order would be reversed. The wife of a man too poor to feed his family on milk was expected to cultivate millet, plantains, maize, and potatoes to supplement the food supply, though as a rule women were not allowed to do any work beyond caring for the milk and the milk-pots, for any work which was tiring or caused them to lose any fat would, by sympathetic magic, harm the cows. Children had to drink large quantities of milk, and were punished if they did not take what was considered enough. A girl when approaching marriageable age was not allowed any food but milk, if enough could be got, and she had to drink as much of that as she could in order to grow fat. Milk was always drunk fresh by men, but women and children might drink it clotted and also drink the whey after churning.

The men of a family would, when they could get it, eat a meal of beef in the evening. The women might also partake of this, but often the whole of the evening's milking was left to them. This meal was eaten at sunset and was followed by beer-drinking which might last till nine or even ten o'clock, after which the men retired to bed and refrained from drinking milk until after the morning milking.

Few men could afford to kill cattle often, but when they did they would dry the meat over the fire or in the sun to preserve it and make it last as long as possible. A man would also send meat to his friends when he killed a cow and would receive meat from them in return when they killed, so that he could keep up a supply of fresh meat. There were recognised methods of distributing meat. The owner of the animal kept the chest and sent the shoulders to his friends. Each member of the family received a little meat, some was dried, the head was given to the servants, and the feet to the dogs. The skin was dressed for clothing or to spread on the bed.

Before a chief ate a meal of meat, a pot of water and a bowl were brought to him; he held his hands over the bowl and a boy poured water from the pot over them. This was done to each person who was to partake of the food. The meat was brought either in a wooden bowl or in the cooking pot; in this it was cut up and a portion was placed before each person as directed by the master. Some might be set aside for his wife and her companions, for women always ate apart from the men. The gravy was placed, in the pot, before the master who invited others to dip into it as they sat round and ate, using only their hands to pick up the food. The person who served the food might not eat with the others, but the master directed that a portion be set aside for him, and some gravy was left in the pot. When the meal was finished, everyone washed his hands and rinsed his mouth.

As the strictness of the milk regulations became relaxed, chiefs began to eat many other kinds of meat, including sheep and goat mutton and buffalo, and, with the exception of two kinds of antelope, they ate almost any wild animal, even pig, hippopotamus, and elephant, all of which were once strictly taboo. Several kinds of vegetable food too came into common use. Plantains were cooked and served wrapped up in their own leaves, which were opened out to form a cloth round which the people sat to eat. Millet-porridge was served in a large pot and other kinds of food in small baskets. For some time pastoral people, though they ate these foods, were careful not to drink milk while any trace of them might remain in the stomach, but one of the effects of the introduction of western civilisation has been a growing disregard of the milk restrictions and the people now eat vegetable food and drink milk on the same day.

The upper classes of the pastoral people wore either bark-cloths or cow-skins which were carefully prepared. The hair was all shaved off and the hide made soft and supple by rubbing and dressing with butter. Women put one end of the skin under the right arm and wrapped the robe round the body from front to back, throwing the other end over the right shoulder. Women of lower rank wore a bark-cloth or skin round the waist and one slightly larger over the shoulders or a large bark-cloth wrapped round the body under the arms and reaching to the feet, but young unmarried women and girls went naked. Chiefs and wealthy men wore bark-cloths or cow-skins passed under the left arm and knotted on the right shoulder and on the feet canoe-shaped sandals of buffalo or cow-hide. Boys went naked and many of the herdsmen wore only small capes of cow-skin round the shoulders or the waist, and sometimes lacked even that.

Both men and women were fond of wearing bracelets, necklets, and anklets, which were made of brass, copper, and iron, and often of hair from the tail of an elephant. Several hairs were put together and secured by an ingenious fastener often made of wood and forming an amulet, which allowed the ornament to expand and contract so that it could be easily put on and taken off. Sometimes fine brass and copper wire, a little thicker than thread, was twisted round the hairs. Women frequently wore ten to twenty anklets and three or four bracelets and, as soon as they cut their first teeth, they began to wear beads on neck, wrists, and ankles. Fetishes and amulets too were decorated and worn as ornaments.

Both men and women of the pastoral classes were careful to keep their bodies clean, and among the upper classes it was usual to have a daily bath, after which perfumed butter was rubbed on the body until no trace of grease was visible. The hair on the head was shaved off entirely every few weeks and the nails were kept short. Hair and nail-clippings had always to be deposited in some safe place where they were not likely to be found and used for casting spells on their owner.

During the early part of the day the greeting given to a friend was, "Oirwota?" (How has the morning passed?), and the answer was, "Ndabanta" (I have seen no evil) or "Ndiho" (I am here). Later in the day they asked, "Ogorobere?" (How has the day gone?) and the other replied with the same word.

When anyone met a friend who had been away for some time, one said, "Mirembe" (Peace) and the other replied the same. The first then said, "Oroho" (Are you well?) and the other said, "Ndiho" (I am well). It was not polite to greet more than one person, a salutation must be addressed to each person separately.

The Kraal

The kraal was the centre of pastoral life and, as all land was free to the cows, a *Muhuma* could settle wherever he considered that the pasturage and general conditions were most advantageous to the well-being of his herd. The kraals built by the herdsmen when wandering about the country with their cows were little more than a few bushes forming a circle large enough to hold the cows, thus preventing them from straying and being attacked by wild beasts, while their own huts, which were built in this fence, were hastily and poorly constructed, being merely a frame of sticks covered with a rough thatching of grass to form a shelter from the fierce rays of the sun and from showers of rain. If a more lengthy stay was intended, or if a kraal was meant for the principal residence of the owner, the fence was made of poles eight to ten feet long, so cut that they would take root and grow, and in the building of such a kraal many taboos and ceremonies had to be observed.

When a man had settled upon the part of the country in which he wished to build, he called in a medicine-man who consulted the augury and found out whether the intended site would be good for the cows. The site was always on a hill and the kraal was built with the gate on the highest side looking up the hill, while on the opposite side was the dung-heap and the gutter for draining the place. As the man might remain in such a permanent habitation for five or six years, it was important not to neglect any precaution, and the process of building, simple in itself, was complicated by the observance of many taboos, neglect of which might result in the loss of all his cows.

If the augury were favourable, the man would prepare to start work on the next day by cutting wood for his gate-posts. He had to be careful, however, that no unfavourable omen appeared during the night or on his way to the forest in the morning. The central fire in the kraal must have burned brightly and not gone out all night, no cry of alarm of fire or of an attack from wild beasts must have been raised, no baby must have been born among his followers, nor must any dog have had pups, nor a hen have hatched chickens; no one must have come to beg or borrow from him, no biting ants must have entered his house, no rain must have fallen, and no one in the kraal must have died. Should all these conditions be fulfilled, he might set out; but if he then met a woman before meeting a man, he had to return and wait until the next day. These taboos had to be observed whenever a man moved his kraal to a new site.

The omens all being favourable, the man went to the forest, where he chose four suitable trees for the gate-posts, for the gate was the most important part of the kraal. The posts had to be of the trees *kirikiti* (*Erythrina tomentosa*), which was the first tree created and therefore the most sacred of all trees, and *omwihoro*, and had to be cut from suitable trees in such a way that they would grow. The man had to cut them himself and assist in carrying them in the afternoon to the new site, where he threw them on the ground and left them.

Next morning, if all the omens were again favourable, he and his men went to the place and dug four holes to hold the gate-posts. These were arranged with two in front, far enough apart to allow the cows to pass between them, and two about eight or ten inches behind them, so that logs could be piled by night across the gateway with their ends between these posts to form a barrier. From the medicine-man the owner obtained some sacred herbs, *olwezo*, *omulembi*, *mulamula*, *muhabula*, and *olihula*. He put a little of each of these in each hole and kept some for the gutter on the opposite side of the kraal. The posts were then put in the holes, and as the earth was rammed down the man uttered a prayer to his gods and his forefathers:

"Mbyaire muti guno omulembe, mbe ne mirembe atalikibi olumula na bakama na batai namajuna onjune kibi kona kitalija omuka muno byosi ekibahiri nekija omuka muno kyose muhagula nempabula entugo kutaha muka muno mpabula oluzala obugudu byona bija muka muno olweza nenyizaka eno abakulu mutaha eka yainu egimu engikozira mundera obusinga."

This prayer, which consists largely of repetition, might be roughly translated as follows:

"Bless this tree, make it grow, let it be entirely a blessing without any evil. Remove all evil, let it not come, but let the good come. Give thy blessing that we may increase in all things and grow wealthy and be free from disease. Let blessing abound."

The man pushed the earth on the top down with his foot so that the posts were firmly planted. He had then himself to cut the first two logs which were put between them to form the barrier by night, and bring them in. These were called *muko* and *mukyola*, and when he had put them in position, his men brought others which were kept at hand and, after the cows had come in for the night, they were piled horizontally between the posts to a height of some five or six feet, which was sufficient to keep the cows from jumping over and to prevent wild beasts from entering the kraal.

The fence and the huts for the calves were built in one day so that the kraal was ready for the cows to come in next morning to be milked, but it was not necessary that the huts for the people to live in should be completed on the same day. On the night before they entered the new kraal the owner had sexual intercourse with his wife to establish it and make it durable.

Early the next morning, if the omens were again favourable, the owner took a little fire from his old kraal and went to the new home. His wife accompanied him, carrying some of the milk-pots, and they drove the cows. They had to reach the new kraal before sunrise and had therefore to start very early. When they entered the man lit a fire in the centre of the kraal; this fire was sacred and might never die out by day or night, nor might it be used for cooking; it was called *Nkomi*, and the fuel used for it was cow-dung or grass refuse from the calves' huts.

While the man was preparing this fire, his wife prepared a rough bed in their hut, or if it was not yet built, on one side of the kraal, and they lay there together. The family, if they had any, and the servants now arrived with some of the goods, and the man called out and asked if it was morning. They answered "Yes" and he asked for water to wash with. Servants brought him water and, having washed his hands, he proceeded to milk a cow, which had to be a young animal with its first calf and both cow and calf had to be in good health. For this milk he used the wooden milk-pot *Kisahi* which was kept for special occasions.

He handed the full pot to his wife who, in accordance with the duty of a wife, presented it to him to drink; having done so he gave it again to her and she drank. No one else might drink this milk, but the man took a short stick of papyrus which had been made perfectly clean, and, dipping it in the milk, he touched the tongue of each member of his family with it. He and his wife then drank the rest of the milk. A second cow was milked for the children, and the rest of the herd for others.

When all the milking was done and the men had had their meal, the cows had to be taken to pasture. A place outside the kraal, called *Isaze*, had been cleared for them to stand, and the owner, holding his spear and staff, squatted beside them as though he were herding them, until the real herdsmen came to take them away to pasture.

When the cows had gone, the women occupied themselves in bringing all the things from the old kraal to the new, after which the old kraal was destroyed. The men built their houses, while the owner's house, if he was a wealthy man, was built by his servants, the agricultural people who were attached to his land. His house was in the fence opposite the gate, with the dung-heap, on to which the refuse of the kraal was daily swept, on the left side of it as one looked in from the gate. In front of the house, slightly to the side, was a calf-hut, and if the herd was a big one, there were other calf-huts at different places in the kraal. On either side of the gate were built the houses of the men who were the special guardians of the herd, and between the owner's house and the dung-heap was a small gate for the calves, which the women also used when leaving the kraal for sanitary purposes in the day-time. The other huts were built at intervals in the fence; they were bee-hive in shape, with one door-way facing into the kraal, and were some fourteen to eighteen feet in diameter and sixteen feet high at the apex. The outlets were never closed by doors, for the men had to be able to see the cows and to rush out to protect them from any danger. The huts were not of much importance, with the exception of the permanent residence of the owner and, as this was generally built by his agricultural followers, it is not necessary here to enter into details of its building or the taboos to be observed. These matters will be dealt with under the work of the agricultural people.

On this first day in the new kraal, no woman who was menstruating might come in nor might such a woman drink of the first milking. She had to wait at the house of some friend that day and enter on the next. The first four days were a special test period for the new kraal. Should biting ants enter during that time, the owner deserted the site and built a new kraal, being careful again to observe all the taboos, for this was a sign that it was not a suitable place for the cattle. Should any wild animal attack and kill a calf, a goat, or a fowl, they had to leave the place, for disregard of this warning might mean the loss of all their animals. Another important point was the health of the cattle: should one of the young bulls die during the four days, they had to desert the place. After the four days were safely ended, the owner had two cows bled, the blood was cooked with salt and mixed with new milk, and the males of the family ate it. No woman was allowed to touch this meal.

On the evening of the first day, when the cows had come

back to the kraal, the owner took his son, or, if he had no son, a slave that he had bought, not inherited, with him to the watering-place. If the water had to be taken from a well, they took a wooden pail (*echura*) and the man went to the bottom of the well, scooped up the water, and threw the full pail up to his son, who caught it and emptied it into the water-troughs which were made for the cows to drink from. These were hollows cut in the earth and smeared with clay to make them hold water; they were about a foot wide and eighteen inches deep, and long enough for ten to twenty cows to drink at the same time.

Four pailfuls of water were drawn in this way by the owner and his son or the slave, who was treated as a son, though he might not inherit the property. After this it might be left to the men to draw the rest of the water required. When the cows had been watered, the wooden pail was given to the owner's wife who put it with the milk-pots on the sacred platform at the back of the house inside. When the cows had been milked that night, the owner had sexual intercourse with his wife to, as it were, set a seal upon the completion of the taboos.

After this the life of the kraal followed its usual course which was a regular routine, each person having his or her task to perform. Rising at cock-crow, that is before five o'clock, the men prepared for the milking. The central fire was blown to a flame and grass added to make a light for the milking. Each milker had also his own fire, made of the grass which was daily swept out from the calves' huts, before which the cows stood and which served the double purpose of giving light and keeping flies from annoying the animals. The principal milking-place was before the owner's hut, but cows which belonged to any of the men were milked before their own huts. There might be five or six men engaged in milking, this work being all done by men: any woman who attempted to take part would be killed with her whole family for her presumption.

Boys and girls had charge of the calves and brought them

out of the huts as the cows came to be milked. The calf was allowed to go to its dam and suck until the milk was flowing freely, when the boy in charge took it away and held it in front of the cow. The milkman squatted down on the right side of the cow to milk.

By this time the women had prepared the milk-pots and the woman in charge of them handed one to the milkman. He milked into it as much milk as he thought it was safe to take from the cow without doing harm to the calf, and handed the pot back to the woman, telling the boy to let the calf finish its meal. Another cow was brought and the woman handed the man a fresh pot for its milk.

The milk and the milk-pots were in the charge of the women. Each house had its raised platform of earth, called *Olubinde*, at the back of which were the fetishes. On this platform stood the milk-pots and each as it was filled and handed back to the woman was replaced there. The woman had to be careful to know which pot contained the milk from each cow, for certain cows had taboos attached to them and their milk had to be put in special vessels and drunk by specially appointed persons. The owner of the kraal and his children might not drink milk from cows which on that day had drunk salt water: it was left for the servants. When a cow had been with the bull, neither the owner nor his wife might drink the milk from it on that day. When a cow had a calf, the whole of the first day's milk was left to the calf, and for seven days no married person might take any of it; it was drunk by a boy appointed for the purpose, who might, during this time, drink no milk from any other cow. For four days the milk was not taken into the house but was drunk outside by the boy as soon as the cow was milked, and none of the milk was churned until the cord had fallen from the calf. The pots from the cows under such special taboos were set aside as they came from the milking. Cows that had lost their calves were milked last, and the skin from the dead calf was held before the cow for her to smell during the time she was being milked.

The calves were allowed to remain with their dams in the kraal while the milk was dealt out, some to be drunk at once and some to go into the churn, while some full pots were hung up in slings over the earthen platform for use during the day. The men drank their share of the milk at once, a meal which had to last them until the evening, and then they turned the cows out of the kraal. The boys in charge of the calves had to see that they did not go with the cows, and should they let any get out they would be punished by the owner.

The men whose turn it was to herd the cows took them off to pasture. Two men, or a man and a boy, went with a herd of one hundred cows and managed them with ease. The animals were accustomed to being directed by word of mouth and readily obeyed the orders of the herdsmen.

The men took it in turns to go out with the cows, and those left behind had to clean up the kraal. The droppings were swept to the dung-heap and thrown upon it, and some of the dung was spread out to dry in the sun for use as fuel for the sacred fire in the centre of the kraal. Dried dung was heaped upon the fire, care being taken not to extinguish it. The owner of the herd had each day to receive milk from it, even if it were so far from him that it took a whole day to carry it and it could only be used for butter. A few herdsmen had therefore to go each day, if the herd was away from home, to the owner's kraal with supplies.

In the evening, on their return from pasture, the cows had to be watered. The men tried, whenever possible, to have a watering-place where the cows could go down and drink; but sometimes this was impossible and the water had to be drawn from a well. Then the men made the long troughs lined with clay which have already been described. Two men, or, if the well was deep, three, were needed to draw the water. One went to the bottom of the well while another stood at the top and, if there were three, one stood half-way down. The man at the bottom filled a wooden pail and threw it up to the others. The one at the top had to catch the pail, empty it into the trough and throw it down again. They became very skilful at the work and could throw and catch a full pail without spilling any. When the cows came to drink one herdsman stood by the trough to guard the animals as they drank and to keep them from putting their feet in the water, while another directed them so that the right number came to drink at one time. The cows soon learned to come as they were told, and would stand and wait until their turn came. Each relay as it left the trough passed on to a fire of grass which was lit near, before the next lot was allowed to approach the trough.

The cows were then taken into the kraal for the evening milking, after which they remained there for the night without further food or water.

The work of the women was mainly the care of the milk, the cleaning of the milk-pots, and the churning. In the early morning the first task was to wash any of the pots which had not been emptied and cleaned after the milking of the night before. The spare milk from both morning and evening milkings was put into churns and made into butter in the morning. The churn was called *Ekisabo* and was a large gourd. This the women rocked backwards and forwards on mats or upon their laps until the butter separated, when it was emptied into a wooden bowl and washed, though not very thoroughly, and then worked a little to free it from water. It was put into special gourds called *Nsimbo* and used for food or for anointing the body.

The rest of the day was occupied in washing and fumigating the different pots. The *Kisahi*, the wooden pot which was always used on ceremonial occasions, such as the birth of a child, the first time he was placed to sit up, the cutting of the first teeth, and marriage and funeral ceremonies, was regularly washed but not fumigated, and the outside was rubbed with butter to keep it clean and smooth. *Mindi*, the commonly used pottery milk-pot, was washed out when empty in the morning with hot water and turned up to dry. Sometimes these were inverted and placed on the ends of upright sticks to drain, and early in the evening, before the cows came in to be milked, they were fumigated. This was done with a small earthen furnace in which a kind of grass was burned and the smoke fanned into the vessel, which was afterwards placed on the platform to await the evening milking. Should any vessel show signs of being sour, it was washed with boiled urine from a cow and rinsed with water. After the evening milking the pots which were emptied were washed out with cold water and set on the platform for the night. Before the morning milking the more careful women fumigated them, but as a rule pots were only fumigated once in a day. *Ekisabo*, the gourd churn, was generally washed out with urine from a cow, rinsed with hot water, and fumigated. *Nsimbo*, the gourd in which butter was kept, was regularly washed with cow's urine, rinsed with water and dried, then washed again with hot water and again dried. Men carried all the water for washing the milk-pots, for the women were not permitted to do any heavy work, indeed few of them were capable of it.

The work of the younger children, both boys and girls, in a kraal was to look after the calves. When the cows had gone to pasture, the calves were allowed to wander about in the vicinity of the kraal under the charge of the children. The smaller calves were turned out for a short time near the kraal, but returned to the huts before the sun grew hot. The older calves were brought back during the heat and went out to pasture again in the evening.

As a boy grew older he was sent out with the herdsmen to learn about the cows, or remained in the kraal to learn a man's duties there. The girls were put in charge of the houses in which the calves were kept by night. They had to clean these out and bring fresh grass for the calves, both for eating and for them to lie upon. The refuse grass was thrown in a heap near the dung-heap, and the men spread it out to dry for burning when they required a fire to light them when milking or to keep the cows quiet and free from flies. As they reached years of discretion, the girls were taught the care of the milk-pots and all about the use of the milk and the taboos connected with it.

The Care of the Cows

It was considered necessary for the health of the cows that from time to time they should have salt. The herdsmen who had charge of the king's cows might procure this from the king's stores, for the king, when he needed salt, sent a messenger to Kibero, where the salt-works were; the messenger took with him a cow and on his arrival the cow was killed at the house of the chief of the place and the flesh cut up into small pieces. These were made into packets with the bones, which were broken up, and the contents of the stomach, and thrown into the houses of the salt-workers with the information that the king required salt. In return each householder brought a large packet of his best salt to the house of the chief. This salt was made into bundles, each weighing about eighty pounds, carried by men to the capital, and put into the king's stores from which his herdsmen obtained it as they required it.

The workers from the salt-works brought salt to the kraals of private cattle-owners and sold it to them, usually in exchange for an animal, three to five loads of salt being given for a goat, according to its size. Sometimes the owner would send to Kibero, giving his messenger meat, butter, grain, or some other article to barter for salt which he carried back to his master.

When the salt had been brought to the kraal, the head of the kraal kept it for one night, and in the morning took it to the watering-place, where it was mixed with water in a large trough and the cows were taken to drink there before going out to pasture. If on the way to the trough they met a woman on the path, they might not drink that day. The cows were fond of the salt water and had to be watched lest they should drink too much, which caused them to suffer from a kind of intoxication. When they had drunk, they were smeared on the head, horns, back, and legs with white clay and driven to pasture, but, owing to the intoxicating effects of over-drinking, it might be some time before they were able to graze. That night the owner and his family refrained from drinking milk from the cows which had drunk the salt water, all the milk from these cows being left to the servants after the evening milking.

When the cows drank salt water for the first time in a new part of the country, the owner sprinkled a little over them, milked a little milk and put it in the water, and then allowed them to drink.

It was usual to bleed the cows when the young grass began to grow after the rains, for it was thought that their blood became heated with the new grass, which tainted the milk and was bad for the calves. Herbs were also administered to remove this taint from the cows.

The value of a cow consisted not in the amount of milk it gave but in the calves it bore: if it had healthy cow-calves, it was considered valuable. A cow which had four bull-calves in succession was first treated with various medicines, and, if these failed to make it bear a cow-calf, it was set aside as an animal to be used for paying a debt or to be sent to the king for an offering at some shrine, or for use in taking an augury.

Cows were said to belong to one great clan *Matabi*, that is, "branches," for they brought all people together from every tribe and nationality. Everyone was concerned with the well-being of the cows. When a cow calved in the pasture, even a passing stranger might not go on his way, but had to stand and wait until the event was over; and a visitor might not leave his host if a cow was about to calve, for he would be called a wizard and, if anything went wrong, would be charged with having used magic.

Though the pedigrees of the cows were not fully known, cows and calves were known by sight as the offspring of certain bulls, and a bull, though it might mate with its own calf, might not mate with its mother. The young bulls were kept tied up so that they might not mate with cows too nearly related to them, and the cows were guarded for breeding purposes. A bull-calf borne by a good cow might at times be

Wife of a former king, said to be over 100 years old.
Muhuma who has lived on milk diet

PLATE XXV

Wife of a former king, said to be over 100 years old

kept in the herd, but more often they were exchanged for cow-calves or killed. Young bulls not required for the herd sometimes underwent an operation which was equal in effect to castration: the scrotum was crushed between two stones, injuring the testicles and preventing any development. The bulls were then allowed to grow up to the age of two years or more and were fattened for killing. A cow-calf might be given in exchange for a good bull, but as a rule it was considered worth two bulls.

A bull was kept in the herd for use until it was quite old and then another was brought to be its heir. All the men of the kraal were called together for the ceremony of killing the bull and eating its meat, and the owner had much beer brewed for the occasion. In the early morning the bull was led out with the young animal that was to be its heir. The old bull was decorated with wild flowers brought by the men, and was led to a spot between the kraal-gate and the sacred fire, where more flowers were strewed upon the ground. There it was struck down by a strong man who drove an axe into the base of its skull behind the horns and killed it with one blow. The cows stood about in the kraal while the dead bull was flayed and the meat cut up and cooked.

After eating meat and drinking beer, some of the men took the cows to pasture, but the feast went on and lasted for two days. The right shoulder with the leg and hoof was carefully cut off and hung over the doorway of the owner's house, and the meat was cut from it to be eaten as he required it. When it was all eaten, the bones and the hoof were left there for months before being taken down and burned.

When there was any difficulty in the birth of a calf, a medicine-man was sent for. He might send an assistant, but if the case was serious and he came himself, he demanded a special fee. The cow was treated like a human being. If it was a case of cross-birth, the limb which was presented was thrust back and the calf turned until the man could get the two fore-legs together and thus bring about an ordinary birth.

When a cow bore twins, there was general rejoicing, especially if both were cow-calves. Should one be a bull-calf, it was feared that the cow would be barren afterwards, and only the cow-calf was reared. Each morning for four days after the calves were born, the cow was marched round the fire followed by the bull and the calves, which were carried by some of the men. This was to impart a blessing to the other cows. Four pieces were cut from the edges of the placenta and tied in a piece of new bark-cloth, which was fastened by strings of the same material from side to side of the hut so that it hung over the milk-pots. The placenta itself was wrapped in the leaves of the *kirikiti* tree and buried between the central fire and the main gate, and the place was daily smeared with cow-dung by the men who cleaned up the kraal. If one of the calves was a bull, it was killed on the fourth day, after the taboos were ended, and men specially appointed for the purpose ate the flesh by the fire. The bones were buried by the central fire and the skin was worn by a child of the family or, if there was no child, by one of the hired herdsmen. When it was worn out, it had to be burnt in the central fire. After the feast was over, the men danced the twin-dance, beating on milk-pots for drums. The milk from the cow had to be drunk by a son of the owner, or, if there was no son, by the hired man who had supreme charge of the cows.

If a cow had a bull-calf and died before the calf was old enough to eat grass, the calf was killed and not allowed milk from another cow, as would be the case with a cow-calf. When a calf died, the skin was held before the cow whilst it was being milked, and should the cow refuse to give milk, the medicine-man came and gave it milk to drink. He also treated it with a medicinal herb, *ngundu*, which was heated over the fire, squeezed into a ball, and dipped in water. This was applied to the animal's eyes, ears, mouth, and nose and thrust up into its womb, which made it yield milk and also gave it the desire to mate. If a cow did not have calves, it was treated by bleeding; the blood was allowed to congeal and was mixed with herbs, and the cow was made to swallow it.

When a cow had had a calf, its milk might not be drunk on the first day, but was left for the calf. For four days it was not taken into the house, but was drunk in the open as soon as the cow had been milked. For seven days it was drunk by a young boy specially appointed for the purpose, who might take no other food during the time. No milk from the cow was churned until the cord had fallen from the calf.

A woman during her menses was not allowed to drink milk, for if she did so the cow's teats would be blocked, its milk would be discoloured with blood, it would cease to give milk, or it would become barren. If a man were wealthy enough, he would permit his wife and daughters at these times to drink milk from an old cow that was past bearing.

If a calf climbed on to a house, it was not allowed to jump off, for that would bring calamity upon itself and the house. A cow-skin was quickly brought, the calf was made to walk on to it, and was lifted to the ground.

Herdsmen had to be careful not to relieve nature where the cows were being herded. During the night anyone might use the dung-heap in the kraal, but during the day they had to go aside into the grass.

Diseases of Cattle

The following were the more commonly known cattle diseases:

Nsotoka, rinderpest. This was new to the country, and nothing was known which would save the animals or stay the disease.

Ejuho, foot and mouth disease. To cure this the leaves of the *mujima* tree were baked and applied hot to the feet and mouth. Grass was picked and the animals were fed by hand; they usually recovered, rarely more than three per cent. dying. The illness lasted about four months, during which time the cows were isolated. No man from another kraal might visit the place, and no one might take one of the cows to any other part of the country. Anyone who entered the kraal might not leave it to go amongst other cows until the illness was over. The milk from the cows might not be used for children, for it would cause them to die; and should a woman with child drink it, it would bring on premature birth.

Kawhola, cough. The leaves of three herbs, *mugina*, *omwenga*, and *nderema*, were dried, powdered, and mixed with water, and the mixture was given daily to the cow to drink.

Musondezi, sleeping sickness. For this no cure was known.

Ebite. This was a contagious disease which caused the cow to twitch up first one leg and then another and shake all over as if from ague for two or three hours, after which it fell down and died. No remedy was known. The meat was eaten after being well boiled, but the water was thrown away and not used. Should any person drink the water, he contracted the disease and died the same day.

Echuma. This was a sickness which caused giddiness, making the cow turn round and round. The sickness lasted a long time, but sometimes yielded to treatment, which consisted of blistering on the head and back with hot irons.

Amaiso. This was an eye disease which attacked cows after a period of drought, and made them blind. The root of the *Musongo* was pounded and the juice expressed was dropped into the eyes once a day for three or four days, and the animal recovered.

Ekitule. The back and neck seemed to stiffen as with rheumatism and the cow dragged its legs. If it fell, it could not rise for two or three days. To cure this it was bled, some three pints of blood being drawn, and after that it recovered. Cows seldom died from this disease.

Omufumbi, a contagious disease which attacked the udder and blocked the teats. Pus was drawn off and the animal recovered. Should such a cow bear a bull-calf and should that gender, the offspring, if cows, showed the same tendency. Bull-calves were therefore killed, but cow-calves seemed to escape and not to transmit the disease. Women might contract this disease from the cow, if they drank the milk while it was ill.

Amakebe, deep-seated abscesses, especially in the glands of the neck. Calves were more especially subject to this and often died, though they might be cured by having the places seared with hot irons.

Kaguru, a foot disease which often killed the animal, though it might be saved by amputating part of the hoof.

Ekyakoha, protrusion of the bowels.

Sheep and Goats

The cow people possessed sheep and goats but these were seldom looked after by pastoral herdsmen. A serf was always willing to look after the sheep and goats of the chief whom he served, for they gave security to his own flocks and herds. No one would dare to rob him even if he had a large flock, if he could claim that they were not his and that he was guarding them for his master. The master, though he would make no fixed agreement with his serf, would repay him for his trouble by giving him one kid or lamb from every third birth among the animals under his charge.

The cow-men used these animals for taking auguries and for sacrificial purposes, sheep being the favourites for their ceremonial offerings, while the peasants more often used fowls or goats. The pastoral people also used these animals for trading and would exchange goats and sheep for young bulls, though a cow-calf would never be given in exchange for goats and sheep alone. Three large goats were given for a bull-calf old enough to leave its dam, and a bull with the addition of one or more goats might be exchanged for a cow-calf.

Sheep were more esteemed than goats. No sheep might be tied with a rope which had been used for a goat, but the rope used to tie the legs of restive cows at milking time might be used for a sheep, and a sheep-rope for a cow. A cow's rope might never be used to tie up or lead a goat.

A sheep might never be tied by the neck, but the rope had always to be put round its body near the front legs. The penalty for infringing this custom was imprisonment in the stocks or confiscation of possessions. Goats and sheep were kept in the houses, where they were tied up in separate places, which might not be interchanged. Sheep-skins might be used by women for dress, but a sheep-skin might not be joined to a goat-skin. If a larger dress than one skin was required, it had to be made from skins of the same kind of animal.

A man might kill a sheep alone, but he had to have someone with him when he went to flay it and cut it up. A sheep, if killed for eating, had to be clubbed to death; but if it was intended for the use of a medicine-man, it was pole-axed just as a cow had to be.

The sheep was held in esteem, and the cow-men kept sheep with their cows, saying that they were akin. It was said that the sheep had taken an oath to Ruhanga, the creator, that it would not cry out when it was killed or when it was caught by a wild animal.

Pastoral people also kept a few fowls, but they did not eat them and what they chiefly wanted was a cock to rouse them to milk in the morning, and a few birds for taking auguries. They did not eat fowls or eggs; and though they would give a fowl to anyone who needed it for an augury, they did not buy or sell them. On the day a hen hatched her chickens no one might go on a journey, though they went out to herd as usual.

CHAPTER VIII

AGRICULTURAL LIFE

The agricultural tribes—the free-men—serfs free to leave their masters—joining a new master—clearing a new field—the first crops—semsem—the first-fruits—the main crop, millet—scaring birds—the first-fruits—harvest—threshing—storing grain—other foods—plantains—honey—brewing beer from plantains and millet—tobacco—domestic animals, goats, sheep, fowls, and dogs—building a new house—entering a new house—interior arrangement of a house—visitors—beds

THE agricultural tribes of Kitara were the original inhabitants of the land, who were conquered by the pastoral tribes and made their serfs or *Bahera*. These serfs did all the manual work of the land, for it was considered injurious to the herds for a cow-man to do anything that did not concern his cows; the serfs, therefore, cultivated grain, plantains, and other vegetables, built the more durable houses, and did all the other labour required. There is no doubt that they were of a far lower type than the pastoral people and have been slowly raised by contact with them. Though I have used the general term "agricultural people" to distinguish these serfs from the pastoral folk, there were among them several distinct tribes differing completely from each other in type and dialect and belonging to different parts of the country. These differences persisted even after the scattered tribes were nominally united under one king, for each small tribe almost invariably clung to its own district and rarely wandered from it. Among the clans which composed each of these tribes distinctions must also be noted, for the iron-workers were a different people from the woodworkers and from the salt-makers, and each of these types, again, differed from the purely agricultural labourers.

For many years the pastoral people of Kitara carefully refrained from intermarriage with the agricultural tribes and treated them as slaves and serfs, though sometimes, if they were sure the taboos would be observed, they would give them milk to drink. In the course of time some of the agricultural people became wealthy and showed signs of ability, or became servants to the king and in that capacity rendered him some special service. Such men were raised by the king to the rank of free-men or *Banyoro*, and it was with this class that there originated the name of *Bunyoro*, which has superseded the real name of Kitara and is now commonly used for the country. When a man had been raised by the king to the rank of a free-man, he was at once considered much superior to his former fellows, and even his parents would kneel to address him.

Though no man of a pastoral tribe would marry a girl from an agricultural tribe, a free-man was at liberty to marry a girl from the lower ranks of the pastoral people, and he would not be backward in seizing an opportunity of thus rising a step in social rank by marrying the daughter of a poor herdsman, who, in her turn, would be glad to exchange a life of poverty and shortage of milk for the more luxurious existence she would lead with such a husband. The sons of this union were free to marry girls either of the agricultural or of the pastoral tribes, while cow-men of the pure stock were willing to marry the daughters. The natural result has been to destroy to a large extent the purity of the pastoral type.

The serfs in a district could be called upon to do work for the king or state by the chief of that district, but he could not summon them directly, for the serfs always attached themselves to some chief who looked upon them as his servants and used them to build for him, to look after his goats and sheep, and to grow what he might require in the way of grain, plantains, and vegetable food. The district chief had, therefore, to call upon the serfs through their own chiefs. The peasant was not forced to stay with any chief and was free to leave whenever he so desired, but as a rule he attached himself to the land, built a fairly permanent dwelling, and did not wish to move. If for any reason one did make up his mind to move and attach himself to another chief, he went to live two days with a friend in the district to which he wished to go. After the two days the friend took him to his master and he was supplied with land, either a field which had been cultivated before or virgin soil on which to start a new field. A chief also gave his serfs from time to time presents of goats, milk, butter, and, when he killed an animal, meat.

The newcomer, having been granted his field, would probably betake himself to some medicine-man to find out by augury or divination whether it was a good place or whether he must seek some other abode. If the augury was favourable, the medicine-man often gave the enquirer a branch of some tree to plant in front of his house for luck, and the man went off to build a temporary hut where he and his wife could settle while the better house was being built and the field cultivated. They were helped with food by friends and neighbours until their own crops had grown.

When the man first went to clear his ground, he had to be careful to observe all the taboos connected with the beginning of any work. The fire in his hut must not die out during the night; no alarm of fire or attack from wild beasts must have been raised; no one must have come to beg or borrow from him; no baby must have been born, no dog must have had puppies and no hen must have hatched chickens; no biting ants must have entered his house; no rain must have fallen during the night, and no death must have taken place. If all was well, he would set out; but if the first person he met on his way was a woman, he had to return and wait until the next day.

The man then went to his field and cut down the trees, tall grass and bushes, and left them to dry. He then burnt the reeds and grass but left the wood for fire-wood, which his wife brought in as she required it. When the ground had been cleared, the woman dug it and probably put in some fast-growing crop, such as sweet potatoes, maize, or dwarf beans, in order to get food as soon as possible. When this crop was ripe, the woman had to prepare a meal of the first-fruits for her husband, and no other member of the family might touch the food until he had eaten this.

The next crop was the semsem, and when going to dig the ground for this, the woman had to observe the same taboos as the man did when setting out to clear the field, with this difference, that she might not go if she met a man on her way. The taboo of the fire going out was most important, for dying fire portended dying plants.

When the land was ready for the sowing of the semsem, the husband, having procured a fetish from the medicine-man, put it amongst the seed, which he gave to his wife in the evening. Again she had to take care that the fire did not go out during the night lest the seed should die. Next day, all being well, she went to sow it, and while doing so she might speak to no one until her husband had come and spoken to her. Should he be unable to do so, she remained silent until she returned home. She took with her to the field some fire from the hearth for her pipe, and this might not be used by any other person; should anyone attempt to take any of it, she snatched it from him and extinguished it. Having sown the seed, she returned home to cook the evening meal and that night had sexual intercourse with her husband to make the seed germinate.

The whole care of the growing crop rested upon the wife, for the husband had work to do for the chief, who might make him build for him, or herd his sheep and goats, or might send him to build for the king or to go out to war.

When the grain was ripe the wife gathered a little and prepared it for her husband, who had to eat it before any of the family might touch it. Should any guest arrive, this meal had to be postponed, for the husband had to eat it alone and etiquette forbade his leaving his guest. That night he had sexual relations with his wife to ensure a good harvest. Should necessity compel the wife to cut and use the grain when he was away from home, she had first to gather some, cook it, and set it aside for him on his return, or the crop would be spoiled.

These taboos ended, the husband built a frame for his wife to dry the grain upon before it was threshed. When it was dry, one head was threshed upon the road, the grain left and the head thrown on it, and any passers-by jumped over it. When all the grain had been threshed, the husband carried it home and divided it out. Some he gave to his wife for the use of the family; of the remainder he tied some up in bundles to be sold, and stored some away to be kept for seed.

The main crop was always the small millet which they called *bulo*, and, when this was to be sown, the man was expected to help and he and his wife worked together. During all the preparations for this crop they had to watch their fire carefully, and no one was allowed to take any from it, for the grain would suffer if they did so.

When the crop had grown to a height of some six to eight inches, the man had to thin it out, and at this time he usually put amongst it some charmed objects which he received from the local medicine-man to guard it from wild pigs and birds. As it began to ripen, children were employed to drive off the birds, which were found to be most destructive in the early morning and again in the evening, their feeding-times. An ingenious method of scaring birds with the minimum of trouble was resorted to by some young people: they fixed, at intervals, stakes, eight to ten feet long, cut from supple boughs, and from the top of each they hung on a rope a collection of shells, gourds, and anything else that would make a noise. A stout rope connected the stakes, and its end was carried to a tree in which the youth made a sheltered seat. From time to time he shouted and pulled his rope, making all the poles shake and the articles hung on them clatter together with a noise which scared the birds. Sometimes, too, people made figures of men, often remarkably good, and placed them here and there to look like men walking along carrying sticks or spears.

When the crop was ripe, the wife had again to prepare some of it for her husband, who must eat alone before the rest of the family might partake. The husband sat by the door looking into the house and, taking a little grain, threw it in front of him into the house, to the right, to the left, and over his shoulder. He ate his meal and then divided out a little of the food to each member of the family, but no stranger might eat any of this first gathering.

Men and women worked together at harvest-time, though the actual reaping was the women's work. With small knives they cut off the heads of millet with three to four inches of stem and dropped them into large baskets or left them for the men to gather up and carry to the threshing-floor, where they were piled up. The stubble was left and the cattle were allowed to wander over it and feed, after which anything still remaining was gathered for fuel.

The threshing-floor was prepared in the field by the husband, who smoothed a piece of ground, beat it hard with a short heavy stick, and smeared it with cow-dung. The woman threshed the grain from the ear by holding the head in one hand and beating it with a short stick. After threshing it lay in a heap until dry, when it was put into baskets and poured out slowly so that the wind carried off the chaff and dust.

The husband then carried the grain to the granary which he had dug in some secret place. He made a kind of well, two and a half to three feet in diameter and six to eight feet deep, and in this the grain was stored in baskets on shelves or platforms made of stout sticks, which were fixed in the sides and extended across the pit. The pit was covered over and the man noted some ant-hill, or some tree which was not likely to be cut down soon, as a mark to guide him. Though sometimes several families would share one cellar, only the husbands knew where it was and they drew the grain from it as it was required. No housewife kept more than a little grain in the house, for there was danger of loss by fire or in war.

Maize was grown in small quantities and it was eaten from the cob or parched, never ground into flour. Sometimes it was boiled, but the majority of the people preferred it roasted in the cob over the hot embers while it was young and tender, and they did not regard it as regular food but as a luxury. They did not store any of it for food, but laid aside some for seed, hanging it in the cob in some place over the fire where rats and insects would not destroy it.

Beans and peas were largely grown and were dried and stored for use in the dry season, when they were soaked in cold water for some hours and boiled. They were never eaten young but were always allowed to mature before being gathered. Beans had to be eaten first by the owner, but there was no taboo of the kind for peas or for the various species of marrow which they also grew.

Three kinds of plantains were grown, and it was their custom to plant a few new trees each year and abandon those which had done badly. *Gonja*, the sweet plantain, was baked by the women for the men to eat when drinking beer. *Mbide*, which they called the male, was used for brewing beer. *Namunyu* was known as the female and was cooked as a vegetable, but it was not grown to any great extent. They sometimes cooked the fruit whole, but this was regarded as a slovenly method and as a rule it was steamed and pressed into a soft paste.

The agricultural people ate honey, which the pastoral people might not eat, though they did so in secret, for they considered that honey taken by bees from all sorts of plants and from dead animals might injure their herds if they ate it. They also said that honey might spread small-pox if the bees gathered it from a place where that disease had been and where the corpses had been left lying unburied.

Brewing

Mbide, the so-called male plantain, was used only for making beer, it was never eaten as a vegetable. The fruit was cut when about to ripen, put into pots, and covered with leaves. Sometimes it was spread over a fire on a frame, so arranged that it got thoroughly heated by the fire without being baked, and grass was heaped over it to keep in the heat and hasten the ripening. When it became pulpy it was peeled, and the pulp was thrown into a large wooden trough in which it was reduced to a watery paste either by working with the hand or by treading on it. This paste was then strained, the sieves being merely bundles of grass shaped into a sort of pocket. When the liquid had filtered through the grass, water was added and sometimes a little grain to make it ferment; after four days the plantain beer was ready for use.

There were two methods of brewing beer from millet. One was to grind the grain to flour and leave it with water in a large wooden trough for one day. The liquor was then filtered through grass and left in pots until the next day when it was ready for drinking. This beer would keep four days, but after that time it became too strong and sour and caused dysentery.

Another method, which was more elaborate but gave better results, was to put the millet, which had to be carefully selected, into a vessel and moisten it well with water. In two days, when it had begun to sprout, it was spread in the sun to dry, after which it was ground and the flour damped until it would hold together when taken in the hand. A hole in the ground was lined with plantain-leaves and the flour was put in, covered with grass, and left four or five days until it was quite sweet. Fire-wood was then collected in large quantities; the sweet flour was baked until it became like sand, and again spread out in the sun. Two small baskets of millet were prepared by wetting the grain and placing it in the sun until it sprouted, when it was ground and added to the dried flour. The whole was put into pots which were filled up with water and it was left two or three days to ferment. Boiling water was added, which made the liquid froth, and it was then ready for drinking. Sometimes this was served in cups, but more frequently it was drunk from the pots through long tubes with filters in the ends. Six or seven men would sit round one pot in the evening, drinking and discussing the events of the day.

Tobacco

Most of the agricultural people grew their own tobacco in small plots and found it a useful source of revenue, for both pastoral people and serfs loved their pipes and the cow-men would barter milk, butter, or meat for the prepared leaf. No information could be obtained as to the introduction of the plant or how it became universally used. Both men and women were addicted to its use, and it was looked upon as natural for boys to smoke as soon as they reached puberty. Women only took to smoking when married, young women who smoked being few in number. Many people also used it for chewing, a habit which was common among princesses and wives of the king. It was, however, strictly forbidden either to smoke or chew tobacco in the presence of the king. Should he come unexpectedly upon a woman who was chewing it, she had to get it out of her mouth quickly or swallow it, for he would make her open her mouth and if any tobacco were seen therein he would punish her severely, in fact to offend the king thus might even cost her her life.

The serfs generally grew their tobacco crop on the dust-heap, which was fertilised not only by the salts from the wood ashes, but also by the goat and sheep-sweepings from the hut. On this the plants grew luxuriantly, often reaching a height of six feet, with large broad leaves.

They did not expend much care on the preparation of the leaf for use. It was dried on mats, the coarse ribs taken out, and the finer parts broken up and dried again, after which it was tied up in small packets for use or barter. The tobacco for the king was more carefully prepared. It was pressed into round cakes two inches thick and four inches in diameter, which when dry were hard like wood and had a sweet scent. It was impossible to discover exactly how this tobacco was prepared, but it was said that cow-dung was smeared upon the cakes while they were being dried.

Animals of the Agricultural People

The most important domestic animals kept by the agricultural people were goats and sheep, which they used chiefly as a means of obtaining wives for themselves or their sons. Cows were chiefly, indeed in former times wholly, restricted to the pastoral people, but in recent years some of the more thrifty of the agricultural people have managed to secure cattle, purchasing them in the first place with goats and sheep and increasing their herds by breeding and exchange. The agricultural people also kept many fowls, and dogs were kept by both cow-men and serfs. A few people kept cats, which were much prized but were scarce, probably owing to the dangers they ran from other animals.

The most popular and common animals were goats because they were easily reared and, being hardy, thrived in almost any circumstances, and they were kept in large numbers by the better-off serfs. The pastoral people also owned goats, but they gave them to the serfs to be herded and looked after. These were always willing to take charge of the goats and sheep of a pastoral master for they could conceal their own amongst them, representing that the whole number belonged to the chief; this ensured them against loss, for no one would dare to rob them of their master's animals and none could be taken from them in payment of debt. As a general rule a peasant who thus herded his master's goats and sheep would receive in payment one out of every third lot of young born under his charge.

The serfs required goats for various purposes. They were the animals most commonly used by them for sacrificial offerings, for the taking of important auguries, and for payment of debts, marriage-fees, and other expenses. Few of them would kill a goat simply for the luxury of the meat, but on ceremonial occasions, such as a wedding, goat's meat always formed part of the feast.

Goats were herded by the children, who took them to any place where grass was plentiful. When the grass was very

Iron smelters preparing furnaces for smelting

Smelting iron, furnace at work

Levering smelted iron from the furnace with tree branches

Cutting iron into small parts for smith while hot from the furnace

abundant during the rainy season, the goats were tethered by the leg to save trouble, and all the attention they required was to have their places changed two or three times each day. During the dry season, however, they had to be herded from about half-past nine in the morning, when the dew had dried from the grass, until nearly noon, when they were brought in and tied under sheds out of the sun until about two o'clock, after which they were again herded until about six o'clock. By night they were tied by the foot to pegs in the floor near the walls inside the house. The kids while small were kept all day in large baskets in the house but were allowed out at sunset to go and meet their dams and get a meal; after playing about for a time they were put back in the baskets for the night and in the morning they were again let out with their mothers for an hour or so.

When a goat was killed, it had to be clubbed to death or its neck broken by twisting its head, so that the blood was retained in the body and eaten and nothing was wasted. Only when a medicine-man required a goat for sacrificial purposes might its throat be cut. Goats were frequently used by the medicine-men for exorcising ghosts, particularly those which were supposed to have attacked a woman with child or whose children died in infancy. The goat was also used when the ghost of some relative had to be persuaded to leave a patient and take up its abode in an animal. A goat which was thus made the home of some family ghost was kept in the house and treated with considerable respect; it might not be killed, and should it die it had to be replaced.

Sheep were also kept by the agricultural people, but they were generally the property of some pastoral chief, for sheep were held by them in some esteem, and they would even at times eat mutton, though no one might approach the king until some time after doing so. Pastoral people generally used sheep for the purposes of sacrifice, augury, or exorcising ghosts.

The rope by which a sheep was tethered must never be put round its neck, but always round its body, and any man found tying a sheep by the neck was liable to severe punishment and loss of property and might even be put to death. A sheep might be tied by the rope which had been used to tie the legs of a restive cow while it was being milked, and the rope might be used again for a cow; but if the rope was used for a goat, it might never be used on a cow again, and no sheep-rope might be used for a goat and afterwards put on a sheep. Sheep were tied up in the house at night, but the places for the sheep and the goats had to be kept apart and might not be interchanged. A sheep-skin might be worn by a woman, but no one might sew a sheep-skin and a goat-skin together; they must be kept each with its own kind.

A man might kill a sheep alone by clubbing it to death, unless it was intended for the meal of some priest, when it had to be killed by striking it with an axe at the base of the skull as a cow would be killed. When the sheep had to be flayed and cut up, however, the man might not do it alone, but must have a second person with him.

Women were permitted to herd both sheep and goats and might tie them up and loose them without fear. They might also eat the flesh of these animals but had to avoid meat from any that were found to have young inside them.

Fowls were kept both by the pastoral and the agricultural people, but the cow-men did not keep many. The agricultural people ate fowls and might eat eggs, and they also used fowls among themselves to buy goats and household commodities.

There were many superstitions connected with fowls. When a hen hatched her eggs the owner might not start on any journey that day, nor might his wife go to dig in her field. They might bring in fire-wood, but do no other work. Among the cow-men, the man might go out to herd, but might not start on a journey. If a hen laid an egg in the doorway of the house, it was killed, for this was a bad omen. If a hen laid on the roof of the house and hatched its young there, it had to get the chickens down as best it could, for no man might go up to bring them down. If a cock crew at seven, eight, or nine in the morning, it was killed, for that again was a bad omen.

Dogs were kept and treated with great care by both cow-men and serfs. They were used for hunting and as watch-dogs for protection and were often very dangerous to anyone who came to the house by night. A cow-man would feed his dog on milk and as much meat as he could secure for it, while a serf gave his potatoes and meat whenever he could get it. When a dog had puppies, the owner had to stay two days with it and see that it had proper food; even if he were on a journey he had to stay where he was for two days before he could go further. On the day the puppies were born, the wife of the owner might not go to her field; no stranger might approach to look at them until their eyes were open; no person might take fire from the house, for the puppies brought a blessing, but anyone removing fire took away the blessing. When anyone came into the house and announced a death, it was said that the puppies opened their eyes even though the time had not yet come for them to do so. Puppies were sometimes sold, but it was more usual to give them away to friends.

A woman might never strike a dog, for if it yapped at her it would bring a curse upon her. Dogs were not allowed to sniff at or touch any food which a man was going to eat. They were kept tied up when there was any infectious disease about, especially if it were small-pox, for they were supposed to visit every place hunting for food and to carry infection with them. Any dog found wandering in a place in which there was disease would be killed at once.

Building

An agricultural peasant had always to make the preparations for building his house himself, but he might call on his friends for assistance in the actual work of building. His first task was to collect and prepare some of the necessary materials. He had to cut poles and make rope for binding from strips of papyrus-stems, or palm-leaf, or plantain-fibre; most of the other necessary materials he brought when the building was about to be started or during the work. When he went to collect or prepare these things, he had to observe the usual taboos—the fire must burn all night, no alarm of fire or attack from wild beasts must be raised, no baby or puppy be born and no chickens hatched; no biting ants must enter the house, no rain must fall, no person must have come to beg or borrow his axe or his hoe, and there must have been no death in the family nor must anyone have told him of the death of a friend. If on his way to work he met a woman before meeting a man, he had to return and wait until the next day.

When the ropes and the poles were ready, he started off one day, all the omens being favourable, and collected reeds for the roof. These he brought to the site of the new house about four o'clock in the afternoon, for this work might not be begun in the heat of the sun. He had already summoned his friends and they came at this time and began to work. Before night they prepared the first three rings for the roof and began to build the roof, working from the apex outwards.

The house was bee-hive shaped with a pinnacle on the top under which was the crown or central ring of twisted creepers, which had to be made by the owner himself. The roof was made of reeds radiating from this crown and bound, at intervals of about a foot, to rings of twisted creepers which increased in diameter as the distance from the apex and therefore the size of the roof increased. The pinnacle varied in height according to the status of the owner, and the greatest house in the land, the king's court-house, had a spear on its pinnacle. The part of the frame of the roof which was finished that night was raised on three poles to such a height that goats and dogs could not jump on it. Should this happen, the work had to be thrown away, for no peace or prosperity could be hoped for in a house built with that roof, and a fresh start was made the next evening, if the omens were all favourable and all the taboos had been observed.

All being well, however, and the omens again favourable, the friends gathered together in the morning and the work went on until the main part of the house was ready. The roof at this time was raised to the necessary height on temporary poles, for the permanent pillars were not put in till later; and there was no thatch but only grass thrown on the frame of the roof to give some shelter from sun and rain.

The man always tried to arrange the work so that he might enter the house between one and two o'clock in the afternoon. On entering for the first time, he took with him his spear, shield, and tobacco bag. He stuck the spear into the floor, laid down the shield and bag, and made a fire which might not be allowed to die out for the next four days.

When the fire had been lit, the man's wife came with a basket in which she had some millet and semsem seed, and sat opposite to him. He took a little of each kind of seed between his thumb and first finger and dropped it in the fire, ate a pinch, threw another pinch in front of him, one to the left, one to the right, and one over his shoulder, saying, "My father built and his father built, and I have built. Leave me to live here in success, let me sleep in comfort and have children. There is food for you." This prayer was addressed to the ghosts of his forefathers who were supposed to enter with him and help him to prosperity in all he did. He then ate a little seed and gave the basket to his wife, who went through the same ceremony. If there were any children they ate some of the seed, but did not go through the ceremony of throwing it.

During the first day no one might take anything out of the house nor might any fire be taken from it. Some people planted two trees or sticks at the right side of the doorway and sometimes also at the back of the house to bring peace and blessing.

The friends worked without ceasing till the afternoon, and after the ceremony of entering the house, the husband directed his wife to bring food which she had prepared, and with the builders they ate the first meal in the house. There was always meat for this meal and a supply of beer, and this was the only payment given to the builders, who then went away, leaving the man to do anything else that had to be done that day alone. That night the husband and wife slept together in the house even though it was still unthatched, for it might not be left until it was finished and the family established in it.

Two days later the woman called her friends to help her and they dug and levelled the floor and then smoothed it, beating it hard. During these two days the husband had prepared the permanent pillars, for the house still rested on the temporary posts. When these were ready, he called his friends again to help him to put them in, which had to be done in a certain order; that in the middle, the main-post, had to be erected first, then one which stood against the owner's bed at the side of the house, and then one by his wife's bed, after which the others might be put in as he wished.

Until the permanent posts were in place the house was not thatched, though grass was thrown upon the roof to make it comparatively water-tight. The women now brought the grass, which was of the kind called *senke,* and did the thatching. That night the man again had sexual connexion with his wife to establish the house.

A wealthy man of the pastoral people, whose house was built for him by his agricultural serfs, did not enter it until it was completed, when he took his drum, spear, and shield, and, placing them by the fire, made an offering of grain and other food and asked for the blessing of his forefathers. He then ate some of the food with his wife and children.

Most houses, whether they belonged to poor or rich men, had the same interior arrangement. The house was divided into two almost equal portions by a reed wall, which was in two parts of different lengths; these overlapped, the shorter portion being set far enough in front of the other to leave room to pass between them, though it was impossible to see from one room into the other. In the second room were the beds of the owner and his wife. A bark-cloth screen was usually hung round these and the wife's bed was often further screened by a low reed wall. At the head of the father's bed a reed wall cut off a portion of the room, forming a bedroom for the daughters, which was thus secluded and could only be entered by passing the parents' beds. The boys of the family, when they reached the age of about seven or eight, had a bed in the front room, but up to that age they slept on the floor.

If an important visitor or near relative arrived, the wife gave up her bed to him and slept with her husband, while a visitor of less importance slept in the outer room, or, among the pastoral people, if he was an unmarried man, he might sleep in a house in the kraal with other unmarried men. Women practically never visited except when quite old, when they might stay with near relatives. A mother might stay with her married son, but this was not regarded as visiting.

Many houses had the dividing wall made only of bark-cloth so that the owner might raise the curtain and, sitting on his bed, talk to his friends who sat on the floor in the main room. Most people were content to sit on the ground, but a goat-skin would be spread for an honoured visitor and a cow-skin for a chief. When the man wished to rest, he would lower this curtain and also the curtain round his bed, so that he was entirely shut off from light and fresh air. His bed was composed of four posts with forked tops fixed on the floor, into which side pieces and head and foot pieces of wood were put. From side to side, to form laths, were laid smaller sticks or strips of papyrus, which were tied to the side pieces. On this frame the poorer people spread grass, on which they lay, covering themselves with the clothing they wore and, if possible, with a bark-cloth, though many men were not diligent enough to make this and went without covering. More careful people made a kind of mat of papyrus-stems tied together side by side, while the wealthy cow-men had a cow-skin on the frame and covered themselves with two or more bark-cloths. The king had a leopard-skin to lie on and bark-cloths for covering.

In the centre of the main room was the fire on which food was cooked by the poorer people, but which was only used for warmth and light by the more wealthy, who built a second house for cooking.

In the houses of serfs short pegs were driven into the earth near the walls, and to these goats and sheep were tied by night. Along the sides, also inside the house, were places where the fowls roosted. The floor was covered with a kind of lemon-grass, which an untidy wife would leave until it became full of vermin before she thought of clearing it out and spreading fresh grass.

Among the serfs houses were built at some distance from each other so that, while a family might dwell in the same plantain patch with others, they were always some little way apart; this was in order that, in case of fire, one house might not set others alight. When a man married a second wife, he built a new house for her at a little distance from his first wife and gave her a field, so that each wife had her separate establishment.

CHAPTER IX

INDUSTRIES

Iron-workers—smelters—kinds of iron—making charcoal—mining the iron—the furnace—smelting—pig-iron workers—prices—anvil and big hammer—the furnace—the smith—his anvil—making his hammer—his tongs—potters—kinds of pots—clay—method of manufacture—polishing and decorating—baking the pots—the graphite mine—carpenters—tools—milk-pots and other vessels—drums—furniture—canoes—salt-making—Kibero—extracting the salt—the salt-workers—the market—the sacred pools—bark-cloth—the bark—its preparation—colouring and decorating—fumigating bark-cloths—skin-dressing—sandals

THE artisans of Kitara all belonged to what we have called the agricultural tribes or serfs (*Bahera*). The most important industries were iron-working and pottery, and in both of these the people of Kitara attained to a considerable degree of skill and produced better work than could be found in the surrounding countries.

(1) IRON-WORKERS

The country of Kitara was rich in iron and for many generations its iron-workers were noted for their skill. There were three stages in the work before the finished article was turned out, and each stage had its own workers, who did only that part and seldom had anything to do with the others except in buying and selling the products of their labours. The first handling of the iron, that is, the quarrying and smelting, was done by the smelters (*Bajugusi*), and the rough molten iron was purchased from them by the pig-iron workers (*Omusami*), who worked it up into pieces of various sizes, roughly shaped for different purposes. The smiths (*Mwesi*) bought this iron and made knives, spears, hoes, and other necessary articles.

The Smelters (*Bajugusi*).

The smelters were drawn from any clan of the serf class, and their work required a certain amount of skill and experience, for they had to be able to distinguish between good and bad stone. There were two kinds of stone in use and in common parlance they were referred to as the male and the female. The male was regarded as better in quality, but it had the disadvantage of being hard to break and prepare for smelting. It was black in colour and was found in the hill Nyaituma, usually on the surface of the ground. The female, or soft, iron was found in Galimuzika Busanga; it was red and lay in layers running into the hill-side.

Before going out to quarry the iron-stone, the smelters had to prepare the charcoal for their furnace, which was done by each man as near his own home as possible. At each stage in the work from the beginning of the preparation of the charcoal until the iron was smelted, taboos were observed and the worker watched carefully for unfavourable omens. When he went out to cut his tree for charcoal, to quarry his stone, or to do any other part of the work, he had to observe all the taboos usual at the beginning of any work and, in addition, if the man himself or a member of his family sneezed, he would not go to work that day, for the sneeze was the means taken by some ghost to warn him of danger, and if he disregarded the warning, he must not be surprised if he met with an accident.

The trees most commonly used by the smelters for making charcoal were *mikola*, *mireme*, and *mirongo*. When a man first went to the forest to cut his wood he brought home two pieces of fire-wood, one to be given to his wife for cooking and one to put on his fire. Until he had done this he might not approach his wife, nor might she touch him, and he had to sleep on the floor. The act of bringing in these pieces of fire-wood removed this taboo, but he had still to observe strict continence and might not have sexual intercourse until the charcoal was quite ready for use. This ceremony with the fire-wood also averted the harm that otherwise would befall him if anyone took any of the charcoal wood for ordinary use, and to neglect this precaution would probably mean that his charcoal would be so bad that it would not melt the iron.

When sufficient wood had been burned and the charcoal had been broken up ready for use in the furnace, the men went out in a body of from ten to twenty to the hill where the iron had to be quarried and gathered, and there they lived together while the work was going on, building grass-huts to sleep in. The first thing to be done was to propitiate the hill-spirit by offerings, that the earth might yield the stone without burying them, and that they might get good iron. On the hill there was a hole, probably of volcanic origin, which had to be visited and covered over, and an offering had to be made to it, lest wind might blow from it and bring rain before they had finished their work. In later times these offerings were made through the chief in whose district the place was, and a fowl or a goat was always killed as a sacrifice to the hill-spirit.

In addition to all the ordinary taboos, none of the men might wash while the work was going on, nor might they approach their wives, and if one met a dog on his way to work, he turned back. Each man had probably also to observe some special omen of which the medicine-man had warned him: while one had to avoid meeting a woman on his way to work, another would have to turn back if he met a man, and should any man's omens prove unfavourable, he would not start work that day.

When mining the stone, they did not dig downwards but generally horizontally into the hill-side, following a seam of stone from the point where it was exposed, and when the mine extended some distance into the hill several men might be engaged in the tunnel. One dug while others gathered the stone into baskets and passed it along from hand to hand until it reached the mouth of the mine, where the good material was sorted out and broken into pieces about the size of walnuts ready for smelting. This was packed in bundles to be carried to their headquarters. The task of digging the stone was dangerous, for no props were used to support the roof of the tunnel and it sometimes happened that the earth gave way and some of the men were buried. Those outside would do what they could to get help and reach the buried men, but invariably some of them would be suffocated before they could be rescued.

The charcoal and iron-stone were both carried to the smelting furnace, which was a round pit eighteen inches to two feet deep and eighteen inches wide, lined inside and covered over with clay which baked hard and did not crumble. A hole in the clay cover or lid served as a chimney and through it the furnace was fed when alight. Four tunnels were cut in the ground round the furnace so that they entered it at an angle a little more than half way down, and blast-pipes were put in them. Before the smelting was started a slow fire of grass and reeds was lighted in the pit to hasten the drying of the clay and warm the furnace. The bellows were clay pots about ten inches in diameter with a nozzle on one side communicating with a blast-pipe. The open top of the pot was covered by a goat-skin, tied on but not stretched taut, so that it could be moved up and down by a stick some eighteen inches long attached to its centre. This was raised to draw in air and on being pushed down forced it through the nozzle, which was connected with a blast-pipe, into the furnace. The nozzles of two pots were attached to each blast-pipe, and one man, sitting between two pots and raising the sticks alternately, was able to keep up a constant blast. When a man was making these bellows, he had to observe continency or they would constantly fill with water and refuse to act.

When the furnace was made and all was ready, the men retired to rest early, for they had to rise at about three o'clock to start the fire in the furnace. This was allowed to burn until the pit was hot, when it was filled up with layers of charcoal and iron-stone and kept full until the smelting was complete, charcoal and stone being added, when necessary, from heaps which were placed near in readiness. There was always a head-smelter who was responsible for adding the fuel and stone, which he dropped in by handfuls through the hole in the clay cover of the furnace. The fire was kept up all through that day and night until about eight on the following morning.

While the iron was being smelted, the workers might not eat potatoes and often they had to refrain from any food but plantain and maize in the cob, which they cooked for themselves over the furnace. Sometimes their wives were permitted to bring them cooked food, but as a rule all women had to keep away from the furnace; a menstruating woman might never at any time come near, and no man might take part in the work whose wife had just given birth. Infringement of any of these rules would prevent the iron from melting.

When enough had been smelted, the men demolished the furnace and with branches or rods levered out the nugget of iron. While it was still glowing and soft they chopped it, with ordinary axes, into lumps which they sold in this rough state to the pig-iron workers.

The Pig-iron Workers (*Omusami*).

The pig-iron workers took the rough iron in lumps as it was chopped by the smelters and worked it up into appropriate pieces, roughly shaped for different purposes, for the use of the smith to whom they sold it, charging him one hundred to one hundred and fifty cowry-shells for a piece to make a spear and two hundred to two hundred and fifty for a hoe; or they might exchange two hoe-pieces for a large and fine goat. These men never made any implements and only prepared the metal for the smiths, but they had to observe various taboos, chiefly connected with the stones which formed the anvil (*Ibala*) and the big hammer (*Muhindo*).

When a man went out to seek for stones for his anvil and hammer the conditions had to be perfect, all the usual taboos of starting work, which have already been enumerated, had to be observed, and he had to avoid sexual relations with his wife during the preceding night. All being favourable, he searched until he found suitable stones and then went to the chief on whose land they were, taking him about three hundred cowry-shells in order to get permission to carry them away. Accompanied by a sufficient number of men to dig and carry the stones, probably about thirty, and carrying a basket containing millet, semsem, and beans, he returned to the place where the stones were. He scattered the grain and beans over the stone intended for the anvil and offered a sheep and a fowl to it, killing them and allowing their blood to run over it. The meat was eaten by the helpers beside the stone and the man asked the stone to accept the sacrifice and prove a useful and remunerative anvil.

The work then went forward and the stone was dug out and covered with the skin of the sheep and two bark-cloths. The hammer was a smaller stone found near the anvil-stone; it was called the child of the anvil and was carried home along with it, and treated like a child. The men slung the two stones on a pole or two poles and carried them along, singing as if they were bringing home a bride. When they reached a point not far from the man's home, he went forward to warn his wife. She dressed herself in two of her best bark-cloths with a wreath of the creeper *luwezo* on her head and taking a small basket with millet, beans, and semsem, went out to meet the carriers. She sprinkled the seeds over the anvil and welcomed it like a bride.

The stones were then brought into the house, the man killed goats or sheep, and the woman cooked a sumptuous feast for the helpers and gave them beer to drink. For four days the stones remained in the house, secluded like a bride, and on the fourth day they were brought out and set ready for use.

This man always worked in the open and had a furnace like that of the smelters but smaller. His bellows were the same as those of the smelters, but he had only two of them and they were worked by one man. In the furnace he had a charcoal-fire, and he put into it the metal which he had to work up. His tongs were the split branch of a tree, into which he inserted the iron when it was hot and carried it to the anvil. His assistant wielded the great stone hammer some eighteen inches long and six inches in diameter, which was always held in a vertical position, being raised straight up and brought down upon the iron, and between them they divided the block of iron into pieces of the size required for hoes, spears, and knives. This metal when it had been worked in the charcoal-fire and hammered into pieces roughly shaped for the required implement made excellent iron.

The Smiths (*Mwesi*).

The smith bought his iron from the pig-iron workers and took it to his own home where he worked under a shed. He kept a supply of charcoal for his own use which he made from *misiso*, *mikindu*, *mukanaga*, and *misasa* trees. He had to observe the usual taboos when cutting the trees and making the charcoal. He made his own bellows and observed the taboo of continency while thus engaged lest they should fill with water and refuse to work. While making the pots for his bellows, he might not go on a long journey until they were perfectly dry and ready for use, for if he did so they would crack. When they were quite ready he had sexual intercourse with his wife, to make them sound and ensure their working well. Some iron-workers made the bowls and tube of their bellows of wood instead of clay, but these were exceptional cases.

He built the hut (*Isasa*) which served him as a smithy, observing while doing so the usual building taboos mentioned in the previous chapter, and scraped a hole in the floor of it for his furnace.

The most important thing was his anvil and he went out to look for a suitable piece of rock. Having found one, he applied to the chief of the district for leave to remove it, paying for the permission two hundred and fifty or three hundred cowry-shells. Taking men with him he went to fetch the stone. If it had to be split from the surrounding rock he took a pot of butter and painted a line round the stone where he wanted it to split. Then, when the butter had soaked into the stone, he heaped fire-wood on and round about it and burned it until the piece he wanted cracked off along the buttered line. If he could not get butter, he used the whites of eggs.

The stone was then secured to one or two poles and carried until it was near the man's house where it was set down, and the smith went on to inform his wife of its approach. The stone was called a bride and the man and his wife, each dressed in two bark-cloths, came out to meet it. The smith took a bark-cloth to cover it as a bride is veiled and his wife carried a basket containing millet, and a bunch of purificatory herbs. The stone was brought in with singing and dancing as in a marriage procession, and placed in the house, whereupon the husband told his wife that he had brought a second wife home to be with her and help in the house and with the family. He took the flat basket with the grain and threw some over the stone and sprinkled it with water from the bunch of herbs, that it might bear many children. The men who had carried the stone were then regaled with a plentiful meal of meat, vegetables, and beer.

For two days the stone remained in seclusion in the house, and when these were ended it was brought out and placed in position in the smithy and the smith set to work and made a knife as his first piece of work on it. This knife might not be sold in the market, but had to be exchanged for millet; this he gave to his wife who ground it to flour and made porridge which the two ate together as a sacred meal, thus preparing the anvil for ordinary use.

To make his hammer, the smith bought two nuggets of iron from the pig-iron worker, and until it was made he might not wash himself nor approach his wife. He might not make his hammer himself but called in two smiths to help him, and he had also to invite his parents to be present. The smiths arrived the night before the work was to begin and in the early morning, about three o'clock, they started work by lighting a fire and heating the iron. The pieces were heated, smeared with clay from an ant-hill, and heated again until white-hot, when they were welded together. The larger end

Exhibition of Carpenters, Potters, and Smiths

PLATE XXIX

Furnace and frame for fumigating bark-cloth

was four inches long, with two flat faces two inches wide and slightly curved sides measuring about one and a half inches. At one end of this a piece six inches long formed the handle of the hammer. When shaped it was handed to the smith's father who dipped it in a pot of water to harden it, for the smith himself might not touch it until it was finished.

When the work was done a feast was made and the smiths who had made the hammer were given four hundred cowry-shells. That night the smith had sexual relations with his wife and the hammer was treated like a bride and secluded in the house for two days. Then the smith took it out and made a knife as his first piece of work with it. With the knife he bought butter, tobacco, or coffee-berries which he gave to his parents, and the next day the hammer might be used for ordinary work.

When making such things as knives, hoes, or spears, the smith used as tongs a stick, into which he drove the prong of the implement he was making, so that he could hold it firmly. When working larger pieces of metal he used the split branch of a tree, wedging the iron firmly in it. His work chiefly consisted of the manufacture of hoes, knives, spears, and needles, though he was at times requested to make iron bracelets or necklets, and on rarer occasions might be asked to work copper or brass wire into wrist, neck, and leg ornaments.

(2) Potters

Both men and women made pots, but the better kind used by the king and more wealthy chiefs were invariably made by men, and the king had his own potters who belonged to a special clan and whose sons followed in their footsteps. A potter who made pots for general sale always attached himself to some chief; he made a pot and took it to a chief as a sign that he wished to serve him, after which he settled on the chief's estate and gave him one from every set of pots he made.

The chief requirements of the pastoral people were milk-pots, which varied in size from those containing a pint to the large pots which held a quart or more, and a few water-pots, which were not like the round pot generally found but were nearer an egg-shape and held a gallon or more of water. There was also a regular demand for cooking-pots, which were like basins and sometimes very large, and great beer-pots which held fully four gallons. In addition to these the potters manufactured the heads for the ordinary tobacco pipes, the stems of which were often made of a kind of stick with a thick pith which could readily be pushed out, leaving a hollow tube.

Two kinds of clay, both found in swamps or marshy land, were in general use, one being white and the other black. The common cooking and water-pots were made from the latter. Each potter procured his own clay, and when he went to get it he had to observe the taboos connected with the beginning of any work. He got men to assist him to carry the lumps, probably weighing about twenty pounds each, to his house, where he put the clay in a hole about two feet deep and a foot wide and covered it with plantain-leaves. At each new moon he had to take millet and semsem to this pit and sprinkle it there that the clay might be good.

When he wished to make pots, he took a lump of this clay, mixed it with water until it was quite soft and then added to it the grit from a piece of broken pot, which he mixed well with the new clay, for he claimed that this made the clay work well and prevented its cracking during drying. The only tools he required were a few bits of gourd and a pot of water into which he dipped these to keep them from sticking to the clay.

To form the base of the pot he took a lump of clay and placed it in the hollow of a bit of gourd or in the bottom of an old pot, working it thin and smoothing the inside with a scrap of gourd. The clay for the sides was made into long rolls and coiled on, worked to the thickness required with the thumb and fore-finger, and smoothed with the piece of gourd. Coil after coil was added, increasing and diminishing the circumference in accordance with the shape required until the sides were high enough, when it was rounded in to the neck; the man had no wheel and all the shaping was done by hand and eye. It did not take him more than an hour to build the pot, and six pots were usually a day's work.

The pot was then placed in the shade of his hut or a shed to dry, after which all rough places on the outside were rubbed off with a smooth stone. If it was for the king, the surface was then rubbed over with graphite from a mine at Kigorobya. This graphite was powdered and all light-coloured stone removed, and it was used in two different ways. Sometimes the powder was mixed with butter and blood and made into balls, which when hard were rubbed on the pot until it showed a bright polish. The usual way, however, was to mix the powder with water and the juice of the bark of a shrub *rukoma* which had glutinous properties; this mixture was painted on the pot and left to dry, and the pot again rubbed with the smooth stone until a fine polish was attained.

After polishing, the pots were dried thoroughly and had then to be baked. For this purpose the potter placed them round a large fire and turned them until the fire began to die down and they were very hot, when he pushed them into the remains of the fire, covered them with the hot embers and then with grass, and left them. When they were cool, he rubbed them again with the smooth stone and the finished article showed a fine silvery-black polish.

The common cooking and water-pots were made in the same way but were not finished off so carefully. They were not polished and the small milk-vessels and some more carefully made pots were plain, but the majority were decorated from the lip to about half way down with markings in a kind of herring-bone pattern, which might be done in several different ways while the clay was still soft enough to take an impression. Some potters used straw, plaited so that the plait had four sides each showing the same pattern; this was about two inches long and each side was about an eighth of an inch across, and it was pressed on the soft surface of the clay and rolled round the upper half of the pot with the palm of the hand. Some scratched the pattern with a pointed stick, while others had a piece of wood cut into ridges which they rubbed along the sides of the pot, pressing it with the palm of the hand, first in one and then in the opposite direction, so that the crossing of the lines formed a sort of herring-bone pattern. After drying the pot was placed under a large fire of grass which was kept up for as long as the potter considered necessary.

Pots had always to be baked in the evening so that they got the night for cooling, and the baking had to be done while there was a new moon, if the work was to be successful. Should any person spit upon a pot while it was being made or touch it with fingers wet with spittle, the pot would break. If a pregnant woman looked upon pots or touched them before they were finished, they would crack.

The mine from which the graphite for the pots was taken is in the side of a hill, and the stone has been quarried for many years from this place. The entrance is only a round hole some two feet in diameter, but inside it grows bigger, until at the end, some twenty yards into the hill, the roof is five feet high and the width some three to four feet.

The graphite stone, which is called *ekipiripyo*, is not very hard, but it requires some instrument to quarry it. When it has been got out, it is powdered and freed from any admixture of light-coloured stone.

(3) Carpenters

In early days there were only two classes of wood-workers, the more important being the men who made milk-vessels, washing-bowls, meat-dishes, and pails for drawing water for the cows, while those of the second class made the canoes which were used upon the river Nile and on Lake Albert. Since communication with other countries has been established another class of wood-workers has come into prominence, the makers of bedsteads, stools, and other furniture. There were also a few men who made drums, but, as there was little demand for these from anyone but chiefs and they could only be made and used by the king's permission, the number of their makers was limited.

The tools of a carpenter were few and roughly made. His axe was a wedge-shaped piece of iron tapering to a point, which was driven into a stout wooden handle eighteen inches long. With this hatchet the man felled the tree, cut it into the required lengths, and roughly shaped the blocks according to the nature of the article required. The same blade fixed in another handle made an adze, and he had a fewlong chisels and two or three long-bladed adzes for hollowing out vessels. His outfit thus consisted of some half-dozen tools, and in spite of its limitations he managed to turn out remarkably good work.

When a carpenter bought a new tool, it might not be used until a fowl had been killed and the tool anointed with its blood; and at each new moon the blood from the comb of a fowl had to be rubbed over all the tools. When a man had no fowl, he used for this purpose the juice from the red seeds of the *ngusura* plant. This precaution not only ensured that the tools did their work well, but it kept them from cutting the man while he was at work.

The most important carpenters were those who made the wooden milk-pots and other vessels, for these were always in demand and the makers found it advisable to keep a good stock of the more commonly used vessels constantly on hand to meet the calls upon them. The vessels were generally sold for cowry-shells and these the artisans exchanged for goats, of which many of them possessed large herds.

The principal wooden vessels were the milk-pots (*Bisahi*), which were used on ceremonial occasions, and the meat-dishes for the king and chiefs, and all of these were made from the wood of the *musoga* tree. Before the carpenter attempted to cut down the tree for his work he had to take to the tree-spirit an offering, generally a basket of millet and beans, though he might take something of greater value, at times even a goat, in order that the tree-spirit might consent to the tree's being cut down, and that the dishes might shape without cracking.

The vessels were cut out of solid blocks of wood which were

roughly shaped and put in the shade where the rays of the sun could not reach them. They were left for only a few days to season and then the man began to work on them with his adzes and chisels, shaping them slowly and watching the wood carefully all the time lest it should crack before he had finished; should it show any signs of doing so, he would sometimes resort to smearing it with cow-dung.

The king had a special carpenter, called *Ababaija*, who was responsible for his drums, milk-pots, and meat-dishes. The drums of the chiefs were also under the control of the king, who alone could give a chief permission to use one and who provided him with it. The drum-makers did not belong to any special clan, but they were all serfs and were all under the direction of *Ababaija*.

The trees used for drums were *kirikiti*, the sacred tree and used especially for royal drums, *mugairi*, and *muhumba*. The drum-maker when going to cut down the tree had to observe the usual taboos and to keep apart from his wife during the previous night.

When he found a tree which seemed suitable, he returned to the king and told him where it grew. The king sent a representative with him to the chief of that district, from whom they got permission to cut down the tree. The carpenter took a fowl, a goat, or a sheep, and, accompanied by a priest, went to the tree, where the offering was killed, cooked, and eaten on the spot. The tree might then be felled and cut into the required lengths, which were roughly hollowed out and carried home, where they were left to season before further work was done.

If the drum was for the king, no woman might come near during the making; but, if it was for anyone else, this taboo was not strictly observed. The maker had to refrain from his wife and from all women during the time he was engaged on the drum.

When the wood was seasoned, the man proceeded to finish the drum. The piece of wood, about four feet long and tapering towards the bottom, was hollowed out until the shell was about an inch thick. The narrow bottom and the top were covered with two skins, which were put on moist and laced together, so that when they were dry they were quite taut; the sides of the drum were almost covered with the strips with which the skins were laced together.

Inside the drums were placed various fetishes, which were the secret of the maker. Those drums of the king which were of most honour and importance had human blood poured into them, while those of less importance were filled with the blood of some animal. Other drums had some fetish, known as *Ikule*, which the maker inserted secretly and the nature of which was unknown even to his assistants, for he would send his men away on some pretext when he was ready to put the cover on the drum; in their absence he inserted his fetish, and when they returned he was busy lacing the skins at top and bottom together.

When western ideas of sitting on benches and chairs were adopted, the number of carpenters whose work was in the nature of furniture-making increased greatly. For chairs and benches they used a soft wood, of which they made a frame standing on four legs eighteen inches to two feet high. The seat and back were made of stems of papyrus-grass or midribs of palm-tree leaves; these were placed side by side, and fixed to the frame by pegs run through them at the ends. They also made some bedsteads in the same way.

The canoes made by the Bakitara were all of the dug-out pattern, and were to be found on Lake Albert, at various points on the Victoria Nile and the river Kafu, and a few on Lake Kioga. On Lake Kioga there were also to be found a few canoes which were built and not dug-out. The keel of such a canoe was made from one sound tree which was rounded underneath and slightly hollowed on the surface. On this keel the boat was built up of planks stitched together with creepers and kept in place by stretchers at intervals of about two feet. These canoes were, I understood, made by Basoga workmen, only the dug-out canoe being the genuine handiwork of the Bakitara.

To make the dug-out canoes a suitable tree was felled and the required length marked and cut off. It was then shaped outside so that the two ends sloped inwards from the top to the flat bottom. The upper surface of the tree was smoothed, and the work of chipping out the wood to form the boat begun. This was a tedious task, for as a rule only native adzes were used, though some men declared that fire was at times applied to hasten the work. The tree was hollowed out until the sides were from three to four inches thick and the bottom generally somewhat thicker. Canoes of this type on the Nile were sometimes large enough to take six cows at a time over the river. The carpenter who made the canoe was often the owner and made his living by ferrying people over the water.

(4) Salt-making

When the kingdom of Kitara was at the height of its power it possessed two important centres of the salt trade, but the salt-works at Katwe on Lake Edward now belong to the kingdom of Toro and the sole remaining part of the salt-works of Kitara is situated at Kibero on the shores of Lake Albert.

Lake Albert, a long narrow strip of water some twenty-five miles wide and one hundred and twenty-five miles long, lies in a saucer among the mountains and is fed at its southern end by the river Semliki flowing from Mount Luenzori, while at the extreme north the Victoria Nile enters it, emerging again as the White Nile. The outlet for the waters of the lake is limited and therefore its level rises and falls rapidly according to the rainfall on the surrounding mountains and the changes in the rivers which feed it. Sir Samuel Baker was the first to make any careful investigation of this lake, though Speke before him spoke of it under its native name of *Muta Nziga* (the locust-killer), a name doubtless given to it because of the numbers of these pests drowned in it when they came up the Nile and tried to cross it.

At one place on the eastern side of the lake, where there is a sandy shore about a mile wide between the lake and the mountains, a river, which in the dry season is some six to eight feet wide and a few inches in depth, runs into the lake. This river drains off the water from a considerable area of the mountains and during the rainy season becomes a wide and powerful stream, covering a great deal more of the shore.

In the dry season when this river is low, the shore for about half a mile on one side of it is penetrated by many saline springs bubbling up through clefts in the rock on to the surface of the ground, which here is a kind of hard black clay. On this the salt-workers have their claims, each marked out with stones or fixed boundaries of some kind. To gather the salt, they spread sand over the surface of the ground and leave it until it becomes impregnated with salt water from the springs, when they scrape it up and wash it. The sand is used again and again, so that in the rainy season, when these claims, with the exception of a few on the higher levels, are flooded by the river and rendered unworkable, the people carry it away and pile it in heaps near their huts where it will be safe until the river returns to its normal condition. Different kinds and qualities of sand are used and many of the workers are able to detect their own sand and distinguish it from that of others, a power which has often been found useful when a case of stealing sand has been brought up for judgment.

When the sand has been scraped up from the ground, it is put into pots which stand in spaces along the rocky walls of the river-bed. These pots have perforated bottoms and are placed in stands over other pots. The sand in the top pot is washed with water which runs through into the lower pot, carrying with it the saline substances from the sand. The contents of the lower pot are then boiled on the spot and evaporated, and the residue, which is the salt, is carried back to the salt-makers' village, which is quite near. During the rains the sand from the few holdings that can be worked is carried to the village, and the washing and evaporating are then done under cover. The salt is cleaner and whiter than that from the Katwe salt-works in Toro, but it is by no means pure.

The salt-makers form a community of between one and two thousand souls, and there are large numbers of children. Their huts are miserable and very dirty, containing nothing but a rough bed, a screen of hides or bark-cloth, a few pots, and here and there a stool or box to sit upon. Some are surrounded by a reed fence, while in other cases one fence encloses three or four houses. Clothing is scanty, and boys and girls up to the age of twelve years go entirely naked. They attempt no kind of cultivation, but most families keep a few goats and sheep, while some have one or two cows, and fowls are plentiful. Recently some attempt at sanitation has been made, and a few people use cess-pools near their huts; but most of them make use of the grass round about for sanitary purposes and all the filth is washed by the rains into the lake from which they draw water for all purposes.

Most of the work of obtaining the salt is done by the women. They scrape up the sand, wash it, and evaporate the water, while the men occupy themselves in bringing fire-wood and building huts. A few men add fishing to their other pursuits and sometimes hunt the hippopotamus, whose flesh is considered a luxury.

In the village there is a large open shed, which is their market place, where a brisk trade is carried on, as people come from all parts of the country to buy salt, bringing in exchange beans, potatoes, plantains, peas and other food, and also cooking and water-pots, animals, fire-wood, and all kinds of things needed for clothing, domestic purposes, and building.

Higher up the river, about two to three hundred feet above the salt springs, there is a sacred pool, *Mukamira*, where offerings were made to the rock-spirits to increase the supply of salt. Above the pool is a rock rising several hundred feet high, from which water falls during the rains into the pool, which is about eighteen feet deep. A priest with some followers had charge of this sacred pool and lived near it. Every year the priest received two goats, of which the king supplied one and the chief of the district the other. One had to be black and the other white, so that, if the king sent a white goat, the chief had to give a black one, while, if the king's was black, the chief's had to be white.

The priest went to the pool in the evening with the goats and a fowl; the goat which came from the king was kept, but the other was thrown alive into the pool, where it swam about trying to find a way out; the head of the fowl was cut off and its body thrown in. The goat found places where it could rest its feet on the rocky sides so that it saved itself from drowning and was invariably found alive in the morning, when it was taken out, killed and cooked. The priest and his assistants, with the chief of the district, then ate the meat as a sacred meal near the pool.

Near the lake, on the side of the river, there was another pool, *Muntebere,* which was also sacred and more important than the one higher up the rock. Another priest and his servants had charge of this pool, and each year the king sent a young slave-woman, two cows, and a white sheep, to the priest. The slave-woman was given as wife to one of the Abasimba clan who was a servant of the priest; and, if she had a child, it was sacrificed the following year when the king again sent the offering of a slave, cows, and a sheep. The child's throat was cut, the blood poured into the pool, and the body thrown in and left there. The two cows were brought to the pool and made to look at the water, and the priest then took possession of them. They were sacred animals, and when killed only the priest might eat their flesh. The white sheep was thrown alive into the pool, and prayer was made for more salt, more children, health and plenty. The people believed that the sheep, if accepted by the spirit, would be taken to the lake by a subterranean passage; to fulfil this expectation the priest's servants took it out of the pool by night while it was still alive, carried it in a canoe out into the lake, cast it in to drown and left the body to be washed up on the shore. The offerings at this pool were for the general good of the country and the increase of the people.

(5) Bark-cloth Making

Bark-cloths have been in use for so long that no one can tell how they came to be introduced. The best kinds of trees for the purpose are *mpwera, ndimwe, kaisuma, ntanga, mgarama,* and *mutuba.* These were grown by the agricultural people, who planted them in their fences, choosing branches from three to four inches thick, eight feet long, and quite straight. They were inserted six inches to ten inches in the ground and grew readily, forming in three years a tree of about seven inches in diameter, at which stage the first bark was removed. A horizontal cut was made through the bark round the base of the tree and another similar cut six or seven feet up the trunk. A vertical cut joined these and the whole of the bark between them was worked off, the instrument used being a blunt chisel-like tool made from the flowering stem of the plantain, which was inserted under the bark and worked along until the whole strip was loose.

When the worker found on first cutting the bark that there was a large flow of sap he had to wash his hands in cold water, not in hot, and he might not smear any fat on his body. He might not drink beer before cutting the bark, and he had to be careful that no perspiration fell on the bark, for that would prevent its working up properly. When the bark had been stripped off, the tree was often smeared over with cow-dung and wrapped up in plantain-leaves to hasten the growth of the new bark, and it would go on bearing for fully twelve years, though the best barks were obtained in the third and fourth years.

After it had been cut from the tree, the bark was rolled up and left for a night, or longer if there was much sap, and in the morning the man scraped its outer side and spread it on his bench for beating. This bench was a log of wood, which was fixed horizontally in the ground, generally under a grass shed, and the upper side was faced, giving some four inches of a flat surface to work on. The man sat by this bench and beat the bark with a mallet not unlike a stone-mason's hammer, but with grooves cut round it. With this he hammered the bark, moving it out from him and back again until he had reduced it to the required thinness, when the size of the cloth would have expanded to some three feet wide and from twelve to eighteen feet long. The worker finished off his work by going over the cloth with a mallet with finer grooves, after which he put it out in the sun to dry. The side which was exposed to the sun took on a reddish tint, while the other side remained lighter in colour.

Next morning the man and a companion set to work to rub the bark-cloth between their hands to soften it and remove all dust and loose fibre. Any holes made by branches or bad places were cut out in squares and pieces were let in and stitched with plantain-fibre, after which it was again stretched out and the stitching smoothed. It was then cut and joined up to make a piece some twelve feet square, when it was ready for ordinary use.

The bark-cloths for better use, however, were coloured by a man who bought them from the makers. Some were dyed a good black on one side by the use of a kind of black clay from a swamp. This was smeared over one side of the cloth, washed off, and the cloth dried. To dye them red, the man used the leaves and flowers of a tree called *mukoro*. These were boiled for a whole day and the bark-cloth soaked in the mixture and then washed and dried in the sun. Those which were not dyed were generally of a brick red or terracotta shade, but one kind of tree bore a bark which was very light in colour, and the cloth when finished was almost white.

The best bark-cloths of the king had patterns painted upon them, and in some cases the patterns were worked with blood by princesses, who drew their own blood for the purpose and spent months drawing geometrical patterns with it.

The only method used to keep bark-cloths clean and free from insects was to fumigate them, and the better classes did this regularly, using for the purpose a wicker frame shaped somewhat like a bee-hive. This was roughly plaited or woven from the branches of a shrub not unlike a willow and measured three to four feet across and two to three feet deep. In it was placed a pot containing a kind of soft wood which, when burned, gave off a sweet-smelling smoke. The bark-cloth was spread over the frame and left until the smoke had thoroughly penetrated into all the folds, when it was turned and fumigated on the other side. It was then folded up and put under the bedding or the pillow to be pressed. Poor people who could not thus cleanse their bark-cloths would spread them in the heat of the sun for a time which would to some extent free them from body-lice, but they always suffered from such pests and after a time the bark-cloths had to be destroyed.

(6) Skin-dressing

The king had his special skin-dressers, the chief of whom was called *Omuhazi we bisato*, and chiefs also employed their own men. The ordinary cow-men were experienced in dressing cow-skins and prepared what they needed for themselves.

When a skin was to be dressed, it was spread out with the inside uppermost, and pegged out with numerous pegs where the sun could beat upon it. The pegs went through the skin into the ground, but the skin was raised on them some three inches above the earth so that the air could pass freely underneath.

When quite dry, the skin was secured to a reed frame like a wall and scraped. For this purpose the man used a slab of wood four inches by three, with pointed iron teeth through it. With this he scraped the skin until it was quite thin and even. This was done in the sun so that the skin bleached white as the work went on. The hair was shaved off and the skin taken down, well buttered, and rubbed until it was quite soft and pliable.

For the special use of the king skins were taken from newly born calves which were skinned before the blood began to circulate.

Sandals were sometimes worn and anyone who wanted them had to supply the maker with a buffalo-skin, from which he cut pieces shaped to the feet of the wearer but rather larger. The edges were turned up and the sandal fastened by a loop round the great toe and a strap across the instep.

CHAPTER X

CUSTOMS OF THE PEOPLE. PART I

(1) BIRTH

Clan-communism in wives—food and other taboos for a pregnant woman and her husband—the husband's mother, the midwife, and other attendants—birth—cross-birth—burying the placenta—treatment of mother and child during seclusion—amulet of umbilical cord—purification of mother, child, and house—naming the child—the nurse—age of weaning—method of carrying a child—ceremony of making a child sit up—test of legitimacy—test for sterility—treatment of a barren woman—treatment of woman whose children die in infancy—premature birth and abortion—death of woman in child-birth—twins—birth—twin drums—placenta put in ants' nests—seclusion of mother and children—telling the grandparents—preparations for bringing out the twins—father's representative—dancing and magic working—bringing out and naming the twins—the ceremonies—placenta put in the forest—death of a twin during the ceremonies—visiting the grandparents—birth of triplets

THE one aim and object of a woman's life was to marry and have children, for an unmarried or childless woman was an object of contempt and scorn and was treated as a thing of no importance whatsoever. It was in her children, especially if she bore a son, that a woman's importance lay.

A woman, unless she was for some reason sterile, generally had children, for any man who was a clan-brother of her husband had the right to approach her bed. Every man in a clan had the right to use the wife of any of his clan-brothers and this was so completely taken for granted that the matter was seldom even mentioned. No husband would think of making any complaint on the subject and no one would think of blaming a woman for allowing her husband's clan-brothers to share her bed any more than for allowing her husband to do so. No judge would condemn such a woman for adultery, for the act was perfectly legal. The woman was, however, restricted to men of her husband's clan, though to them she could only deny herself on the plea that she was unwell. Her husband in the same way was restricted to the wives of his clan-brothers, and if he took any other woman he was guilty of adultery.

Among the Bahuma there was little need for many food-taboos for a pregnant woman, for, as far as possible, her food would always be milk. She was free to eat beef when it was to be had and might also take millet-porridge. Her husband would do his best to supply her with milk from a healthy cow which did not lose its calves; and she had to avoid milk from one which had lost a calf, from one that had drunk salt water, and from one that had been with the bull less than four days previously. Among the agricultural people a pregnant woman had to be careful to drink a little water before eating, and she might eat no salt except what had been cooked with her food, for it would cause her child to be born blind or to have skin-disease. Beans and a kind of wild tomato, *njagi*, were forbidden and she might eat no hot food nor drink hot water lest her child's hands and arms should be scalded and show white patches.

There were a great number of other taboos to be observed, most of them belonging properly to the agricultural people but to a large extent adopted by the pastoral people also. A woman might not eat her food with anyone except young children or old women who were past the age of menstruation. Any food she left had to be eaten by a small child. Deformed persons and certain animals, such as monkeys, were kept as far as possible out of her sight, lest they might affect conception. She had to be careful not to sit on a bed or stool that had been used by any other person, and no man but her husband might sit on her bed. She might not touch the clothing of any man but her husband, and no one might touch hers. She might never sleep on her back, and if she wished to turn over in bed she had to sit upright and then lie down again on the other side, for otherwise the child would die or there would be a miscarriage. She had to keep her breasts and stomach covered lest any person should see them and by magic cause some evil to enter her and injure her offspring.

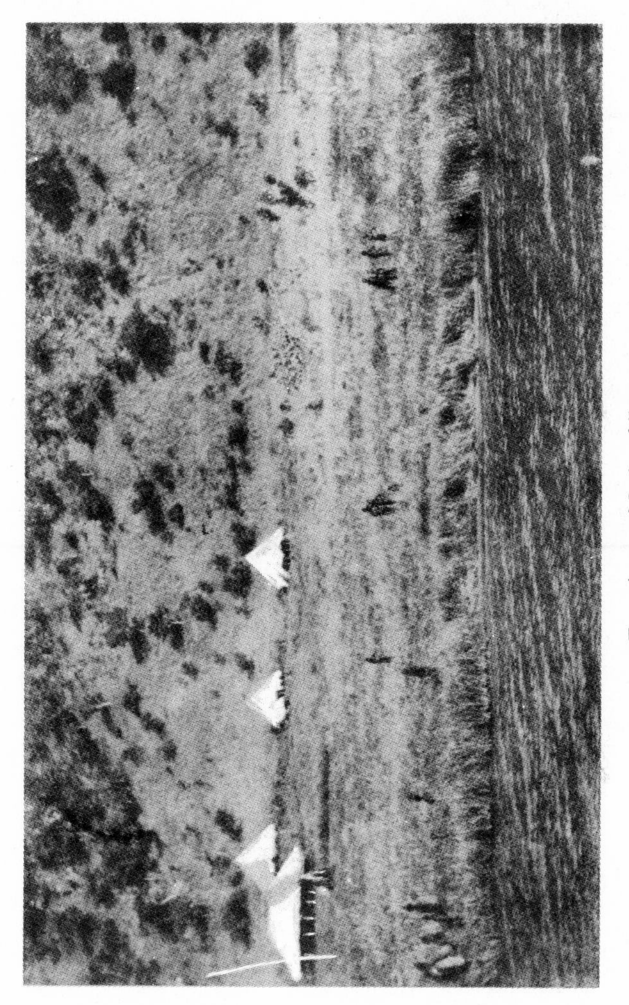

Foreshore of Lake Albert

Lake Albert. View of salt-works at Kibero

Lake Albert. Salt-worker gathering up sand
for washing out salt at Kibero

When she went to relieve nature she took with her a gourd with a long spout, which was placed so that a stream of water mixed with certain herbs ran over the organs as she evacuated and prevented evil from entering her. When she went along the road, if a tethered goat or sheep crossed in front of her and its rope lay across her path, she might not step over the rope but had to go round the animal or step on the rope, for otherwise her labour would be difficult. If she encountered black ants on her path, she had to spit on them or throw a little grass on them before stepping over them, or the child would either cut its upper teeth before the lower, a most unlucky happening, or have sores in its ears. Should she commit adultery by having sexual intercourse with any man not of her husband's clan, she would experience retarded labour and her own life or that of her child would be lost. Her husband also had to avoid having sexual intercourse with the wives of any but his clan-brothers, and for him this taboo continued as long as his wife was nursing her child. Should he transgress, the child would suffer from pains in the stomach and might die. The husband might never take a long journey when the time for birth approached, and during the time of labour he had to be at hand in order to go for help if required.

Among both pastoral people and serfs a woman's mother-in-law was the person who took charge of affairs during pregnancy and at birth. It often happened that the man lived in the same kraal as his parents, and then his mother was always near to advise the wife. If, however, she lived at a distance, she would come and stay with her son as the time for her grandchild's birth drew near. Among the agricultural people another woman of the husband's clan was also appointed to attend to the wife and see that she took medicine daily and that she observed the necessary taboos. In both cases all the women who assisted her were of her husband's clan.

Women always continued to go about and to perform their ordinary duties until the time of delivery. When labour commenced the preparations were of the simplest. A little fresh grass was spread upon the floor near a post in the inner chamber of the house, and upon this the mother stood in a stooping posture, holding the post. In many pastoral clans, and sometimes among the serfs, a midwife was called in who was not related to either the mother or the father, but the man's mother was always present to see that all was done for the safety of her son's child. Many children were said to die at birth, and, more especially among the serfs, a wife, if she had some grudge against her husband, would seek to kill her child by pressing on it, or even by sitting upon it. Should a woman bear a child whose paternity was doubtful, the midwife often strangled it at birth.

The midwife, whether she was the mother-in-law or not, stood in front of the patient, and the women who were called in to assist stood behind and supported her as she crouched holding on to the post. Should the mother be nervous, she was admonished, and should she cry out in pain, her mouth was held or a bark-cloth was thrown over her head and she was whipped to make her brave. Little mercy was shown to a fearful woman, though women-doctors sometimes gave their patients a herb to chew, which was supposed to assist labour.

When all went well, the child was delivered on the grass and the midwife or the mother-in-law washed out its mouth, eyes, and ears, and started respiration. The baby was seldom removed or the cord cut until the placenta had come; but, if this was delayed, the midwife tied the cord with grass in two places, cut it between them with a piece of reed from the roof, and passed the child to some attendant to hold.

Head-presentation was the only form of birth liked. Foot-presentation, which was known as *Khabona* (an evil thing), was a particularly bad omen and would cause the parents to die. When this took place, any people who were in the house were sent out, a food basket was brought, the bottom of it cut out, and the child was passed through this head first to reverse the order of birth and avert any evil. Offerings were also made to the gods and ghosts to prevent evil results.

If the case was one of cross-birth and the midwife was unable to press the child back and right it, she called the husband and sent him for a well-known medicine-man, called *Omusehenga*, who was an expert in midwifery. The husband took with him a young cow or its equivalent in cowry-shells, that is one thousand shells, to make the man come quickly. As he came the medicine-man watched for omens, and should the first person he met on his way be a woman he would turn back and nothing would induce him to start out again that day. When he arrived he pared his nails, washed his hands with hot water and rubbed them with fat from a cow before examining the patient, who lay with her face covered. He passed the limb which was presented up into her womb gently, and seeking either the neck and head or the other hand or foot tried to turn the child and bring about ordinary presentation. He might even endeavour to bring about foot-presentation, if that were the easier course. If he failed in his attempt and the mother's life was in danger, he proceeded to dismember the child and save the woman. It was seldom that a woman died in child-birth, though she might be kept two days in labour. Among the agricultural people, if a child appeared to be still-born the midwife beat with a stick on an iron hoe over it to awaken it to life.

Should the placenta not come away at once, the same medicine-man was called in. Taking hold of the umbilical cord he followed it up into the womb, and working the placenta free brought it out.

The father dug a hole in the floor of the house near the door, on the right side if the child was a boy, and on the left for a girl. This he lined with the leaves of the *kirikiti* tree, and the mother placed the after-birth in the hole and covered it with more leaves and sometimes also with the flowers of the same tree. Among the agricultural people and a few pastoral clans, plantain-leaves were used for this purpose, the leaves from the kind of tree used for brewing being taken for a boy and those from the tree used for cooking if the child was a girl. The husband then filled up the hole with earth and beat the place hard.

After this the wife went to bed, for four days if her child

was a boy, and three if it was a girl. The midwife washed her and the child every day. Warm water was poured over the child and it was well rubbed with the palm of the hand. There was no towel, but the friction soon dried the child and butter was rubbed over it until no trace of grease was left.

If the child was a boy, the husband gave the midwife a leather strap which he used when milking to tie the legs of restive cows, and this was used as a belt for the woman. If the child was a girl, a piece of bark-cloth was used. During the four days no one except the midwife and the husband was allowed to see the woman.

Among the peasants women often continued to work in their fields until labour commenced, and they would sometimes bring it on by lifting a water-pot or a bundle of fire-wood. When there was not time to reach home and the child was born in the field, the woman would call for assistance and the midwife or mother-in-law would be summoned, the cord cut and the child washed on the spot. The placenta was carried home and buried in the usual way, and the woman went to bed for the proper time.

During the days of seclusion after birth, nothing might be taken from the house in which the woman lay. Should anyone have left anything in the house or lent the husband anything and insist on having it back, the husband had to make arrangements to borrow a similar article from someone else in order to satisfy the demand, for to take anything from the house would harm the young child. The husband brought in one of the logs forming the gate and put it on the fire, which had to burn brightly all the time and might not be allowed to go out, for the child's life might go out with it. No pipe or grass might be lit from the fire and no fire might be taken from the house.

When the stump of cord fell from the child, the mother put it into the small stem-end of a bottle-gourd and made it into an amulet which the child often wore in infancy but which was afterwards kept by the mother in her special basket of treasures with the child's teeth and such things.

When the period of seclusion was ended, the mother was taken out and purified by being washed from head to foot, her nails were pared and all the hair on her body even to her eyebrows was shaved off. She then shaved the baby's head and pared its nails. Among the pastoral people the hair and nail-clippings of child and mother were made up into a ball and stored away or buried in the dung-heap where no one was likely to find them and use them for magic. Anyone might cut the hair of a child, but he must give it to the mother to keep. When a man grew up he hid his hair-cuttings, for to leave them about or throw them away was dangerous and caused headaches, and if either they or his nail-clippings were found they might be used to cast some evil spell upon him.

Among the serfs, the nail and hair-cuttings of the mother and child were placed in the mother's bed, but no further care was taken of them and they found their way to the floor to be swept up with the dust of the house. Among some clans this ceremony of shaving the child's head and paring its nails did not take place until it was four months old. Then the child was washed with water in which millet had been soaked, its hair was shaved and its nails pared, and the clippings placed in the mother's bed.

When the mother and child had been purified, the room was swept out and the sweepings thrown by the pastoral people on a special place in the dung-heap. Among the serfs the sweepings were thrown at the root of a plantain, the kind used for beer if the child was a boy and that used for cooking if it was a girl. The fruit on the tree at the time was afterwards made into beer and drunk, or cooked and eaten, according to its kind, by the midwife and members of the family; no outside person might partake for that would injure the child. For some months afterwards the sweepings of the house were thrown at the root of this plantain and the fruit was generally guarded for the use of the family, though it would not injure the child if others partook.

When purified the mother and her child might be seen by visitors and the husband's relatives came in numbers to see the new addition to the clan. The name of the child was then pronounced by the grandmother before the assembled members of the clan. The name was usually that of some ancestor who was noted for his long life and good character, who had had a large family and had been a prosperous man. The spirit of this ancestor was then said to guard the child from evil and to have a great influence on his welfare.

Among the pastoral people a nurse of the father's clan was appointed for a child as soon as it was born, and the mother had little to do with it save to suckle it, which she did whenever it would take nourishment. As a rule a child was not weaned until between two and three years old, but it was given cow's milk to drink at an early date, and if the husband wished his wife to return to him, she would leave the child to the nurse, who fed it entirely upon cow's milk, and would return to her husband. As cow-men had only one wife, the woman usually became pregnant again soon and according to custom could not nurse a child when she had conceived again. Even in recent years a child of a pastoral family was fed on cow's milk alone until it was quite big.

Much child-sickness and many deaths might be attributed to the nurses, who had complete charge of the children. Often through over-anxiety and a desire to help the child, they gave it, for slight ailments, herbs and drugs to such an extent that its life was in danger from poisoning. This is not surprising when we consider how little was known of the power of the drugs used or of the methods of preparing them. The nurse usually chewed the herbs to be administered or moistened them with her own saliva and spat them from her mouth into that of the infant. In this way the child often contracted other diseases, especially venereal diseases, from which so many of these women suffer.

Among the serfs a woman nursed her child for at least two years and lived apart from her husband lest she should conceive again, for she might not suckle the child when she was pregnant. If she were found to be with child again before her former one was a year old, the husband was censured by the members of the clan, for such a state of affairs was considered to be injurious both to the born and to the unborn child. The baby was taken away and fed on artificial food and the mother was carefully guarded. After the first three months of a child's life, it was taught to take artificial food, stewed plantain being a favourite dish. When it was weaned the paternal grandmother generally looked after it.

Until a child was four months old, it was not allowed to sit up but lay on its back. Among the serfs the mother carried her child about with her in a sling on her back. This was made of goat-skin which was dressed with oil or butter and rubbed with the hands until it was quite soft. Strips of skin were attached to the upper corners and the two lower corners were tied round the waist to fasten in front. The mother took the baby and, stooping, placed it on her back and threw the sling over it. Then, bringing the thongs at the upper corners over her shoulders, she crossed them in front and tied them round her waist. From this sling she could bring her child to the breast to be suckled and when it had been fed it was thrust back into the sling without untying it, so that she could go on with her work.

When a boy, whether of the cow-men or serfs, was four months old, his father put him to sit on the floor in a bark-cloth ring, steadying him for a few moments until he could sit alone, after which the mother was at liberty to let him sit up. A girl baby was made to sit by her mother and father's mother. In both cases the child received from its relatives presents of beads, which were made into strings and put on its wrists. There was great rejoicing and the father made a feast. Among the Bahuma he often gave the child a cow; if it was a boy, the cow became his own property, and if it was a girl, the cow was hers until she married and left the home. After this the mother took the child on a round of visits to relatives.

There used to be among the pastorals a custom which has long fallen into disuse, for discovering whether a child was legitimate or not. The child was placed on the ground in the gate-way of the kraal when the cows were leaving it in the morning. If it was illegitimate the cows trod it to death, but if it was the owner's own child the cows avoided it and it was unharmed.

If within a reasonable time after marriage a woman did not conceive, her husband would call in a medicine-man who prescribed a medicine to be drunk after a period of menstruation. If this failed, the medicine-man resorted to a trial to see whether husband or wife was the cause of sterility. The man and his wife, both naked, sat side by side on a bark-cloth and were given some medicine to drink. They sat there an hour and if the medicine took effect and caused either of them to urinate, that one was the cause of barrenness. Should they both be able to retain the medicine, they would be able to have children.

There were a number of women doctors who professed to be able to make barren women conceive. If one of these was called in, she gave the patient a potion of certain herbs to drink after menstruation had ceased and also gave her an amulet consisting of a string with knots tied in it to wear round her waist, resting over the pubes. The medicine-woman would test whether the woman was able to bear children by making her sit naked on a bark-cloth and drink water with a certain herb in it. If it caused the woman to urinate unconsciously she could not have children, but if she retained it she might hope to become a mother. The medicine-woman then made her a medicine of the flowers of some herb mixed with the urine of a bull. After her next menstruation period she was given another dose and she would thereafter bear a child.

The medicine-woman could inform such a woman how many children she would have. She gave the woman three pieces of the plant from which her medicine had been made. On these the woman smeared some of her menstrual discharge and gave them back to the medicine-woman. They were inserted in a ball of dung from a bull and put in a safe place in her field. On the third day she examined the ball and foretold the number of children from the number of insects she found eating the menstrual discharge.

In later years should one of the children, who had thus been magically foretold, die and the mother fear that the sickness was contagious, she sent for the medicine-woman, who went to the place where the mother's special medicine-plant grew. She had to cut the shrub with one stroke of her knife and from it she made an amulet for the mother to wear to protect the other children from the disease. This woman also shaved the heads of the children when necessary and was given a small present each time she did it. She gave them amulets to wear, and when they grew up, the mother gave her a bark-cloth.

When a woman who had been childless, more especially if she were of the serfs, found she had conceived, she summoned a number of children to dance before her. Her husband sat beside her and, as the children danced, suddenly turned to her, shouting "Ah!" to frighten away any ghost which might be hovering round to steal away her child.

A woman who had been childless had to wear amulets during the period of gestation, and no person might pass a tobacco pipe behind her, as they usually did when passing a pipe from one to another across a third person. The pipe must be passed in front of such a woman or she would remain barren.

If a woman had had two or three children who died in infancy, she visited a medicine-man who gave her drugs to drink after menstruation and an amulet to wear round her waist. If she did not conceive after the first time of drinking the drug, she was given more after her next period of menstruation and was sure to conceive. When she had her child the medicine-man came to place it sitting on the floor and to name it. He also shaved its head and pared its nails. If she had more children she sent for the medicine-man to shave their heads and cut their nails, which was done for the first time at four months old, not at four days as was the usual custom. The man was rewarded by the gift of a goat or a sheep. Special names were used for these children and were given to them by the medicine-man.

Premature birth and abortion were said to be due to ghosts and a woman who had suffered thus was treated in the same way as any other sick person from whom a ghost had to be driven. Afterwards the medicine-man visited her frequently and gave her special food to help her to conceive again and carry the child the proper time.

When a woman died in child-birth leaving children, her relatives gave the husband another wife who became mother to the children. If a wife, however, died during her first confinement, the relatives did not help the husband, unless she was staying with them at the time of her death, when they restored the marriage-fee or gave him another wife. If both mother and child died, they were buried at one place side by side but in different graves. Even if a woman died when she was with child, the foetus was removed and buried in a separate grave.

Birth of Twins

Twins were said to be the children of the god of plenty, and special ceremonies were observed at their birth. It was a joy to the parents if the twins were boy and girl, for should both be boys, the god was thought to favour the father and have some grudge against the mother and her clan, while, if both were girls, the father and his clan were thought to be in disgrace. The party thus shown to be out of favour had to make offerings to pacify the god and remove his displeasure.

When a midwife perceived that there were twins she dismissed all the women who might be present except those she really required to assist her. She then by a sign enjoined silence until the second child was born, for the sound of a voice or an ejaculation might cause the twins to die. This silence was called *kwase*, and the midwife might only speak if it was necessary to summon the medicine-man, and even then she must on no account mention the word "twin." When both were born she raised a peculiar shrill cry which made the event known to those outside. Special twin drums were hung on a *kirikiti* tree, which had to be planted if there was not one near. These were sounded and songs begun, while the husband went off in haste to bring a special medicine-man. If he lived at a distance, the children's eyes, mouths, and ears were washed and respiration started, but they might not be moved or the cords cut. The mother had to lie beside them on the grass and nurse them there until the medicine-man arrived. When he came he severed the cords and gave permission to move them and wash them.

The father was next despatched to bring two nests of the black ant (*mpiki*), which were mounds of earth about eighteen inches high and a foot in diameter. The inside of each nest was scooped out by the father, and the medicine-man lined them with the leaves and flowers of the sacred tree *kirikiti* and put in them the flowers of the herbs *luweza*, *kasekera*, and *ruira*. He then put the placenta of one of the children in each nest, covering it over with leaves, and smeared the outside and filled up the hollow and the opening with potter's clay, which was mixed and handed to him by the father. Each lump was decorated with the creeper of the wild gourd *bombo* and placed by the fire to dry and harden. Instead of the ants' nests peasants frequently used water-pots, which had to be quite new. They also usually kept a white fowl in the house after the birth of twins.

The medicine-man closed the front door and, if the house had not another entrance, a door was cut at the back and a fence built round it to form a courtyard for the mother and to prevent people from coming into the house. Dancing began outside and was continued well into the night.

The mother was given two bark-cloths which she wore like a man, one knotted on each shoulder. She also wore a wreath of the gourd-creeper *bombo* round her head. The father had also to wear two bark-cloths, one knotted on each shoulder, and a wreath, to show his new position as one favoured by the god. A special bed was arranged for the mother and her children, for she must not sleep on her husband's bed.

Each morning and evening when the mother nursed the children she had to sing while drums were beaten and the people danced outside. Among the cow people the drums were beaten each evening by the herdsmen after the cows had been milked and they had had their meal of milk. Peasants or serfs beat their drums soon after sunset and kept it up for an hour or two.

When the stumps of umbilical cord fell from the children they were decorated and made into ornaments which the children wore round their necks.

A man was allowed to tell his own father what had happened, even if they lived in different places. As a rule, however, they were in the same kraal, and there was no need for him to make a journey for the purpose. The father of the twins however was not allowed to go to his father-in-law to inform him, but had to let him know indirectly. He had two emblems made for the twins according to their sex, the emblem for a boy being a needle and that for a girl a knife. Peasants frequently used two short sticks instead of the needle and knife. When these emblems were ready, the father found some friend and asked him to take them to his parents-in-law. The friend had to be an active man and able to run, for he had to place the emblems in the house and escape without letting the inmates know his errand. There was a certain amount of responsibility and danger in his task for if he were caught he suffered punishment. He went as an ordinary visitor, bearing the emblems wrapped in bark-cloth, and greeted the people and talked to them to disarm any suspicions they might have of his object. During conversation he slipped his parcel into some place where it was not noticed, took his departure, and, when he had reached a safe distance, called, "Your daughter has twins," and fled. They gave chase and if caught he might be roughly handled; in fact it was even permissible to kill him. If they failed to catch him they shouted after him, "If we had caught you, we would have killed you." This method of treating a captured messenger was later given up and a fine imposed. The grandparents had then to wear two bark-cloths and creeper-wreaths. They purified the emblems by sprinkling them with water in which herbs had been placed, before picking them up and placing them with their sacred treasures.

During the next four or five months, or in the case of poorer people for as long as two years, preparations were made for the great festival which had to take place when the twins were brought out from seclusion and shown to the relatives. During this time the mother remained in seclusion and the father either had to stay with his wife himself day and night or else, if he were a poor man who had to see to the preparations himself, he provided a substitute who was chosen by a medicine-man by augury and was known as *Sabalonga* or *Salongo Muto*, the "little father" of the twins. This might be a younger brother of the husband, or in some cases a slave would have to undertake the duties, which were not strenuous, consisting merely of constant presence in the hut with the midwife and the mother and children. He was purified and wore a wreath. Some peasants were too poor to secure even the services of a boy for this office, so the father would place his walking-stick in the house and call that his representative.

The father had to get all things ready for the feast, and a poor peasant would ask his master to assist him with a goat or two and beg his relatives to help with other food or beer. The wife's parents also collected from her relatives. When all had been prepared the father of the twins went to the medicine-man and asked him when the children might be brought out from seclusion, and the day, which had always to be the second or third day of a new moon, was fixed. The father made known the day to all concerned, and engaged a band of drums and wind instruments for the occasion.

The relatives on both sides congregated at about four or five in the afternoon of the day before the dance, the husband's relatives meeting near the house, while the mother's relatives met a short distance away. During the night there was much noisy dancing and a great deal of magic-making, for each party brought its medicine-man, who was busily employed during the night seeking to outstrip the other in making magic in order to ward off from his own party and transfer to the other any evil which might be attached to the twins. The rivalry amounted to serious hostility, and should a member of one party wander to the other, there was danger of a fight and broken limbs. The whole night was thus spent by both families in dancing to please the god of plenty and in seeking to influence the unseen powers so that evil might be averted from their own and transferred to the other party. When the twins were boys, the maternal party made strenuous efforts to cast off the evil and displeasure which the god was threatening against their clan; if they were girls, the paternal party had to show the greater diligence in their efforts towards the same end.

About five o'clock, with the first signs of morning, the chief medicine-man brought four branches of the sacred trees *merembe*, *mulamula*, and *nkoni*, and planted them in the ground between the two parties. The place thus marked was called *Ekibarekya lubanga*, and grass was laid upon the ground and covered with a bark-cloth. The twins and the clay lumps containing the placenta of each child were brought and laid there. It was the duty of the grandmothers to bring the children out of the house in the early morning and place them with the placenta on the bark-cloth. During the whole ceremony the grandmothers had to wear creeper-wreaths. The boy-twin was carried by the father's mother and the girl-twin by the mother's mother. If both were boys, the paternal grandmother carried both and the maternal grandmother was excluded, while if both were girls the rule was reversed. The medicine-man was always present to supervise the ceremonies.

The children were then given names by the grandmothers. A boy was called *Sengoma*, and, if the second was a boy, he was called *Kato*. A girl was called *Nyagoma*, and a second girl *Nyakato*. The father of the twins was known as *Salongo*, and the mother as *Ṇalongo*.

Hostilities now ceased and the two parties danced round the twins for some time. The parents of the twins and all the grandparents were dressed in two bark-cloths knotted one on each shoulder, and wore newly-made wreaths of the creeper *bombo*. They and the near relatives had their faces painted with white clay, while other friends smeared their faces with grey ash from the wood-fire. After the dancing had proceeded for a time, the two parties separated, the father placing himself at the head of his relatives and the mother at the head of hers. The father sprinkled the maternal party with a mixture from a gourd-vessel which contained water and certain powdered herbs, mixed at times with urine. The mother sprinkled the paternal party with a similar mixture from her gourd. This was to bestow a blessing on each party and to remove any remaining evil. The people usually covered their faces, for the liquid ought to fall on their backs and shoulders. It was supposed to bring blessing and all wished some of it to fall on them.

When this part of the ceremony was ended, the medicine-man, with the parents and grandparents, carried the clay lumps containing the afterbirths to the outskirts of a belt of trees or a forest near and placed them where they would not be disturbed by anyone coming to make a garden or a field there. The place was first purified by being sprinkled with water by the medicine-man, and after the lumps were put down the people danced round four times singing, then left them and returned to the scene of the festivities.

The parents and the grandparents then had their heads shaved and their nails pared, and members of the father's clan shaved the head and cut the nails of a boy-twin while members of the mother's clan performed the same service for a girl-twin. The hair and nail-parings were made up into a bundle decorated with a wreath of the creeper, and were carried in procession and placed with the afterbirths near the forest. The peasants also took the sacred trees to this place.

The two families had a sham fight to obtain ashes from the fire which was always lit near the children and the mother took a bit of cloth, which she rubbed in the ashes, and wiped her tongue with it.

Should a twin die during these ceremonies, the medicine-man took the body, bent it up, and put it into a water-pot which had to be lined with flowers, leaves, and herbs like the nest for the placenta. The mouth of the pot was sealed with clay and it was deposited on waste land. No mourning was made for the child.

After these ceremonies, among pastoral people, milk was distributed to the guests, while the agricultural peasants gave meat with vegetable food and beer, and dancing continued during the day; the parents were congratulated and the twins, who were placed in state with their nurses in some conspicuous place, were admired and presents were given to them.

The person (*Salongo Muto*) who represented the father of the twins was given two bark-cloths, and sometimes a sheep or a goat, and returned home. The maternal grandparents sent their son-in-law a present, which might be a cow, a goat, a sheep, or a fowl, and he had to send a similar present in return.

The parents of the twins had to complete the festivities by sexual relations, without which the blessing of the twins would be lost.

After a few weeks, when the mother's hair had grown again, she visited her parents, taking the girl-child with her, and her father shaved her head and that of the child. The paternal grandfather at the same time shaved his son's head and that of his grandson at the door of their house. The parents then went about amongst the kraals of their friends and gave them a blessing, in return for which they received a meal.

For some years, if the father met a relative whom he had not seen for a time, he took the man's hand, and spat into it; the man rubbed his hand on his forehead and did the same to the father. The mother also did this to any of her relatives, for it brought blessing.

After the ceremonies the twins were treated like ordinary children, but both had to fare exactly alike, lest the ghosts of the father's or the mother's clan should be made jealous.

Lake Albert. Hot springs at Kibero from which salt is obtained

Lake Albert. Sacred pool for human sacrifices at Kibero

PLATE XXXIII

Lake Albert. Washing sand for salt at Kibero

Thus, during childhood, if one of the twins did wrong both were punished, and if one received a present the other had to receive a similar gift.

If a woman bore triplets, it was regarded as a dreadful event and most unlucky, bringing with it all kinds of evil. The king sent some of his personal guard, who took the mother with her children and her parents to a desert place at some distance, where they speared them to death and left the bodies for wild animals to devour. The father of the triplets had his eyes gouged out so that he could not look upon the king at any future time, for his gaze would bring evil upon the king.

(2) CHILDHOOD

Cutting the first teeth—learning to walk—teeth, hair, and nails—up-bringing and training—clothing—pastoral children and the calves—games—teaching boys the duties of herdsmen—initiation ceremony—boys of agricultural families—marriage and the marriage-fee—work of the girls—initiation—fattening before marriage—milk taboo during menstruation—girls of agricultural clans

A child of the pastoral people when it had been weaned was left entirely in the charge of its nurse, though it did not leave the kraal in which its parents lived. The age of a child was never calculated by years, but by its size and strength and by the natural episodes of its life, such as the cutting of its first teeth, and later, if the child was a girl, the growth of the breasts.

After the ceremony of being made to sit alone, the next great event in a child's life was the cutting of its first teeth, which were watched for with great anxiety. If they appeared in the lower jaw, all was well; there was much rejoicing and the family were called together for a feast for which the father killed some animal. The child was given presents and its father would give it a cow, placing it to sit on the animal's back. This became the child's property and the milk might not be drunk by anyone else. On the day of the feast the child was kept in the house and the relatives visited it.

If, however, the teeth appeared in the upper jaw, there was consternation, for it was a very bad omen (*Khabona*), and might be the cause of deaths in both the father's and mother's clans. Offerings were made to the gods and ghosts to atone for the evil which must have been committed to cause this and to avert future ill-luck. As far as possible the parents kept the fact secret, sending for the medicine-man, who extracted the offending teeth as soon as possible. He gave the child medicines and the parents danced round it to purify it and take away any evil. No presents were given to this child for only shame and disgrace were attached to it, and whatever its rank might be, it might never enter the presence of the king.

After the appearance of the first teeth the child was allowed to crawl and to try to walk. To encourage it to walk bells were fastened to its legs that the noise might tempt it to move them; each leg must therefore have its bell or bells, for if they were put on one leg, the child would move that leg only and the object of the bells would not be attained. The bells had to be removed at night lest the noise might attract snakes or draw the attention of ghosts who might steal the infant.

When the first teeth were shed, they were given to the mother who placed them in a special basket and treasured them with other relics, such as the stump of the umbilical cord and, later, the teeth which were extracted at puberty. She also had to look after the hair and nail-cuttings of the child which, among the pastoral people, had to be thrown on a special place on the dung-heap, and among the agricultural people under a plantain-tree. Among the pastoral people it was the duty of a wife, mother, or sister to cut the hair and nails of a man or boy, but the serfs had no such rules.

Until they married, both boys and girls lived in their parents' house. The girls slept in a small enclosed space at the head of the parents' bed, which could only be entered by passing the bed, while the boys slept on the other side of the house, sometimes on a bed but in their early years on the floor. Children received little moral training or discipline and were free to do much as they liked until they were old enough to be of some use. Respect for their parents was insisted upon and a child telling lies or using obscene language was rebuked, but no punishment was administered beyond a scolding or a slap on the arm if the child refused to drink its proper amount of milk. There was no reticence before children on matters of sexual relations and birth, but their open discussion apparently awakened no sense of curiosity and the early separation of the girls from the boys, combined with early marriages, prevented the growth of sexual desires.

It was customary during childhood to wear no clothes at all, but children were provided with amulets which were hung in numbers round neck, waist, and ankles. At about the age of six a boy of the cow people would wear a calf-skin or a scrap of cow-hide over his shoulders, tied on the right shoulder, and later on he might wear two skins. When he had been initiated he wore a skin round his loins. A pastoral girl wore nothing until she was quite big, when she might wear a small apron or a skin as a loin-cloth and sometimes also a skin over her shoulders, but girls often went naked until they were married, even when full-grown. The serfs wore even less: at about the age of six boys wore a scrap of skin round their loins and a full-grown girl would wear one or two goat-skins tied together to form a loin-cloth.

Pastoral children, both boys and girls, at about the age of five or six years were set to herd the smaller calves, which were allowed to wander round in the neighbourhood of the kraal while the cows were out at pasture. It was a task which called for only casual attention, and the children were able to play together while the calves grazed.

There were many games, the favourites being make-believe games, in imitation of the doings of their elders. They played at going out to war, fighting battles and capturing prisoners and cattle and bringing the spoils to the king; they married and built their kraals, observing taboos as their elders did; they bought, sold and exchanged cattle and tended them, healing them of various diseases. Miniature bows and arrows were favourite toys and a kind of nine-pins or skittles, while wrestling was enjoyed by both old and young. Besides these outdoor games, they had many of a quieter kind. One was played by spinning the stones of a wild fruit, like a plum, on a plantain-leaf; two spun their stones together, and the owner of the stone which knocked the other down was the winner and confiscated the fallen stone. Guessing games were also popular. One child would go outside and in his absence another would rise and touch some object; the returning child had to guess in a certain number of attempts who had risen and what he had touched. Another game was for one child to hold something concealed behind his back while another guessed in which hand it was. Sleight of hand tricks too were practised. The performer had his two little fingers tied behind his back and a stone was put in one hand. He was left alone for a few moments and then appeared before the others with the stone on his head.

At about ten years old, a boy was removed from taking charge of the calves, for he had to begin to learn the duties of a cow-man. His first task was to hold the calf in front of the cow while it was being milked, and then he was taught to milk. He was told that milking had to be done on the right side of the cow and he had to learn how much milk it was safe to take from a cow without depriving its calf of the amount necessary for its nourishment. He had to go out with the cattle to pasture and learn how to herd. Then cattle sicknesses had to be studied and the various kinds of herbs, the quantities to be used, and the methods of preparation and of administering them to the animals. He had also to be taught the general treatment of the cows, how to water them, when to give them salt and so on.

At the age of seventeen or thereabouts the boy should have mastered the duties of a herdsman and should show signs of reaching puberty. It was his father's duty to see that the boy came forward for the initiation ceremony at the right time. This ceremony consisted of the removal of the six front teeth in the lower jaw, and boys of all classes, pastoral and agricultural, had to undergo it.

Up to this time a boy of the agricultural classes had been occupied in herding goats and sheep and in learning any other duties which would fall to him. At the age of puberty he had to come forward like boys of the upper classes and have the six front teeth in the lower jaw extracted. The operation marked him as fit to marry, and until he had undergone this he was not admitted into the adult membership of the clan.

The chief of the kraal arranged for the presence of a medicine-man and a special operator with his assistant, and the other parents brought their sons, many of them in great fear and crying bitterly, to the place appointed. The special operator was not paid but was given beer and meat.

The dentist's assistant sat down and the boy to be operated upon sat between his legs. The man put his legs over those of the boy and clasped his arms in his. The instrument for extracting the teeth, which was merely a round pin of iron, six inches long and a quarter of an inch thick, with a pointed end, was given to the medicine-man, who ran it along the gums of the teeth to be extracted, a magical action to ensure success. The dentist then took the instrument from the medicine-man and took his place to operate. It was believed that if the boy was afraid and tried to catch the dentist's hand, the man would die; he would therefore tap such a patient on the head, saying, "You wish to kill me; may you die!" Sitting on the boy's legs, he forced the instrument down into the gum below the first of the teeth, beginning on the right side, levered it out and went on to the next until all six were out. He then pressed the bleeding gums together and gave the boy some water to wash out his mouth.

The teeth were picked up, counted, and given to the father, who took them to the boy's mother to put in the basket with the other treasures. The boys all went to a special house where they were nursed until the gums healed. On their way they had to spit only over the right shoulder and in the house they were each given a special vessel into which to spit the blood until bleeding stopped. This was emptied in some place where no person was likely to step over it, for should such a thing happen the boy would die. Among the pastoral people, boys drank only milk for the first four days after the teeth had been extracted, but the agricultural boys had to eat porridge.

Relations and friends came to see the boy have his teeth extracted and brought him presents to help him to obtain a wife. His parents also gave him some gift, among the pastoral people probably a calf, and the youth when healed sat in the lap first of his father and then of his mother. Among agricultural people it was usual to test whether the gums were healed by giving the boy a bean to bite. If he could bite it in half he was well.

Up to this time the life of the son of a well-to-do cow-owner and that of the son of a poor herdsman differed little. The course of training was the same in all cases and little distinction was made between classes. Now, however, when the question of marriage arose, the pinch of poverty made itself felt, for the poor boy had to trust to himself to provide the marriage-fee. There was very little real hardship in this for the boy would hire himself out as herdsman to some cow-man and would be supplied with a sufficient number of cows to feed himself and his wife, when he got her. These cows were looked on as his, inasmuch as he might use the milk, so that by selling butter and by borrowing he would be able to get himself a wife.

For the girls of a family the mother was specially responsible. Among the Bahuma a girl was usually betrothed in infancy, but she knew nothing of the arrangement. The girls played about with the boys and herded the calves until they were about seven or eight years old, when they were considered old enough to have some responsible work and were given the task of keeping the huts of the calves clean. The huts had to be swept out each morning and clean grass brought for the calves to lie on and for them to eat.

As a girl grew older she no longer went freely among the men, and she began to learn a woman's duties of looking after the milk and the milk-pots. She had to learn how to keep the milk-pots clean and fresh, how and when to churn, and all the taboos connected with the milk.

As she approached a marriageable age she was kept more secluded from men and had to drink more milk and grow fat before her husband came to claim her. Like a boy she had her six front teeth in the lower jaw extracted and her mother took charge of them, keeping them separate from those of her sons. Before she married she was confined entirely to the house and forced to drink as much milk as she could, in order to go to her husband as fat as possible.

When she had her first menses her mother concealed the fact from everyone, sometimes even from her husband. She provided special food for her daughter, for during this time she might not drink milk but lived on gruel and porridge and sometimes plantains, and drank beer and water. If a girl or woman in this condition drank milk it would harm the cow, for either blood would come with the milk or the cow would go dry or bear no more calves. If possible, the father would supply his wife and daughters during this time with milk from a cow too old to bear again. A woman at this time was not permitted to eat hot food but had to eat porridge which had been made the day before and left over-night to get cold. She might not touch the weapons of her husband lest they should be contaminated and useless in battle. Husband and wife might sleep on one bed, but they might not have sexual relations.

After the first menses the fact was not kept secret and the girl might be claimed by the man to whom she had been promised.

Among the serfs, girls, like boys, were sent to look after goats and sheep as early in their lives as possible. Even infants accompanied their elder brothers and sisters during the early part of the morning, and when the animals returned at noon they would go to sleep until the heat of the day was over. At a very early age the girls were taught to carry pots of water and bring fire-wood and to attend to the fire for the cooking. Later a girl went with her mother to the field and learnt to dig and to plant the various crops. When preparing for marriage the *Bahera* girls, like the *Bahuma,* were expected to get as fat as possible, but their parents could not supply them with milk, and fed them on the best they could obtain, usually porridge, and meat when they could get it.

(3) MARRIAGE

Clan exogamy and blood relationships—monogamy and polygamy—communism and adultery—inter-marriage of classes—marriage ceremonies among the pastoral people—marriages arranged in infancy—herdsmen and the marriage-fee—settling the marriage-fee—the wedding-feast—receiving and bringing home the bride—milk-drinking as a marriage-pledge—purifying the bride and bridegroom—departure of the bride's friends—consummation of marriage—departure of bride's aunt—seclusion of bride—learning a wife's duties—the husband's visit to his parents-in-law—marriage among agricultural people—not arranged in childhood—negotiations with girl's parents—beer-drinking—the marriage-fee—wedding-feast—bringing home the bride—making porridge—the marriage-pledge—purifying bride and bridegroom—feast—consummation of marriage—the bride's aunt and sister—seclusion of the bride—learning a wife's duties—fire-wood and water—bride's mother and sister taboo to her husband—entering a new house—the fire-stones—her husband's pipe—unfaithfulness and divorce

Among both the pastoral and agricultural tribes of Kitara, with the exception of the royal family, clan exogamy was enforced, and it was a criminal offence for a couple who belonged to the same clan to form an alliance. The guilty pair would be condemned by all the members of their clan, with the complete assent of their respective parents.

Blood relationship was also carefully considered, for a man might not marry into the clan of his parents or of his grandparents, though he might marry into the clan from which any of his great-grandparents had come. The totem was the chief guide as to relationships.

Among the upper classes, although monogamy was the rule until recently, it became customary during the reigns of the three kings who preceded Kabarega, the present king's father, for the wealthy cow-owner to follow the example of the king and have more than one wife. Before this a member of a pastoral clan only took a second wife when he found that his first was sterile, and frequently a sterile wife would advise her husband, if he were wealthy enough, to do this. Sometimes a man would put away his first wife before taking a second, but, if he could afford it, that is if his herds were big enough, he would keep both and they lived together in one house.

Members of the agricultural clans rarely married more than one wife, for, though there were no restrictions as to their doing so, and women, being in excess of the men, were easily obtainable, few men were wealthy enough to pay two marriage-fees or to keep two women. If a man of the agricultural class had two wives he built them separate houses and each carried on her own establishment.

One point in the marriage-laws is of special interest. The relationship between members of the same clan was of such a character that any man's wife was common to him and the other members of his clan. It was perfectly legitimate for a man to have relations with the wives of the men he called his brothers, that is, his clan-fellows, and such action was not looked upon as adultery. A man might use his influence with his wife to make her refrain from such action, and might be annoyed if she admitted to her bed a member of the clan with whom he was not on good terms, but he could not accuse her of unfaithfulness for so doing. Adultery lay in admitting to her bed a man of some other clan than her husband's.

No member of a pastoral clan would marry a member of an agricultural clan, and for long the pastoral people of Kitara kept themselves free from any admixture of negro blood. Later, however, the kings, as described in a previous chapter, began to honour members of the slave class who had become wealthy or had done them some signal service, by making them free-men or *Banyoro*. This raised them to a station much above their original rank, though still inferior to the pastoral people. Such a man might marry the daughter of a poor herdsman of the pastoral class and the children of such a marriage might marry into any of the pastoral clans, with the exception of a few who kept themselves apart from such unions. These mixed marriages raised up in Kitara an intermediate class of people who were looked up to by the serfs but were not on an equality with the pure cow-men.

The marriage ceremonies and customs practised by pastoral people and serfs differ very considerably and it will therefore be wisest to deal with them separately.

Marriage Ceremonies of the Pastoral People

A well-to-do cow-man and his wife would take care to seek out a wife for their son while he was yet an infant. When they heard of the birth of a girl of suitable family they would visit her parents, taking with them a pot of beer for each. The acceptance and drinking of this beer by the girl's parents was a sort of pledge to which the boy's parents might refer in after years should any question as to the engagement arise. The boy's parents might then send one or two cows to supply the girl with milk. These were sent more as a loan than as part of the marriage-fee. They were exchanged for others from time to time as their milk ran short, and at the time of the marriage the particular cows in use were returned to the boy's parents.

The children were allowed to grow up without knowing anything of this arrangement. They might know each other and, if they happened to be neighbours, they might play together in childhood, but as a general rule they never met until they married. When the boy was old enough to understand what marriage meant, his parents told him what they had arranged and informed him who the girl was and where she lived. He then had to make the acquaintance of her parents, though he was not supposed to see the girl herself. He showed his interest and satisfaction by sending gifts, however trifling, from time to time to his future parents-in-law, while he waited for the girl to grow old enough to marry.

Parents were never in any hurry to part with their daughters when they came to marriageable age, and the youth had to see to it that his bride was not kept from him longer than was necessary. When he began to think she should be ready for marriage, he would go to visit her parents, taking with him a female relative who would see and examine the girl. His parents would then provide him with the marriage-fee, which generally amounted to from ten to twenty cows, according to the status of the bridegroom, and the marriage would take place.

A poor herdsman, however, could not make these arrangements for his son, for it was all he could do to provide food to feed his family. The boy, therefore, had to wait until he was grown up before he could become engaged, and often he had to work hard in order to procure the sum required for a marriage-fee. His parents might be able to help him to some extent: perhaps the marriage-fee received for a daughter would be kept to help in the marriage of a son, but probably the most they could do would be to supply him with two or three cows, while a marriage-fee usually amounted to from ten to twenty cows. The father of a boy who could not afford to pay this would take his son to one of the ruling chiefs, or even to the king, and explain his case, begging that his son might be given the amount necessary. In return he would promise that the boy would become a herdsman to his benefactor. If the request was granted, the son would give his father one cow and with the rest pay the fee and secure his bride. It might be that he could not pay all the fee at once, for his master might simply give him cows to herd and leave him to earn what he required by selling butter and looking after the cows. Then the boy would pay part of the fee at once and his bride would be kept for him for a time varying from six to eighteen months, until he could earn or borrow the remainder.

This marriage-fee was not considered as purchase-money paid for the girl, but as a kind of recompense to the parents, who had had the expense and trouble of bringing her up. It was divided among the relatives, the larger portion going to the father's clan, though the mother's relatives also got a share.

When her parents declared that the girl was old enough to marry, the promised husband sent one of his friends to visit them. This man, who was known as *Mukwenda,* had to arrange with the parents the amount of the marriage-fee, the date on which it had to be paid, and the day of the marriage. He then returned to the bridegroom and informed him of what he had arranged. It might be some days or even weeks before the boy could collect the animals necessary for the fee. Even if his father was a rich man and could supply him with the cows, he and his son would find it difficult to agree in their choice; some would be too good for the father to give and others too poor for the bridegroom to offer.

When the cows were ready the bride's father was informed and he sent a messenger to examine them before they were allowed to go to him. This man would reject any he did not think good enough, and these had to be exchanged. When both parties were satisfied the cows were driven to the kraal of the girl's father, accompanied by a party of the bridegroom's friends, among whom were *Mukwenda* and another special messenger known as *Mugurusi,* who was sent to receive the bride and bring her to her husband. He was often a brother of the bridegroom and, if not, had to be a clan-brother.

This party had to go to fetch the bride when the moon was new, and the bride's father made a feast for them. During this feast, for which a cow was killed, the *Mukwenda* might not ask for meat, but he expected his needs to be attended to. He took a stick with a sharp point and, placing it in the ground near the fire on which the meat was cooked, sat down beside it and ate the pieces of meat which were put on it for him. The animal killed for the feast had to be divided up and distributed in a certain way, and it was the bride's duty to see that this was properly done and that everyone got the portion to which he or she was entitled. A special piece, which was called "the skin" and was cut from one side along the ribs from the leg to the shoulder, was sent to the bridegroom; the bride's father and his relatives were given the right shoulder and the tongue; the bride's mother and her relatives the back; and a portion went to the bride's sister.

The people who had been sent to carry the bride home might not approach the house until permission was given by the bride's father. While they waited outside the kraal, he might send them tobacco and fire that they might smoke.

Meanwhile the bride had for some weeks been prepared for marriage by special feeding to make her fat and by anointing with butter to make her skin as soft and smooth as possible. All the hair on her body was shaved off except that on the pubes, which was plucked out by her mother, a painful proceeding which often took a week to accomplish.

The father then arranged who should form the party to conduct her to her new home. The most important member was his sister, or sometimes his mother: she was known as *Mukaikuru,* and had to go with the bride to instruct her in all the duties of marriage. A younger sister of the bride and some of her girl friends also accompanied her, and with them went two men who acted as her witnesses and were called *Mukwenda* and *Mugurusi,* like the messengers of the bridegroom.

When all was ready the messenger of the bridegroom, *Mugurusi,* came to receive the bride from her father. The bride first took leave of her mother, sitting upon her lap, and then sat upon the knees of her father, who presented her to the messenger, saying that she went from him pure and must be well treated. He then mentioned the special name by which she was known in the clan, adding "This is her true name which may not be changed. Should anything displease her husband and cause him to wish to get rid of her, she must be returned to her home with this name." This is the only ceremony in which this secret clan-name is mentioned, and what exactly it implies is not clear. *Mugurusi* knelt and kissed the hands of the father, which indicated a promise that the bridegroom accepted the girl and would fulfil his instructions.

The girl was completely veiled in bark-cloths so that she could not see, and was carried in a litter made of a cow-hide. Her aunt, *Mukaikuru*, was also carried, and the procession left the bride's home at a time which would allow them to reach the bridegroom's kraal at sunset when the cattle returned from pasture, for a bride, in order to bring luck, must enter with the cows.

In preparation for the bride's coming, grass was usually laid on the path outside the kraal-gate for a little distance, and also inside, from the kraal-gate to the house of the bridegroom's parents. When the bride reached this grass carpet she was allowed to alight from her litter and walk to meet her husband, who came from the kraal when he heard the procession approaching. He drove two heifers before him and was accompanied by a party of his friends. The bride, being veiled so that she could not see, was led by the hand by her aunt, *Mukaikuru*, and, if possible, a brother walked at her other side.

When the two parties met, someone from each gathered a handful of grass. That picked by the bride's friend was taken to her mother, and the bridegroom's tuft to his mother; both tufts were put away with the fetishes in the respective houses, for they were supposed to ward off magic. The friends of the bridegroom stopped the other party and took their spears from them, and the bridegroom, who carried a spear, fell in behind the bride and her conductors and directed them where to go. The two heifers were driven in front of the party back to the kraal.

On entering the kraal the bride was handed a small basket of millet and scattered some of the grain on the ground to ensure fertility in the home and among the cattle. The bridegroom directed her to the house of his parents, where they were sitting on their bed awaiting her. No word was spoken, but the bride's aunt presented her niece first to the father-in-law, who received her in his lap like a child and embraced her, and then to the mother-in-law, who did the same. The bridegroom stood outside the door and did not enter until his bride had thus been received into the family.

The bride was conducted into the chamber which had been prepared for her at the head of the parents' bed. In some instances an old woman would stop the way, standing in the doorway leading into the chamber, until she had been given some cowry-shells to let them pass. The bride's aunt and her friends entered with her and the bride was allowed to lie on the bed and rest, to recover from the fatigue of the journey, until the cows had been milked.

The milk from a healthy young cow that had a calf alive and well was put into the special wooden pot, *Kisahi*, and the bridegroom's mother brought it in and handed it to the head of the house, who drank a little and handed it back to his wife, saying, "Give it to the boy." The bridegroom, who had now entered the house, went into the bridal chamber and sat on the bed by the bride; his mother handed the milk-pot to him, and, first drinking a little himself, he passed it to the bride, who drank from it. This constituted the covenant of marriage and was binding. Should the bride refuse to drink, no further step could be taken until her consent had been obtained. When she had drunk, she handed the pot to her mother-in-law, who put it with the milk-pots until the early morning when she finished the milk herself; no other person might drink any of it because, being the marriage-pledge, it was sacred. If it was taken from a cow which had lost its calf or was sickly, the couple would either have no children or those they had would die in infancy or be delicate.

The bridegroom, sitting on the bed by the bride's side, put his hand on the inner side of her thigh, between her legs. This, though nothing was said, completed the marriage covenant.

The friends of the bride and bridegroom had meanwhile remained outside the kraal, but some of them now entered. The bridegroom rose and went to the door, whereupon one of the men in the kraal crowed like a cock. The bridegroom asked, "Is it morning?" and they answered, "Yes." One of the servants brought water and he washed his hands and face and went out to join his companions, who were drinking beer, singing, and dancing outside the kraal. By this time it was about eight or nine o'clock and he remained with them drinking beer and rejoicing until midnight, when he returned to his bride. No sleep was allowed that night and the marriage was not consummated, but the bridegroom sat on the bed beside his bride until dawn while the friends outside came into the kraal and danced and sang at the door of the house.

At dawn the bride and bridegroom came out to a spot in the kraal where grass was spread. There they stripped and sat naked, surrounded by their relatives, who held bark-cloths to form a screen. The man's mother brought a pot of water which she gave to the bride's aunt. This was placed on the bride's legs and her aunt, taking a bunch of purificatory herbs, dipped them in the water and passed them from foot to head and head to foot four times over the bridegroom and four times over the bride. This removed any evil that had attached itself to them during their youth and enabled them to commence life as a married couple in perfect conditions.

The marriage party then broke up and those who had accompanied the bride from her home were given a fat cow to take with them in order to celebrate the occasion on their return. The aunt of the bride remained longer, and her visit might last any length of time from two days to a month. Her departure had to be on a day which fell on an even number counting from the day on which she arrived, for odd numbers were bad for the young people. She slept on the same bed as the newly married couple and on the second or third night directed them how to consummate the marriage. Should the bride be afraid and resist the bridegroom's advances or leave the bed, it was the duty of the aunt to instruct her by giving her the example of sexual intercourse with the bridegroom.

When the aunt was satisfied that the marriage had been consummated and that the bride was settled in her new life,

Potters at work for the king

Potter finishing a small cooking-pot

PLATE XXXV

Type of potter of artisan class with small beer pot

she prepared to leave. The young husband made her some suitable present, usually a cow and calf, and she took with her the bark-cloth on which the marriage had been consummated, and which bore the signs of the bride's virginity. These signs were eagerly looked for by her parents when the aunt reported to them how she had left their daughter.

For four days after the marriage the bride did not leave her room, but remained in seclusion and might not even speak in a tone which could be heard outside. On the fourth day her mother-in-law came into the room, bringing her son's milk-pot, and handed it to the bride, who had to wash and fumigate it. The mother-in-law supervised the work as if the bride knew nothing about it, and when the milk-pot was cleansed she brought a churn and explained its use. The girl was then considered to be a fully trained wife and might leave her seclusion.

Many of her relatives came to see her and wish her happiness on the occasion of her first leaving her room, but she might not speak to any of her husband's brothers until they had given her a present of a few cowry-shells.

If the husband was one of the herdsmen in his father's kraal, as was usual, the young couple would live with his parents until their first child was born before preparing their own house. If, however, the husband had another kraal or had a house of his own elsewhere, he would take his bride to it shortly after the marriage and they would settle down at once.

The husband was expected never to leave his wife for a night for six months after the marriage, and for some months they had always to sleep face to face and never back to back. He was also expected to pay a visit to his wife's parents shortly after the marriage, when he was received by them as a son and sat in their laps. On this visit he might take with him a friend, who had to be received with honour and given a goat. After this formal visit he might go to see his wife's parents as often as he liked.

Marriage Ceremonies among the Serfs

Among the agricultural clans parents could seldom afford to arrange a marriage for a son, and it was as a rule left until the boy was of marriageable age. Sometimes the boy himself would wish to marry and he would then ask an elder brother or his father to arrange the matter for him. Sometimes his mother, thinking he was old enough, would speak to her husband about it and he would question the boy as to whether there was anyone he wished to marry or whether he would leave the matter to be settled by his parents. If it was left to the father, he took counsel with his wife and one or two relatives and chose a suitable girl. The qualifications for a good wife were diligence in field-work, ability to cook, and a good temper with no tendency to quarrelsomeness. She had also to be of another clan from that of the boy and not of the same clan as his parents or grandparents.

The boy's father or a chosen messenger went to see the parents of the girl and, if they seemed satisfied with the proposal, he took them two large pots of beer, one for each parent. The beer had to be in two pots, for, should there be only one, the wife would declare that she and her family had been left out and slighted, and she would not permit the engagement to take place until the omission had been rectified. When the messenger took the beer, the boy accompanied him and was seen by the girl and her parents, so that they might judge of his suitability. In some instances a youth might himself take the initiative and send his own messenger, instead of doing things through his father.

The father of the girl might object to the marriage on the ground that, at some past time, the boy had spoken unkind things of him, used abusive language to him, or called him bad names. Before any negotiations could take place the boy had to apologise and pay a goat as compensation to the father.

Sometimes a boy and girl who knew each other might agree that they desired to marry, but the boy would have to visit the girl's parents and go through the regular routine. At times, but this was very seldom, they would elope and the girl would be hidden in the house of some friend or relative of the boy. After a short time the boy would go to the girl's father and confess what he had done, taking with him a goat to allay the man's anger. There could be no marriage ceremony without the consent of the parents and all the usual steps of bringing beer and collecting and paying the marriage-fee had to be taken, though the youth might be living as a married man all the time.

When a girl's parents had accepted a youth as a prospective husband for her, the question of the amount of the marriage-fee had to be considered. The bridegroom came again, bringing beer, and the girl's parents called together their relatives to talk the matter over. They first asked the bridegroom for a goat, which had to be supplied before anything further was done.

At the time of this beer-drinking, the girl was present and was asked whether they might drink the beer. Her reply to this constituted her consent to the marriage, and after the beer had been drunk she was considered to be engaged, and was kept in the house and fed with the best her parents could obtain to make her fat. She underwent daily bathing with warm water and was rubbed with butter or vegetable oil to make her skin soft and a good colour.

The usual marriage-fee was a cow worth five goats, but the relatives might ask for a cow and two or three goats in addition, while at times they asked for as many as six cows. Payment would usually be made in goats or shells, a goat being valued at from two to four hundred cowry-shells. As with the pastoral people, the marriage-fee was divided among the relatives, but in a few agricultural clans the parents kept the whole of it and the relatives were satisfied with a share of the wedding-feast.

It might take the youth several months of bartering and begging from his clan before he could supply the necessary fee. His father would assist him as far as possible, and if a daughter of the family had been married, some of the fee which had then been received would be reserved for the son's wedding; in fact the marriage-fee of a daughter was looked upon by the peasants as the chief means of getting a wife for a son. Such help not being available or being insufficient, the boy might go to work for some chief, who would pay the marriage-fee for him or would give him a wife in order to retain his services, and the boy would then consider himself bound to work for that chief.

When the marriage-fee was made up, the man who had formerly acted as messenger and who was called, as among the pastorals, *Mukwenda*, went to announce the fact to the bride's parents and to ask for a time to be fixed for the wedding. The bride's parents sent their messenger, also called *Mukwenda*, to examine the animals collected for the marriage-fee and to arrange the day. He was empowered to reject any animal that was not in good condition, and he always asked for a goat as his own perquisite before he would declare himself satisfied with the animals offered.

When at last the fee was sent many things would have to be added to it, for the messenger would ask for bark-cloths for the parents, for a goat to make a feast on his return home, for salt to eat with the meat, for a knife to kill the goat, and so on. It was impossible for the bridegroom to refuse what was asked, and if he had not got the articles he was expected to pay their value in cowry-shells—four hundred shells to buy a basket to carry the things, three hundred in lieu of a stick to drive the animals home, one hundred to have his bride's head shaved, and so forth. He also sent to his bride one hundred cowry-shells as a gift and one hundred to induce her to come to him. In some instances the bridegroom would arrange to pay in cowry-shells a sum sufficient to cover all demands.

A day as soon as possible after the appearance of the new moon was fixed for the wedding and the bridegroom's messengers, *Mukwenda* and *Mugurusi*, with a number of his friends, accompanied the bearers of the marriage-fee. They spent a night at the house of the bride's parents and made a feast with the relatives and friends. An animal sent by the bridegroom for the purpose was killed for the feast, and as in the case of the pastoral wedding-feast, it had to be cut up and distributed in a special way. The piece called "the skin," that is, a piece cut from one side along the ribs from the leg to the shoulder, was sent to the bridegroom. The bride's father took the right shoulder and the tongue, her mother the back, and her sister also had to have a piece. Her brother had no special piece, taking his share with the general company, but the sister of the bride's father, who went with the bride to her new home, was given a special piece. As with the pastorals, *Mukwenda* might not ask for any meat, but the bride gave strict orders that he should be kept supplied with pieces, which were put on the end of a pointed stick beside which he sat. *Mukwenda* also bore another name—*Kibonomuko*—he who hands over the gifts, and he and *Mugurusi* were the bridegroom's witnesses should any question about the marriage arise later.

Similar customs to those of the pastoral people were followed when the bride left her home. Her mother took her into her lap and took leave of her, and then she sat on the father's knee and *Mugurusi* received her from him with instructions to look after her. The father mentioned the secret name which was her clan-name and must be kept free from taint or scandal, and said that if she was not acceptable to her husband she must be returned to her home. *Mugurusi* kissed the father's hands on receiving the bride.

The bride was veiled with a bark-cloth and was as a rule carried, though with some of the poorer people she had to walk. With her went her father's sister, *Mukaikuru*, her own sister, *Mpedia*, and, if possible, a brother. Her two witnesses *Mukwenda* and *Mugurusi* and a number of other friends also accompanied her.

The procession carrying the bride started in the afternoon in time to reach the bridegroom's house at dusk. As they were about to start the younger sister of the bride, if she had one, cried because her sister was going, saying, "Who will look after me and nurse me now?" and had to be soothed with a present of a goat, and the parents were given a pot of beer to console them. The *Mugurusi* had also to pay a goat or one hundred cowry-shells to have the door opened that he might pass out with the bride.

The company went along singing and dancing, and when they reached the path that branched from the main road to the house of the bridegroom's parents the litter was set down and the bride alighted. At this point the aunt often pleaded weariness and had to be bribed with one hundred cowry-shells to go forward. She had to see that the bride's veil and garments were properly arranged and, as the bride thus veiled was unable to see, the aunt had to lead her by the hand.

The bridegroom advanced down the road to meet them and accompany the bride back to the house. At the spot where they met members of each party plucked grass, which was taken, as in the pastoral ceremony, to the respective mothers, who put it with their fetishes. The bride, however, did not throw grain as she entered the house.

When the door of the house was reached, the bride's aunt refused to enter until another gift of one hundred cowry-shells was given to her. Then she presented her niece to her parents-in-law, who took her into their laps and embraced her, after which she was taken into the chamber at the head of the parents' bed where the aunt, her sister, and her special friends accompanied her and sat with her. As she entered she avoided the bed and walked to the opposite side of the room where she sat with her friends upon mats.

The bridegroom's mother placed a pot on the fire and produced some millet-flour which the bride sprinkled into the water as it boiled. The mother handed her a long wooden spoon, and she and the bridegroom stirred the porridge together until it was cooked. When it was ready, the mother gave each of them a little and they ate it together. This was the first part of the marriage-pledge.

The bridegroom then went and danced with his friends outside until midnight, when he returned to the bride's chamber and sat on the bed. The bride rose from the mats and sat beside him. The bed was covered, if possible, with a cow-skin and had coverings of bark-cloths. *Mukaikuru* conducted the bride to the bed, covered her with the bark-cloths, and loosened her loin-cloth. The bridegroom placed his hand on the inner side of her thigh and her friends pulled the hand away and wiped it with a sponge. This was the second part of the marriage-pledge.

After this they might lie together on the bed. In most cases the marriage was not consummated the first night, though in some instances this was done, and the bridegroom remained with the bride till morning.

The guests went on dancing and singing all night. A special house was placed at their disposal, but they generally preferred to sit outside to rest when tired with dancing. There was abundance of food and beer for all, which added to the attraction of dancing and merry-making.

The ceremony of washing the bride and bridegroom (called *amagita*) was performed the next morning by the aunt, as in the case of the Bahuma, but the sister of the bride accompanied the couple and was washed with them. Should the bridegroom have been previously married he did not sit but stood holding his spear during the washing. This was said to remove all evils which might have been contracted by the couple from youth until this time and thus enabled them to begin married life free from ill.

The guests were given a goat, which some of them killed and cooked, while the others continued dancing. Unless the animal was a large fat one it was rejected with scorn, but this seldom happened, for the bridegroom was anxious to obtain the good opinion of his guests and probably also to outdo some friend who had been married not long before. Furthermore, any meanness in this respect would be remembered against him by his friends in the future. In the afternoon the bride's friends returned home, carrying some present from the bridegroom to the bride's parents.

If the marriage had been consummated on the first night,

the bride's aunt returned home on the second day, taking with her the bark-cloth on which were the signs of the bride's virginity. If the marriage was not consummated the first night she waited until it was, so that she might take the bark-cloth with her. If it was found that the bride was not a virgin, the husband cut a hole in the bark-cloth and sent it thus. In this case, if he so desired, he might send the girl back to her parents and demand the return of the marriage-fee.

The bride's sister remained with her for the first month of her married life, and slept on the same bed as the bride and her husband. As this girl was usually marriageable, the bride had to be careful that her place with her husband was not usurped.

For the first four days after marriage the bride remained in seclusion, seeing no one but her husband and her sister. Her husband spent much of his time with her, but she might not leave her chamber nor speak in a tone which could be heard beyond it, and no one but the husband and sister might speak to her.

At the end of the four days her parents sent a supply of food and her mother-in-law gave her a pot, water, and a stick for stirring the porridge, and explained to her, as if she were a child, how to use them and how to cook the food. The bridegroom provided a goat and this meat was also cooked under the directions of the mother-in-law. A number of friends and relatives of both parties came together to eat the first meal the bride cooked and to visit her, and they were then told whether she had been a virgin or not. When she came out from seclusion she might not speak to her brothers-in-law until they had given her a present of cowry-shells. When the meal had been eaten the wife went to the well with a small pot and brought water and a few sticks for the fire, thus completing the marriage ceremony. From this time she was free to do her proper work as a married woman, but for some days she never left the house by the path in front of the door, but stole out at the side of the door and followed a side-path. After a few days, the father-in-law asked, "Who is this who brings fire-wood and water and steals away to dig in secret? We have not stolen her." He took a string of one hundred cowry-shells and threw them out by the door down the path. The young wife was told that these were hers, and she put on her best clothing and went out to pick them up; when she had done so, she was free to enter and leave the house by the ordinary way. The shells she kept to take to her mother.

After a month the bride's sister went home, and from that time she was taboo to her brother-in-law. He might never meet her and had to leave the path if they happened to be on the same road. His mother-in-law was also taboo to him and, if he had to hold any communication with her, he had to do so from a distance or from the outside of the house in which she was. If he met her in the path he retired into the grass and looked the other way until she had passed. Should he by any chance see her breasts, he had to atone by sending her a bark-cloth to cover herself.

For some four months the newly married couple lived in the house of the man's parents, but by the end of that time the man would have built himself a house in the neighbourhood of his parents' field. Relatives gathered to escort the bride, and her mother came bringing uncooked food, a pot of beer, and a goat. In the early morning the food was cooked and a feast made for the relatives. Before the bride could enter her new house she had to go with her mother and mother-in-law to find suitable stones for the cooking-pots to stand upon. Each house had three of these stones and the three women carried them in and set them in position. The mother and mother-in-law then took the bride's hands and placed them upon each of the stones, explaining to her how to light the fire and keep it up and how to cook food to please her husband. The care of the fire was an important part of a wife's duties, for it might never be allowed to go out and she would be very perturbed if it did so during the night. The fuel was usually wood and the thick stems of grass or millet which, being easily ignited and giving a fair heat, were used for emergencies. Until this ceremony of the cooking-stones had been performed, the wife might not cook in her own house. Should one of the mothers be unable to come for a few days after they had entered the house, the bride had to cook outside or in some other house.

When food had been cooked on the new fire-stones, the husband and the two mothers ate it, the husband being given a portion in some place where he could sit without seeing his mother-in-law, who was taboo to him.

A husband usually gave his wife after marriage one or two goats, two bark-cloths, two water-pots, two cooking-pots, and two small vegetable-pots. The goats were left to her to herd and were used for meat, should her father or mother come to visit her. She might not kill, sell, or exchange any animal which her husband gave her, without his permission. He also handed over to her his pipe, which she had to have ready for him when he came in. If he wished to get her into trouble and had no definite cause of complaint, he would put his pipe in some place where she was likely to break it. She might avoid it for a time but he would persevere, and in the end she was sure to break it. He then refused food and slept in another house until she, in despair, went to her mother to ask for help. There she remained a few days until her parents were able to supply her with beer, food, a goat, and another pipe to pacify her husband. He at first pretended not to want the gifts, but at last accepted them and called his friends to eat a meal which his wife cooked. The people who had brought the wife back from her mother's house then returned, and the wife was reinstated in his favour.

Some Marriage Customs common to Pastoral People and Serfs

If a husband found that his wife was unsatisfactory, perhaps because she could not cook or was incapable in some other respect, or if he had constant quarrels with her, he would try beating her, and if this did not have the desired effect, he would send her home and demand the return of the dowry.

The only man except her husband from whom a wife might

receive a gift was one with whom her husband had sworn brotherhood. If any other man wished to give her anything, it had to be done through her sisters or sisters-in-law, and such gifts were usually in connexion with some intrigue.

Every man, rich or poor, when he went on a journey or to war, left his wife in the charge of a representative who had to supply her with what she needed and to buy salt and other things for her. If the husband intended to be away for some time, he made his wife take an oath to be faithful to him. She took a handful of grass from the floor and placed it with the fetishes, which was equivalent to saying that no man should cross the floor to her bed during her husband's absence.

CHAPTER XI

CUSTOMS OF THE PEOPLE. PART II

(1) ILLNESS

Preliminary treatment—summoning a medicine-man—reading the augury—causes of illness—treatment of illness caused by a family ghost—treatment of illness caused by a hostile ghost—treatment of illness caused by magic—madness—small-pox—syphilis

WHEN a man fell ill, his wife first exercised her own skill on him, cupping him or using herbs which she knew or which he wished to try. Should these fail, she had to lose no time in summoning his friends and relatives to come and see him, that they might advise her what to do and assist in the nursing. This was important lest it might be said that she had used magic to get rid of him, a crime of which she would certainly be accused if she acted alone and the man died. On consultation they might resort to cupping, which was especially used for headache, and sometimes they blistered the patient over the place where the pain seemed to be greatest, another method used for headache and also for colds, for which the patient was blistered on the chest. Numbers of friends would come to see the patient and offer sympathy and suggestions as to the treatment, for, if they stayed away, it was possible that they also might be accused of having used magic against him.

If, however, none of the remedies tried had the desired effect, a messenger was sent, bearing a small preliminary fee, to call a medicine-man who, no matter how early in the day he was sent for, came in the evening. A hut was prepared for him and on his arrival he was given either a fowl or a sheep, according to the seriousness of the case and the wealth of the patient. This animal he kept near his bed until morning, when he took it outside and, after washing and going through certain ceremonial preparations, cut its throat and watched the flow of blood. He then proceeded to open the body (cutting a bird from the underside of the beak to the tail and a sheep from the throat down), took out the entrails with the liver and lungs, and examined them. By various markings he was able to tell the cause of the illness, and whether the patient would die, have a prolonged illness, or make a speedy recovery. It sometimes happened that the augury did not satisfy him and another fowl or sheep would be demanded to make a second examination for the confirmation or correction of the first. This delay meant that the patient had to wait another day before being treated, but that was a minor matter when his life was considered to depend on the result of the augury.

When the second augury had been taken, the medicine-man was able to declare his findings. The illness might be due either to ghosts or to magic, and the medicine-man had to declare what was the cause in order that the proper means of dealing with the case might be used. If the augury proved the illness to be due to a ghost, the medicine-man had also to declare whether the ghost was hostile and intended to destroy the person or whether it was the ghost of some member of the patient's own clan, for the treatment differed according to the nature of the ghost. It was generally on women that ghosts exercised their powers and few men were ever troubled in this way. The most common cases of ghostly possession were those of women whose children were either prematurely or still-born.

The medicine-man who discovered the cause of the illness never prescribed the treatment but told the people whom they should employ, after which his part of the work was ended and he was paid for his services.

The people then sent for the medicine-man who had to carry out the treatment and administer any necessary drugs, paying him in advance. He also came in the evening and was given a black or white goat, female if the patient was a woman and male for a man. If the ghost causing the trouble was a member of the patient's clan, the goat was tied by the foot to a peg in the floor near the bed and was attached to the sick person by a string. The ghost was besought by the medicine-man to pass from the patient to a new abode in the animal which was presented to it. After the prayer of the medicine-man the animal was left there all night and any droppings or water from it were caught and thrown over the patient. Next morning the ghost was pronounced to have passed into the goat, which thus became sacred and lived near the bed ever afterwards. It might not be killed, nor might any person strike or ill-use it. Should it die, the owner must replace it with another at once. If it had kids, and the ghost's possessions thus increased, the man had to ask the ghost's permission before he might use any of the animals to buy a wife or a cow, and one had always to be left for the ghost.

When a ghost would not accept an animal, an offering of a girl or woman-slave was made. When the medicine-man found by the augury that a slave was required by a ghost, he made the presentation and the woman took the place of an animal, slept all night near the bed, and was said to receive the ghost, after which she became a favoured member of the family. She might not be sold or sent away, nor dared they ill-use her, because of her connexion with the ghost. She always ate her meals by the bedside and from time to time she would demand a goat or some animal for food and it had to be given to her, for the family would suffer for a refusal. Should the patient again fall ill, the slave was given a goat, for it was said that the ghost was not being treated with proper respect.

These family-ghosts seem invariably to have attacked women and I have never heard of a case of a man's illness being treated in this way. When the ghost had left, the medicine-man treated the woman with drugs or other means according to her symptoms, and she was given a special amulet to wear to protect her against a return of the ghost.

When the ghost was of another clan and hostile, the medicine-man took a black goat which he kept with him all night, and in the early morning he made his preparations to capture and destroy the ghost.

The patient, wearing a black bark-cloth, lay on a bed near

the door and the medicine-man prepared a heap of herbs near the bed. The black goat was thrown on its back on this heap and killed ceremonially by having its throat cut. The throat and stomach were washed with water and the meat was cut up for cooking. All this had to be done on the heap of herbs. Then a fire was made near the bed and pieces of the meat were placed over it on long wooden spits to cook. When a little was cooked it was put into a pot near the bed, and some blades of grass were arranged over the mouth of the pot in such a way that the least disturbance of the air moved them. Some of the patient's friends were set to watch this pot, with instructions to inform the medicine-man if the grass moved. The reason for these preparations was that ghosts were supposed to be shy creatures who objected to being exposed to the light of day in the presence of spectators. A place of retreat in the pot was therefore prepared. The medicine-man sat on the other side of the fire, chanting incantations and using his rattle to persuade the ghost to come out of the patient and eat the meat. Smelling the savoury odour, the ghost came out and looked about for some place where it could eat unseen. It discovered the meat in the pot and entered, causing the blades of grass to wave. The watchers told the medicine-man, who at once seized a skin he had placed ready, put it over the mouth of the pot, and tied it down, securing the ghost inside. Sometimes the medicine-man was a ventriloquist and then the ghost would call out from the pot. The medicine-man smeared clay over the skin to make quite sure it was safe and took it to waste land, where he burned pot and ghost, or threw them into running water, though the latter method was dangerous, for the pot might break and the ghost escape and return to the sick person. The medicine-man then went back and treated the patient with drugs according to the symptoms. The meat and the skin from the animal sacrificed were taken by the medicine-man as part of his pay.

Another method of dealing with ghosts which were hostile was to smoke them out. The patient, wearing fetishes, was placed on a bed and a pot with hot embers was put on the floor near by. Sheep's wool or cock's tail-feathers were thrown on the embers together with some medicinal herbs, which caused the place to reek with foul smoke. Sometimes a bark-cloth was spread over the patient and the pot with the smouldering ingredients put under it. When at last uncovered, the patient would be perspiring freely and more dead than alive, but free from the ghost, for when the patient was nearly suffocated, the ghost escaped and sought some other abode. The medicine-man then detected it in some part of the room and made frantic efforts to catch it, chasing it about with a pot in which he sought to entrap it. Sometimes the ghost escaped from the house and the man rushed after it, screeching and hitting about in the air and trying to drive it back so that he could catch it. The struggle lasted for some time, but in the end he was successful and covered the pot, in which the struggling ghost cried as it tried to escape. It was taken to waste land and burned and the patient and his clan were thus freed.

In some cases the first medicine-man pronounced the sickness to be due to magic and gave instructions that a special medicine-man should be sent for to treat it and remove the cause, which must be got rid of before drugs could have any effect.

A hut was prepared and in front of it a tree or branch, or, if the right kind of tree was unprocurable, a stout reed was stuck in the ground. A goat was brought and kept by the medicine-man during the night, when he made it swallow some of the patient's saliva. Next morning it was killed beside the tree and the blood was caught in a vessel. The sick man was now carried out and placed a little way from the tree, which stood between him and the new hut, while the members of his family came and stood near him. The medicine-man took the bowl of blood and with a bunch of herbs which he dipped in the blood, he touched the man on the forehead, the front of each shoulder, and the legs below the knees; he then, with a wave of his bunch of herbs, sprinkled the members of the family. The tree was also touched with blood and the

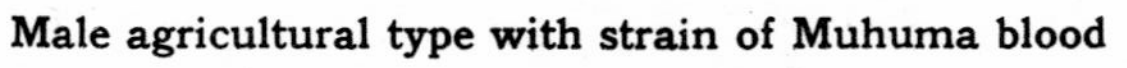

Male agricultural type with strain of Muhuma blood

Male type of Muhuma with serf blood by mixed marriage

house sprinkled. The tree or reed, which must be chosen of a suitable size, was then split from a few inches below the top to near the bottom and the slit held open by sticks. The sick man was told to rise and walk through the slit and enter his new house. As he went through the tree he allowed his clothing to fall off and passed on into the hut naked. He might not look behind him but kept his eyes fixed on the door of the hut, into which he entered and found a bed made ready for him and new clothing to put on. Sometimes the medicine-man was provided with two goats, and then the second was secured between the tree and the new hut. As the sick man passed it he put his hands on its head, or cut off an ear, or simply passed near it. The goat was then driven through the split tree the reverse way to the path of the sick man, and the medicine-man took it away with him and kept it alive. It bore on it any remains of the sickness caused by the magic.

Another means of curing illness caused by magic required that two goats, of colour stated by an augury, should be given to the medicine-man on the evening of his arrival. In the early morning he killed one goat on a heap of sacred herbs, caught its blood, and sprinkled the sick man and his family with it from a bunch of sacred herbs. Sometimes a cow was used, and the people were then washed with the blood, while the meat of either animal was taken by the medicine-man. He then took a bunch of herbs, rubbed them over the patient, tied them to the neck of the other goat and drove it away into the wilds. It might be taken by any person who had the courage to keep it, but the herbs identified it as an animal that was bearing away magic, and people, being afraid of the evil influence, would not allow this scapegoat to come in with their herds, so that it was more frequently caught by wild animals and devoured.

Yet another method of dealing with magic was to rub herbs over the sick man and tie them round the neck of a goat; this was then driven to waste land, its legs were broken so that it could not move, and it was left to die and be eaten by wild beasts.

When a man went mad, his clan put him in the stocks and sent for the medicine-man to prescribe treatment. This varied, but one method often followed was to cut a tunnel through an ant-hill and draw the patient, after he had been well rubbed with medicinal herbs, slowly through this, giving the ants plenty of time to bite him even to the extent of drawing blood. He was then guarded and fed until he recovered or died. The madness was thought to be the work of an evil spirit or of some powerful magic-worker, perhaps a medicine-man, who had been insulted or offended or even struck by the patient.

There were many diseases for which certain treatment was regularly adhered to. Inoculation, as a preventive of small-pox, has been practised for some fifty years. This method became known in the early years of Kabarega's reign, having been learned originally from the Sudanese by the Madi on Lake Albert. Hearing of its beneficial effects, Kabarega sent for a man who knew how to practise it. Whenever the scourge attacked a district, they took as many young people as possible and brought them to a place where there was a sick person. The medicine-man made two or three slight incisions on the arm of the healthy person and, piercing the pustules of the sufferer with a thorn from the acacia tree, smeared the pus on the incisions. If the application caused swellings in the arm-pit and groin shortly afterwards, the medicine-man was satisfied that the treatment had taken effect and, administering some simple potion, left the person to get well. No consideration was paid to the possibility of the presence of impure blood in the patient's veins, and thus many other diseases besides small-pox were spread.

Syphilis has been treated by old women for years. When a child was born, in order to render it immune, they placed it with a person already suffering from the disease, or wrapped it in a bark-cloth which had been used by such a person. A woman with child was given certain herbs to drink to protect the child from it, and when it was born they gave it medicine in milk. If the woman was poor and could not get milk for her child, she smeared her breasts with the medicine and the child sucked it in with the milk.

Enemas were known both for children and adults. To administer the medicine to a child, the mother blew it through a little gourd tube into the child's bowel, while a large tube was used for older people and the medicine allowed to run through it into the bowel.

(2) DEATH

Death of a chief—duties of the heir—preparing the body for burial—the widow's leave-taking—the grave—mourning—introduction of the heir—announcing the death to the king—purification—settling claims—the widows—the kraal—death of poor herdsmen—death of women—death of twins

When a chief died, the first intimation of what had happened was the sound of the death-wail, which was raised by the widows and friends in attendance. His people said, "Ahire omukono omungabo" (He has no more strength to serve the king). His drum beat, "Bekereza nkaba taliga basala ensale nkabe taliga" (The sick man cries out for all kinds of things and fetishes to prevent death, but death says, "It is useless, you must come").

The dead man lay in the house until evening. If he died during the night no one in the house might sleep, and even the children were kept awake to wail. A daughter-in-law might never enter the house where her husband's father lay dead, and no one whose father was alive might look upon a dead man.

No one thought of washing a dead man, but his chief widow shaved the man's head and pared his nails, and the heir was summoned to perform the last rites. A young cow with her first calf was brought from the dead man's herd, and a little milk was taken from her and put into the dead man's mouth. Sometimes the cow was killed after being milked and her skin used to wrap the body in, but this was only done in the case of a wealthy man; more often the cow was given to one of the herdsmen, for it might not remain in the family. A sheep was also brought and killed, and the heir took the raw skin and placed it between the dead man's legs and over the lower part of his stomach. This skin was called *Mbindisisi*, and was so sacred that the most solemn oath a man could take was by the skin he had placed on his father's body. Some millet, or a few dwarf beans, or some pumpkin seeds were put into the right hand of the dead man and the heir took them out with his lips, chewed them, and puffed them out over the floor.

The dead chief's legs were then bent up under his chin in the squatting attitude and his hands were folded together under the right side of his head. The body was tightly bound in a bark-cloth or, if he were a wealthy chief, in a cow-skin.

When it was thus bound ready for the grave, the chief widow came, wearing a new bark-cloth which had been given to her for the purpose. She lay down by the body, threw part of the bark-cloth over it, stretched herself beside it as if in bed, and remained there a few minutes. If the death had occurred during the night, she lay thus until morning. When she rose, the bark-cloth was cut into two pieces, of which one was worn by her during the mourning and the other was wrapped round the body. This was regarded as taking leave of the dead and she thus shared with him her last gift. On the day the mourning ceased the widow either gave the bark-cloth to one of her children to wear or burnt it. Among the agricultural people, who followed the ceremonies of the pastoral people, the widow, when she was shaved at the end of the mourning, wrapped the hair in the half bark-cloth and threw it on the grave.

The chief was buried in the dung-heap on the right side of his house as one looked from the door. The grave was dug in the deepest part of the dung and was made only deep enough to reach the earth, below the surface of which it might not go. Amongst the agricultural people, if a man had several wives dwelling in their own houses, his grave was dug in the ground near the house of his chief wife, and her hoe was used to dig it. Trees were planted round it to keep the children from walking over it, which would be bad both for them and for the ghost.

At sunset, after the cows had come into the kraal, the body was taken and buried, lying on its right side and looking away from the house. Among the pastoral people the heir and the chief relative threw the first two lots of dung into the grave with the right hand, and each widow and child did the same. Among the agricultural people the first earth was pushed in with the elbows, and the people said, "We have finished using our hands for you; we take leave of you with our elbows." This was done because they feared that in the future the ghost might be angry with them for having buried the body as if anxious to get him out of the way. They felt that the fact that they had not buried him with their hands was something of a safeguard against the wrath of the ghost. No man whose father was alive might help in the burial or eat any of the meat of the funeral feast.

None of the cows in the kraal were milked on the night of the burial. Sometimes their calves were allowed to take all the milk, but often the calves were kept in their huts and not allowed to go to the cows, so that their cries and the lowing of the cows added to the noise of mourning. The bull of the herd had its scrotum tied with string, which caused it to low with discomfort and prevented it from mating with the cows. It was not allowed to gender with the cows again, but was kept to be killed after the heir had been installed. No one was allowed to sleep all that night, but they sat outside by the kraal-gate, where fires were lit, and wailed. In the morning the cows were milked and the milk given to the children, for the mourners might not drink any.

Mourning was carried on for at least four days, though the period might be much longer if the dead man was an important chief. During that time the mourners drank beer, which was supplied by the relatives of the dead man, and ate meat, the full-grown bulls of his herds being killed to feed them. They might not wash or shave or pare their nails, and in the old days they wore special garments of dry leaves or fibre which were left on the grave at the end of the mourning; these, however, have not been used for some time. They might not scratch their bodies with their nails or the tips of their fingers, but had to use the back of the hand, or rub the irritating place on some other part of the body.

Among the agricultural people those who lived at a distance and desired to do so might leave, after washing, shaving, and cutting their nails, on the second day, but those who could stayed the full four days.

At the end of the mourning period all the mourners washed, shaved their heads, cut their nails, and put on new clothes. All this was done by the grave, the hair and nail-clippings being laid on it and the water used for washing poured over it, while the pots which had held the water were broken and put on the grave.

The head-man of the clan then introduced the heir, placing him before the assembled mourners and pronouncing him to be the true heir to the property.

The heir or the head-man of the clan had to send messengers to inform the king of the death, a ceremony which was called *Kubika*. Two or three members of the clan, chosen for fleetness of foot, started before dawn and drove a bull towards the royal enclosure. When it had reached the entrance they shouted, "Afulire mukama ayihongire Nyamionga" (He—naming the man—has left the king and gone to the king of the dead). This cry was an insult to the king, for it declared that the king of the dead had been too powerful for him and had succeeded in robbing him of one of his subjects. When they had shouted it the men fled, leaving the bull. The guard of *Bamuroga's* men, who kept the royal gate and guarded the sacred drums in the court, gave chase, and if any of the messengers were caught, they were liable to severe punishment and might even be killed. The guard, however, did not follow far, for they had to catch the bull, kill it, and cook and eat some of the meat before the sun rose. Whatever was uneaten by the time the sun appeared had to be buried quickly in a pit, which had been dug by some of the guard while the others killed the bull and cooked the meat, for the sun might not be allowed to shine upon it. They dared not try to hide any away and eat it later, for not only would their chief punish them, but the ghost would be revenged upon them if they ate any of it in the sunlight.

In the case of men of less importance and among the agricultural people, this ceremony did not take place. The chief of the district or the chief under whom the man served might be informed but no bull or cow was used in announcing the death.

In the kraal of the dead man the purificatory ceremony now took place. All the pots and vessels were brought from the house and set before the door, and those which had any flaw or crack were broken and cast upon the grave. A pot in which was water mixed with white clay was given to a sister of the heir, and with two bunches of purificatory herbs she sprinkled this over the members of the family and all the household goods. Among the pastoral people many people came to look on at this ceremony, but they were not sprinkled as onlookers were in the case of the king's death. The sister took something, it might be a cow or only a bark-cloth, from the dead man's goods as payment for this service.

On the next day the bull of the herd was killed, and a young bull which the new owner brought with him was declared to be its heir.

On this day the heir sat at the door of his house with his mother or the chief widow, and anyone who had a claim upon the estate of the deceased had to appear, for after this day no claims were recognised. The heir was carefully guarded all day and had to remain at home lest he should injure himself in any way, an event which would be harmful to the estate.

The heir took possession of the widow or widows and might take any of them to wife, though they were all free to return to their homes on condition that the marriage-fee was refunded. If there was a young childless widow, he might take her to wife, but must give her parents a cow or a goat, or, if she preferred, she also might return to her home and the marriage-fee paid for her had to be refunded to the heir. The head-man of the clan received a cow, or, if he so chose, a widow from the estate.

The heir generally remained in the same kraal for some six months until it was thought that the body was decomposed, when he built a new kraal and the old one quickly became overgrown with grass and shrubs. While it was in use, the dung was daily thrown upon the grave.

When a man of the pastoral people who had no kraal of his own died, he was buried by his relatives in the earth somewhere near his master's kraal. Those who had no relatives to do this for them were simply cast out into the grass and the wild animals devoured the bodies. The king's cow-men were forbidden to bury their dead in the dung-heap and had to dig the graves outside and bury them in the earth. No special attention was paid to the burial of poor men, for their ghosts would not be powerful and were not feared. No attention was paid to a ghost unless the man was powerful and the medicine-man considered that his ghost might be dangerous. Then a shrine was made in the new owner's house near his bed and milk was daily placed there for the ghost.

The wife of a wealthy man was treated with some respect. Her ornaments were removed, her head shaved, her nails pared, her legs bent up, and her hands placed under the left side of her head. No milk was put in her mouth, but the body was wrapped in bark-cloths and buried on the left side of the house. Mourning lasted four days. The grave was marked by the planting of a few sticks of euphorbia, which took root and grew.

The house in which a wife died was immediately destroyed, but the material was not damaged and was used to build a new house quite near the old one. No attention was paid to the ghost, for a woman had no property and her ghost was not dangerous.

Death of Twins during the Dancing Period

If a child that was a twin died during the period of the dancing, before the children had been brought out to be seen by the relatives and named, the medicine-man was sent for. He took the body before it was stiff, bent it up, and thrust it into a large new cooking-pot. The pot was lined with bark-cloth and when the body was put into it, the bark-cloth was folded over to cover it and protect it from contact with the potter's clay with which the medicine-man filled up the pot, smoothing it over the top.

No detail of the festivities might be curtailed or delayed, and no mourning took place for the child. Even if both the twins died, the festivities had to go forward and be completed before any notice might be taken of the deaths.

The pot with the body of the child was kept in the house, and when the placenta was taken to the forest it also was taken and placed there but was not buried. After the dance round the placenta was performed, the people left the place and no further notice was taken of the dead child.

(3) INHERITANCE

Inheritance among chiefs—the king's messenger—visit of condolence—heir summoned to court—augury of the red cattle—visit to the king—anointing the king's toes—admission to the Sacred Guild—the sacred milk—assembly of chiefs—greeting the king in the seventh courtyard—the stool and the crown—*Mulanga* and the sacred milk—drinking beer—kissing the king's hands—the king's gifts—leaving the royal enclosure—visit of *Mulanga*—chief's visit to the country—inheritance among pastoral people other than chiefs—the widows—slaves—agricultural people—women

The killing and eating of the principal bull of a dead man's herd usually marked the end of the mourning ceremonies and the heir, though he had already been recognised by the clan, had then to be formally installed with the approval of the king, and, if he was heir to a chief of the Sacred Guild, he had to be admitted into that body. A chief of the Sacred Guild when he died was called *Kiro* and his heir *Karongo*.

After the purification, when the next new moon appeared, the king sent a messenger who was called *Nsomerano*. He went nominally to sympathise in the king's name with the heir for the loss of his father, but he had also to see whether the chosen heir was a suitable person for the post; he had power to reject the man, should he see reason to do so, and elect a more suitable son or member of the clan. He had to be received and treated with honour, and was given a cow and one or two slave-women. Having completed his task he returned to the king, gave a report of the heir, and told what gifts he had received, whereupon the king gave him his hands to kiss as a sign that he might keep the gifts.

The king sent the messenger back to tell the new chief when he might come to court. On this visit, the messenger placed the chief on his father's stool and gave him his father's drum and spear, and he was permitted to beat the drum as chief. He had a temporary enclosure built, and moved from the kraal of his father to take up his residence in it. He had, however, still to be confirmed in office by the king.

A few days later, the king's messenger again came to take the chief to court. He brought a red heifer, a red bull, and a water-horn, which in the early morning were led before the door of the chief's house. The animals stood there for a short time, and if they urinated it was a good omen. The water was caught in the horn and some was sprinkled over the family and the house. If, however, the animals made droppings first, it was a bad sign, and the chief might expect to be removed from office or to suffer some other calamity.

The chief, accompanied by his relatives, then went to the king, taking with him a cow and a calf and the horn containing the urine. When he entered the king's presence he knelt and touched the underside of the king's great toes with the urine. If the king did not wish to give him the chieftainship he refused to allow him to touch his toes and announced that some other son or clan-member was to be chief. This nominee of the king then came forward and touched his toes with the urine. All the other chiefs of the Sacred Guild had to be present to see the touching of the king's toes, which was supposed to preserve him from the infection of death. The new chief rose from his knees without touching the ground with his hands, and, backing out of the throne-room, returned to his own house.

The king's messenger accompanied a chief of the Sacred Guild back to his home and told him what to prepare for the next ceremony. He had to gather together and take with him cows and sheep and a liberal supply of cowry-shells, for he was expected to distribute gifts lavishly.

When the day came on which the new chief was to be installed, the king ordered that a special milk-pot, *Kisahi*, should be filled with milk from his sacred cows, for the man had, by drinking this milk, to be admitted into close fellowship with the king. The ceremony was one which caused the chief much fear and trembling, for it was a solemn affair and he dreaded lest some mistake would lose him the favour of the king and even rouse the royal anger.

The new chief, who had to remain silent all day, came to the royal enclosure, escorted by his relatives, and joined the other chiefs of his rank, who assembled outside the enclosure beside their special entrance to the court of the seventh hut, where the sacred cows came to be herded. The chiefs wore their best bark-cloths and, with the exception of the novice, all wore their crowns.

The king, when he had drunk the morning milk and gone through the usual morning duties, went about eleven o'clock to the seventh courtyard where he "herded" the three cows. When he had finished he sent for the new chief who came, attended by the others, through the special gate and greeted him.

Having met his chiefs, the king returned through the seven huts, and when he reached the queen's reception-room he sent the messenger to summon the new chief to the throne-room. The chiefs left the sacred courtyard by their own gate and came to the court outside the throne-room. When they arrived there, the chief's stool, which had been made for him from the sacred tree *kirikiti*, was placed before the king, with the chief's new crown upon it. The king told him to sit on the stool, whereupon the crown was removed and placed upon a rug before the throne.

The chief was accompanied by a man who had charge of the distribution of his gifts. This man told the king's messenger that the chief had brought a cow and a calf in order to drink milk, and the messenger informed the king. The king then instructed one of his wives, who was called *Mulanga*, to bring the sacred milk and told the chief to go to drink it. For this purpose the whole company proceeded to another house, *Kitogo*, where the chief stood supported by his companions as if he were about to faint. *Mulanga* held out the pot which the chief took in both hands, and she then guided it to his lips. He took nine sips and put it away; the king told him to drink more and again he took nine sips, making eighteen in all.

The company then returned to the throne-room and the king sent for a special pot of beer with two mouths in which were two straws or drinking tubes, taken from the plants *musinga* and either *kigulagasani* or *kisekiseki*. The novice was bidden to drink and again took nine sips.

Stocks made of a log from the *kirikiti* tree and a rope were brought, and the king informed the chief that if he attempted any rebellion or insubordination he would be bound and put in the stocks.

The king ordered one of the chiefs to place the crown on the man's head and he did so, raising and lowering it eight times and the ninth time leaving it on his head. The man was then raised from his stool and supported to where the king stood. The king presented both hands placed together palms upward and the man kissed them, which was the final confirmation of his chieftainship. The other chiefs led him away, walking backwards from the king's presence.

The king sent a cow and a calf as gifts to the man. As in all cases where the king gave a cow to anyone, if it urinated on the way home there was general rejoicing and the urine was caught and the fetishes were sprinkled with it. Should there be droppings first, it was a bad omen; they made a little fire with the dung and said that the king had given a gift of perpetual fire. Should a woman who had been received as a gift not have a child, or should a cow not bear a calf, they explained it by saying that they had had droppings first.

Music sounded and songs were sung while the new chief, with his drum beating, was conducted out of the royal enclosure to his new house. He was stopped at every turn. Triumphal arches had been placed ready at each gate and the man had to give presents in order to be allowed to pass. He gave a cow and a calf to the woman who brought the milk, and bulls, sheep, and cowry-shells were doled out to those who barred his way. He might not speak as he was conducted home and indeed had to remain silent until sunset.

When he reached home, his stool was placed for him in front of his house and he was put to sit on it four times, being raised each time he sat down. His "little father," a brother or clan-brother of his father, came and took his crown from him and put it in a box. The chief then sat on a rug by the stool, and the king's wife *Mulanga* came with the pot of milk which was left over, and gave it to the chief's "little father" and his wife. *Mulanga* remained with the chief a few days, living in great luxury. A cow was promptly killed that she might be supplied with meat, and a special house was placed at her disposal. She was treated and waited upon as if she were of the royal family.

People came and went all the day, congratulating the silent chief and receiving presents from the man in charge of the purse. When the cows returned from pasture in the evening, the chief called to one of his trusted servants, "So-and-so, that is your cow and calf," naming the cow by name. The servant kissed his hands to show that he would be a faithful servant and never leave him, and after that the chief might talk.

He next had to go to bed with his wife to complete the ceremony and confirm it. After a short time the servant came to the door and crowed like a cock and the chief said, "It is morning," got up, washed, and went about his duties of the evening. This had to be done before jackals began to bark near them, for, if they began before the ceremonies were finished, they would bring evil.

During this day the chief had to go all day without relieving nature. He might urinate, which was a good sign, but to relieve the bowels would bring evil upon him.

During the next four days the king's band played at the man's house and he had to entertain them and other friends as they came. On the second day he had a cow killed for them to eat. On the fourth day he took a cow and a calf to the king, who received him and gave him his hands to kiss, and this ended his installation as chief of the Sacred Guild.

He then asked permission from the king to go to the country to build a new house and settle all his affairs there. He was received and acknowledged as the chief of the property and stayed a month, during which time all his people came to see him and bring him presents, in return for which he had to give them presents. He returned to the capital after a month and built himself a new permanent residence there, burning down his temporary one.

If he was an important chief, *Mulanga*, the king's wife, went with him to the country and stayed there with him until he came back to the capital. She then returned to the king, being given a cow and a calf before she went. She told the king all that had passed and he permitted her to kiss his hands as a sign that she might keep for her own the cow and the calf.

From this time the chief had always to come before the king wearing a bark-cloth of good quality, bracelets and anklets, and a string of beads round his neck. He might never again drink milk before the king, and he had to be careful in his behaviour and conversation.

The ordinary pastoral people, who were not chiefs but who inherited property, were first installed by the head of the clan and it was he who announced to the king the fact that a certain man or child was heir to property. The king sent his messenger who confirmed the appointment and summoned the heir to the king. When he went, he took with him a cow, which was given to the king when he was announced. The king gave him coffee-beans, which were called the milk, and which the man took home. He gave some to his "little father," i.e. either a real or clan-brother of his father, who received him on his knees, gave him some of the beans back, and told him to sit by his side on a mat. The rest of the beans the heir kept for his own use. During the early part of the morning, before he went to see the king, he kept silent, but after he came home he might speak.

After two days he again visited the king and kissed his hands, and the king gave him a cow, which became his most valued animal. This cow from the king was the witness that he had been received and confirmed in office. He gave presents, usually sheep and cowry-shells, to the relatives who came to see him and who brought him gifts.

The heir to any property also took the widows of the dead man. Should one of them be his mother, as was usual, for the heir was nearly always a son of the dead man, she became an honoured inmate of his house, while he took the others to be his wives. Any widow was free to return to her clan, provided her relatives consented and returned the marriage-fee. Should there be among them a young childless widow, he had to pay her clan a cow or a goat, unless she chose to go back, when the original marriage-fee was refunded.

The man probably also inherited slaves as part of his property, and inherited slaves were treated differently from those who were bought or captured. They were regarded almost as members of the family and were never sold. A man often married an inherited slave-woman, and when she bore children to her master she became free. Should he marry another wife, who was a free woman, her children and not those of the slave-woman inherited his property; but the children of a wife who had been a slave inherited before the children of a widow whom he had inherited and taken to wife.

Among the agricultural people, a man who became heir to any property had first to be recognised by the head of his clan, and then he went to his master, whether it was the king, a chief, or a wealthy cow-man. The master gave him the coffee-beans, which he took home, whereupon he was recognised by his clan as the owner. Among the agricultural people, the heir might talk on the day of his installation, but he had to be careful not to run any risk of hurting himself.

Sometimes it happened among the agricultural people that the eldest son, who was the rightful heir, had grown up and, having his own house and establishment, did not wish to be heir to his father. In that case he would agree with the head of the clan for a younger brother to take his place and would take for himself merely a few cows or goats, or a wife, or a portion of whatever there might be. The younger son then inherited the widows and children and cared for them.

Women seldom inherited, but, if a cow-man from some other nation came into the land and died, leaving no son, he might bequeath his property to his daughter, who then became a slave to the king.

Women, having no property, had no heirs. If a wife died leaving children, her clan sent another woman to take her place. This woman was known as the dead woman's heir and the husband generally married her. She took possession of any articles the other had owned, and looked after her children. If there were no children, the man might take another wife from the same clan, but he had to pay for her, unless his wife had died while visiting her relatives, when they sent him another woman.

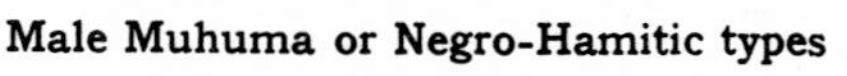

Male Muhuma or Negro-Hamitic types

PLATE XXXIX

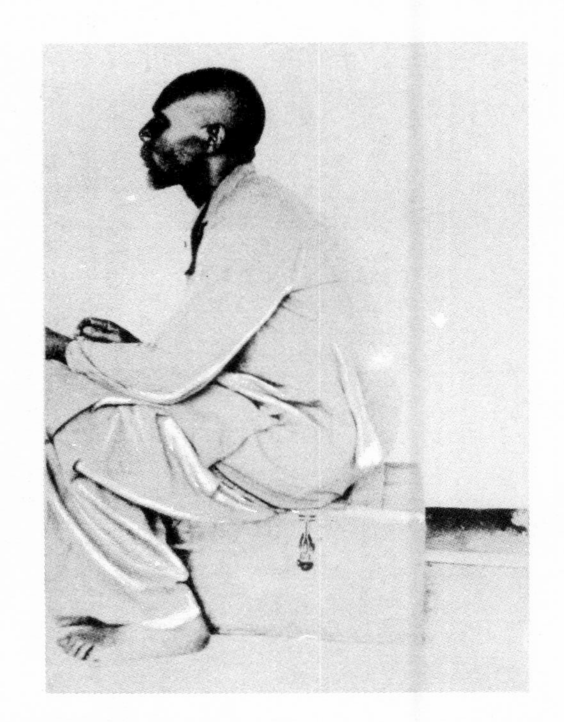

Male. Agricultural class of better type

CHAPTER XII

WARFARE

Pastoral people and the aborigines—king used to lead the army—chief enemies the Baganda—consulting auguries—the *Mutaka wa Manda* of Bunyaga—the leader of the army—gathering an army—duties of women—weapons—spies and secret agents—omens before setting out—magic-working against the enemy—the attack—treatment of the enemy's dead—the first prisoner offered to the fetishes—the division of the spoil—purification—reporting to the king—punishment for cowardice—purifying a man who had killed an enemy—an unsuccessful leader—rebellion and civil war

THERE can be little doubt that, in the early days of the Bakitara nation, the king and the pastoral people revelled in fighting and were keen and energetic warriors. When the pastoral people came into the land, the aborigines were agricultural people who lived in small detached communities or villages, formed each of some twenty to forty huts, sometimes enclosed by a rude fence or stockade of growing trees but more often unprotected. They had no settled form of government, but each village had its chief, to whom the people looked to settle all local differences and act as arbitrator in matters which concerned the whole community. In their personal affairs, the members of each clan looked for advice, direction and counsel to the head of the clan. These scattered communities found it wiser to give way and become subservient to the pastoral people when they appeared, rather than to attempt to carry on hostilities.

The pastoral tribes were a more united people, all looking to one man, their king, for leadership, and they probably did not find it difficult to subdue the aborigines, into whose lands they pushed their way in search of pasture for their great herds of cattle. They treated the subdued people leniently so that they settled down contentedly into the position of serfs to their conquerors and did for them all the work which the pastoral people might not do without harming their cows.

They also joined the invading armies of the pastoral people as they spread further, thus adding to their numbers and their strength.

In these early days, the Bakitara went out to war under their king, who led the army in person. Later, however, as his territory and the number of his subjects increased, the king became so engrossed in directing affairs at home that he seldom left his enclosure and would nominate some chief to lead the army. The warfare with which we have to deal here was carried on under this later regime, in the time of the last three or four kings of the country.

For many years the chief opponents of the Bakitara were the Baganda, whose kings, realising that the Bakitara were powerful enemies, sought to take their land from them. There was much fighting between the two nations, but there were also periods of peace when the kings were friendly and exchanged presents to prove their pacific intentions. These periods, however, did not last long, for they were brought to an end by the cupidity of some border-chief, who would either make a raid on some neighbouring territory and capture insufficiently guarded cattle, or would send to the king to inform him of the presence of such herds and excite his desire to possess them.

When the king made up his mind that an expedition was advisable, or when some information or rumour made it necessary to prepare to attack or to be on the defensive, he had first to discover what steps he should take to ensure success. This could only be done by consulting auguries; so the king, after a conference with some of the chiefs of the Sacred Guild, would summon his medicine-man.

The chief of the medicine-men was always in the royal enclosure ready for the king's summons, and it was his duty to consult the augury on any question which the king wished to have decided. According to the gravity of the question a fowl or some kind of animal was chosen, its throat was cut, and the flow of blood watched. The body was then cut open and the markings on liver and intestines examined. Either to begin the taking of this augury or to confirm it, a second medicine-man took an augury over water.

There was another important medicine-man to whom the king applied in such cases. He was called *Mutaka wa Manda* of Bunyaga and was so famous as a medicine-man that, from time immemorial, he and his forefathers lived on their hill immune from robbery. Even the Baganda would not plunder his goods or lands, for his fame was known to them. The king sent to him for advice on military matters, but he never appealed to an augury. The hill on which he lived was his shrine and on the top of it the victim, which had to be a white or white and red cow, was offered. The animal was killed and eaten on the spot and the medicine-man kept the skin. When the sacrifice was over, he beat his drum and sent a message to the king that he might proceed with his plans, for all would be well.

Auguries and prophesyings all being favourable, the next matter was the choice of a leader for the army. This too was done by augury taken by the king's medicine-man, and the chief named as leader (*Mugabe*) was sent for to receive his instructions. He came to the king, took an oath of fidelity, and was given a spear, a shield, a drum, and some special fetishes, after which he had to leave the capital without spending a night there.

For the purpose of gathering together his army he settled down a few miles from the capital and waited for people to come to him. He would not have to wait more than a few days, for chiefs and their followers flocked to join him, eager for plunder and the excitement of fighting. There would be a little more delay while the men got their spears sharpened and visited their clan-priests to obtain their blessing. They had no clothing to trouble about, and the commissariat department did not exist, for the men helped themselves to what they wanted as they went along, both in their own and the enemy's country. The only desire of the warriors was to set out and move as quickly as possible, so that they might reach the place where they were to attack or plunder the enemy before word could reach him of their approach.

Some of the important chiefs would take women with them to cook for them and to nurse them if wounded or sick, but it was seldom that a woman witnessed a battle, and they were never permitted to take any active part in the fighting. The wives who were left at home had to do their part by observing strict laws of chastity and by attending to the fetishes. Should an accident injure or disable a man, he would feel sure that his wife had been careless or unfaithful.

When a man went out to war he wore many amulets and fetishes on his neck, his wrists, and his shield. He carried spears, and a shield made of soft wood which grew hard with exposure. It was leaf-shaped, some two to two and a half feet long and eighteen inches wide, and was curved to go round his body. It had a boss in the centre and was covered with laced or plaited reeds. With this the man was able to parry a spear-blow or catch arrows, if the foe used such missiles. He also carried a goat-skin bag slung on his left shoulder, in which were his tobacco, his pipe, and invariably one or two more fetishes.

The king's medicine-man and some assistants joined the army in order to give help and advice to the leader and to any other men who could afford to consult them.

With the army there also went a secret agent of the king whose duty it was to watch the doings of the leader and his forces and send independent reports to the king. The leader was aware of the presence of such a person, but did not know who he was.

The leader and the medicine-man, as chiefs of the force, had also their special agents who were sent ahead into the enemy's country to spy out the land and report on the whereabouts of the enemy or of the cattle which the expedition was sent to capture. When possible, a few trusted warriors would be sent out to capture the cattle quietly by night, or to follow them up, if their guardians had heard of the approach of the raiders and were moving the herds away. Spies were often sent into the enemy's country weeks before an invasion took place. They went as traders, selling salt and other things from Kitara, and as they went about the country they found out where food was stored and where there were weak points and good places to attack. These men would act as guides to the army when it crossed the boundary into the enemy's country.

When all was ready, a day was chosen for the beginning of the expedition. On the previous evening, the medicine-man killed an animal to see if the augury was favourable for the start. He ate some of it, and the blood was sprinkled over the warriors. Sometimes he might order that a cow or sheep be killed and pieces sent to different places as offerings to ensure success and blessing, or he would throw the meat in different directions, saying, "I give this meat to avert evil and that my men may fight victoriously." This throwing of the meat was supposed to save the men from being made prisoners. If rain fell that night, the army might not start the next day, but had to wait until the omens were propitious.

When the army was about to set out, the medicine-man made them all jump over the body of the sacrificed animal, or over a stick, or he touched each man with a stick dipped in the blood of the animal.

When the foe was reported to be near, or the leader learned that a force was on its way to meet him, he consulted the medicine-man about making some special offering to ensure divine favour before going forward to the attack. The medicine-man took auguries every day, but on this occasion he often called for the sacrifice of a human being, who had to be blind; or he might be satisfied with a blind cow, a puppy whose eyes were not yet opened, or a bird or wild animal blinded for the purpose. This offering was taken by night, maimed to render it unable to move, and placed with many magical objects in some path by which the foe was sure to come. The blindness was supposed to confuse the enemy and make them perplexed about the right way and about the strength of the other army, so that they were not able to act together and organise their forces, and thus were easily routed. A ceremony similar to this one is described in *The Northern Bantu*:

Ceremony to prevent war. Should a report arise that an enemy was about to invade the country, or when some portion of the country had been raided and some people killed and others carried away into slavery, the medicine-man procured a blind cow, a puppy with its eyes still closed, and a basket of food which was carefully wrapped up so that no one could tell the kind of food it contained. The animals were killed and cut up into small portions and the food was also divided into a corresponding number of portions. These were taken and buried in every road by which it was possible for the foe to enter the country. This was supposed to be sufficient to ruin the powers of perception of any expeditionary force, when the members of it stepped over the hidden portions of food, minced cow, and minced puppy in the road.

When enemies raided the country the alarm was given by the beating of the war-cry on drums, and the army collected together to repel the invader. There was usually fighting, for the invaders would not retire after their first raid, but would seek to follow up their advantage and capture more cattle and people for slaves. If the Bakitara were the invaders, they too could not resist going forward into the enemy's country to find more spoil, and they would follow a defeated enemy until help came and the pursuers were faced by a fresh army.

There was no method in the marching or mode of attack. Each chief led his men as he thought best, and the men hung back or rushed on the foe as they felt inclined. Matters usually ended in one man's rushing out from one side to attack one of the other side. This would lead to several hand-to-hand fights, and when the champions of one side were wounded or killed, their companions, in dismay, would flee, leaving their wounded behind them to be killed by the companions of the victors, who would seize this opportunity to attack the fleeing forces.

When a man killed one of the enemy, he adorned himself with a band of grass as a crown. In the early days this was shown to the leader at the close of the day as proof of the deed, but later this was not thought sufficient, and it was ordered that a hand or the private organs of the dead man should be brought to the leader as a proof, before the soldier received the honour of the deed.

It was customary to mutilate the bodies of the dead and leave them to strike terror into the hearts of their fellows, should they attempt to return to the attack. Sometimes the stomach was ripped open and the bowels thrown over the face, or a spike was run through the body with the point turned towards the direction from which help might come, or the head of the dead man would be severed and stuck on a pole looking towards his fellows.

The first prisoner taken was brought to the leader and in the presence of the king's fetishes his heart was torn out and offered to them and the body was cast aside. The medicine-man who accompanied the army had to make daily offerings of animals to these fetishes, smearing them with the blood, while he and his assistants ate the meat.

When the leader considered that he would gain little by prolonging the expedition, he recalled the chiefs and their men by beating the retreat on his drums. After this no man went further into the enemy country, though they might continue to rob and plunder as they retraced their steps. The spoil had to be brought before the leader, who decided what should be kept for the king, what he would take for himself, and what the chiefs and their followers might retain. Women, when captured, were not put to death and were not ill-used, but they and the children were brought before the leader, who picked out some as slaves for the king and some for himself. The chiefs and the men who had captured them took the rest. Careful watch had to be kept on the animals which were being taken back, for there were many risks, and a man who wished to steal some would ascribe their loss to death by disease, or by wild animals, or by drowning when crossing rivers, and so on. No excuses were accepted by the leader; the animals were counted daily, and any that were missing had to be made good by the men in charge.

As they neared the capital the leader ordered the king's spoil to be separated from the rest, and this the medicine-man purified. Other medicine-men also came from the royal enclosure and again purified the cattle and slaves intended for the king.

The king then appointed some place where he would meet the army and receive the report of the expedition. A medicine-man came to the king there, bringing two goats, one black to remove darkness, and one white or coloured to take away evil. These were killed, and with a bunch of purificatory herbs dipped in the blood he touched the king on the back between the shoulders, on the cheeks and elbows, and below the knees. The leader then came at the head of the army and knelt before the king to recount their doings and tell what spoil they had brought. He returned the fetishes, drum, and spear and the spoil was marched past for the king to see. The king was quite aware that much had been retained by the leader and the chiefs, but nothing was said about it, and he commended the leader, who in return thanked him for his favour.

The king then ordered cattle to be killed and a feast to be made with beer in abundance, and there was general rejoicing. The leader and the chiefs ate apart from the rest of the army. Should the leader accuse any chief of cowardice, he was given an opportunity of explaining his conduct and, if he could not satisfy the king, he was degraded before the other warriors by being made to wear the dress of a slave-woman, wait on the others while they feasted, and sweep up when they had finished.

Any man who had killed one or more of the enemy was rewarded by the king with a slave, a wife, or a cow. Though he had already been purified from the evils of death on the battle-field by the medicine-man and also when the spoil was purified before entering the capital, he had to undergo a third purification, when the priest passed fire over him and he was washed, before he partook of the feast with his comrades. When he went to his own home, he was sprinkled with millet and given a special meal of porridge made from millet-flour. He sat in the lap first of his father and then of his mother, who received their son as re-born, before he might return to his wife. After he had done the deed he might not, for the rest of the expedition, sleep with another man, nor might he go near any woman until he had been purified, and then he had to go to his first wife.

After the feast the leader asked permission to go home and rest, but the king ordered him to remain for two days until he had received the reports of the other chiefs, who had been with him. He had to pay liberal fees to the medicine-men who went with him, and also to the bearers of the drum, spear, and fetishes of the king; this he did willingly, for he ascribed his success to their influence. He had also to satisfy the demands of many friends and relatives, who would clamour for gifts from his share of the spoil; and by the time he had distributed cows, goats, sheep, and slaves as lavishly as was expected of him, there would be but little left for himself.

If an expedition failed, the leader, instead of returning home, would betake himself to some place of safety and send urgent messages for help. He would then make a fresh attempt to capture some spoil, for unless he could make some show of success, he would be degraded and deprived of all his property, if indeed he escaped death at the hands of the irate king.

A prince would sometimes plunge the country into civil war by raising a rebellion against his brother, the king, and attempting to secure the throne. Before doing so, the prince would persuade certain chiefs to promise him their assistance, and it was important to have the support of the chief who was his guardian and responsible for him. If a chief discovered that a prince under his charge was hatching a rebellion of which he did not approve, he would inform the king and seek help to put down the rising before it could assume serious proportions. The king then appointed another prince to attack and destroy the rebel, and gave him the royal spear as leader of the army. The aim of the expedition was to kill the rebellious prince rather than to destroy his followers, who were not even punished after their leader had been killed and the rebellion crushed, for it was said that they had obeyed their leader as a woman obeyed her husband.

If any ordinary man succeeded in killing the rebellious prince he at once sought the leader of the king's forces, who came with the royal spear and ran it through the body. This was called "killing" the prince, though he might in reality be already dead, for no ordinary man might shed royal blood, and the prince's ghost might be a dangerous enemy to the man who had done such a deed.

The most serious and widespread internal conflicts took place when a king died. It was seldom that a prince was allowed to ascend the throne without having his right contested by one or more of his brothers, and the rival princes fought until only one was left alive. During this time no property was safe; the armies of the princes robbed and plundered wherever they went and only superior power could restrain them, for, the king being dead, there was no government and no one to punish the robbers. Chiefs had to see that their cattle were well guarded and had to keep their herdsmen informed of the position of the contending forces, so that the herds might be moved, when necessary, to places of safety. The agricultural people naturally suffered more than the pastoral people, and if the warfare lasted longer than about a month matters became very serious throughout the country, because of the loss of life and the shortage of food. The pastoral people could move their herds away and keep them safe, but the agricultural people, except in the outlying parts of the country, were prevented from looking after their land and the fields were left uncultivated. Their stores of grain soon became exhausted, and it was in such times that the underground food-stores were of value. Even these, however, did not last long, and if they had not been able to plant their next crop or if it had been destroyed by lack of attention or by the troops, the outlook was very black.

CHAPTER XIII

HUNTING

The priest of hunters—elephants—spears, traps, and pits—the hippopotamus—lions and leopards—buffaloes—hunting with dogs—small game—birds and monkeys

HUNTING was carried on mainly as a means of obtaining food, but also for sport and for the protection of the herds. If cows were being attacked by lions, it was the duty of the chief of the district to organise a hunt and get rid of the animals. The men who chiefly took part in the hunt were of the agricultural class, who would eat any kind of meat they could procure, but the pastoral people also joined in the sport.

There was a special priest for hunters, who supplied them with fetishes and who had a shrine and consulted the oracle to find out where game was to be found. He also informed them what taboos they must observe in order to hunt with success. Whenever the hunters succeeded in killing an animal, a special portion, consisting of the back or the loins with the sirloin, was given to the priest. The jaw-bones of elephants and the heads of other animals were brought and placed near his shrine.

Both pastoral and agricultural people kept dogs for hunting. These were poor animals, not far removed from the wild dog, and they were kept half starved to make them keen. They were used in hunting big game, more especially buffaloes.

Elephants were for many years hunted for their meat, but the ivory was little in demand, though some was used for ornaments. Later, when communication with other countries was opened up, the trade in ivory led a number of men to become professional elephant-hunters.

Several methods were employed, but the most popular was to spear the animals as they came to drink. The favourite drinking places were invariably sheltered by trees, and two or three hunters would conceal themselves over the path among the branches. Each took with him two spears, one of which he prepared for use by attaching it by a strong rope to the tree. The spears were made with a strong, heavy shaft, into which was fitted an iron blade some eighteen inches long. The other hunters concealed themselves in the neighbourhood in readiness to follow up any wounded animals. As the elephants passed beneath him, the man in the tree aimed his spear at one, trying to hit it between the shoulders and penetrate the lungs. If his attempt was successful, the elephant fell at once, but if it was only wounded it would strive to get away, trumpeting with fear and pain. The rope might drag the spear out of the wound, when it could be used again, and the animal, if severely wounded, would be followed up and killed. Sometimes the rope would break, and the elephant would carry the spear away sticking in the wound. They were said to be very clever at withdrawing spears if they could reach them, and a wounded animal had to be followed up without delay. Elephants, when killed, have been found to have a spear embedded in the bone of the skull, and the iron of the shaft has been bent round close to the head, showing that the animal had tried to extract it and failed. In some cases they must have gone about for years with the spear sticking in the bone.

At times some of the huntsmen would act as beaters, and drive the elephants under the trees in which other men were hiding. The men in the trees would select one or two and devote their attention to them. When one man had wounded an elephant and it was rushing off, another would attract its attention and it would turn to attack him. In this way they would bring it under the trees where others might aim their spears at it until it fell. If it escaped wounded, it was followed up until it got separated from the rest of the herd and could be killed.

There are many stories of the sagacity of these animals and the ways in which they help each other. One such story, for the truth of which I cannot vouch, though, from what I have heard, there is not much reason to doubt it, tells how, when one was wounded, two others placed themselves one on either side of it and supported it, while others formed a guard so that the men could not come near. In this way the wounded animal was helped along for many miles, until it reached a quiet spot where it could remain until it recovered or died.

Another commonly adopted method of snaring elephants was by the leg. A ring was made of strong creepers large enough to encircle the foot of an elephant. In this wooden spikes, two or three inches long, were fixed so that they would not move. Several of these traps were placed in the path of a herd and fastened to trees by strong ropes. Each ring was placed over a hole in the path and was covered so that the animals did not notice anything. When an elephant trod upon one of these rings the covering gave way and its foot went through. The spikes entered the flesh of its leg and it could not withdraw its foot. The more it tried to free itself the deeper the spikes entered, and the rope held it until the hunters came up and speared it. Sometimes these traps were set without ropes, for the pain prevented the animal from keeping up with the herd and from going far away.

Another kind of trap was formed by suspending a spear, weighted with a heavy log, in a tree. This was attached to a cord, which was arranged in such a way that an elephant going along the path released a stick-spring and the weighted spear dropped on the animal's back.

Pits were also used to snare elephants. While a hunter was engaged in digging a pit, he might not sleep on his bed nor wash until it was done. The pit was dug big enough for an elephant to fall right in, and it narrowed towards the bottom so that, when an animal fell in, its own weight wedged it firmly and it was unable to move. The mouth of the pit had to be very carefully covered with branches and grass and earth to resemble the surrounding ground, for elephants were said to be very suspicious and very ready to detect unsafe places. When a herd passed over one of these traps one of them was almost sure to fall in, and the huntsmen came up and speared it.

In one part of Kitara it was usual to attack elephants while in the water at a point where there was a deep stream. At such a place the elephants would walk through the water with their bodies entirely submerged and their trunks raised above the water in order to breathe. The hunters, armed with large stones, to each of which was attached a short rope with a running noose, waited in light canoes. When the animals had got well into the water, they paddled up to one of them, slipped the noose over its trunk, and dropped the stone into the water. When its trunk was thus drawn down, the animal naturally drowned, unless it could free itself or get to the bank. When the herd had gone on, those which had died in the water were found and towed to some point where it was possible to get the tusks and cut up the meat.

Sometimes the animals were speared with weighted spears in the water, the hunters guiding their aim by the trunks and striving to hit between the shoulders. Wounded animals would then be followed up until they could be approached and killed.

The jaw-bones of an elephant were taken to the shrine of the hunters' priest. The right tusk was the perquisite of the chief on whose land the animal was killed, while the left tusk went to the hunter who drove his spear into the animal. The meat was divided among all who took part, and they sold it or took it for their own use as they wished.

The hippopotamus was hunted by certain fishermen, mainly about Kibero on Lake Albert and on the banks of the river Nile, who made this their business. It was a hunt full of danger, but the flesh, though it is almost entirely fat, was much prized by the people.

Before setting out the hunter prayed to his fetishes, and his start had to be made between midnight and four o'clock in the morning. Should he meet a woman, or should a frog jump over his path, he returned home and did not hunt that day.

A favourite method was a spear-trap over the path. It is a well-known fact that hippopotami dislike having to climb over a bank or any obstacle. The men, therefore, made rude fences which led the animals, as they left the water, to some narrow opening. Here a roughly constructed arch would be made, high enough to support a weighted spear. A cord on the path, when touched, released a stick-spring and the spear fell. The huntsman was always at hand to despatch the animal, should it not be killed outright.

Another method was to lie in wait in the early morning and spear the animals as they returned to the water after feeding on the land. The weapon was a kind of harpoon to which was attached a rope with a float, and the animal when struck rushed into the water, carrying this with him. The hunter followed in his canoe and kept the animal in sight until he thought it must be dead. He then summoned his companions and, paddling up to the float, they pulled at it, keeping themselves in readiness to paddle away or use their spears if the animal was still alive and rose in anger. Sometimes two or three canoes would be lashed together, to make it easier to attack the animal without upsetting them. If a hippopotamus attacked a canoe it could smash it entirely, but few men ever seem to have been killed by them, though the risk is considerable.

The head with the tusks was placed in the shrine as an offering to the god. One shoulder went to the owner of the canoe and the other to his assistant, while the hunter took the remainder of the animal. Both flesh and skin were eaten.

When a lion attacked cows or people, the chief of the district had to organise a hunt and kill it. He summoned the men by beating a drum, and from two to five hundred gathered together, all armed with heavy clubs. These were their only weapons, for spears were forbidden, lest in the excitement of the hunt they might wound each other. The whole company surrounded the place where the lion was said to be concealed, and advanced, singing and shouting and beating down the grass as they went. They went on narrowing their circle until they came upon the animal, which, terrified by the noise on all sides, cowered down and seldom had time to realise what was happening and make a spring before it was despatched by a shower of blows.

Leopards were hunted in the same way when they attacked people, but neither they nor lions were ever hunted unless they became dangerous. The skins and claws of both animals were sent to the king, for they were royal beasts and none but royalty might use them.

Both the pastoral and the agricultural people hunted buffaloes and kept dogs for the purpose. They trained them to track the animals by scent and drive them, when found, towards their masters. The men went out in parties with the dogs on leads, one or two of them wearing bells tied round their bodies so that their whereabouts might be known. When they were in the district where they knew game to be, the men surrounded the place and let the dogs loose to follow the trail. When the herd was found, the dogs set upon one of the buffaloes and, as it fought, the men closed in and speared it.

When dividing the animal, the hunter who first threw his spear took the left shoulder and the head; this he had to cook outside the village, for it might not be taken into any inhabited place. He cooked it and then called his companions to eat it with him. The bones of the head were placed near a shrine outside the village and left there. The owner of the land on which it was killed took the right shoulder and the skin, and the rest of the meat was divided among the assistants. The stomach was cooked with vegetables and given to the dogs.

A ring-trap, like that used for elephants, was also sometimes used for buffaloes and for antelopes, the size of the ring varying according to the nature of the animal to be trapped. The trap was occasionally secured to a log instead of being

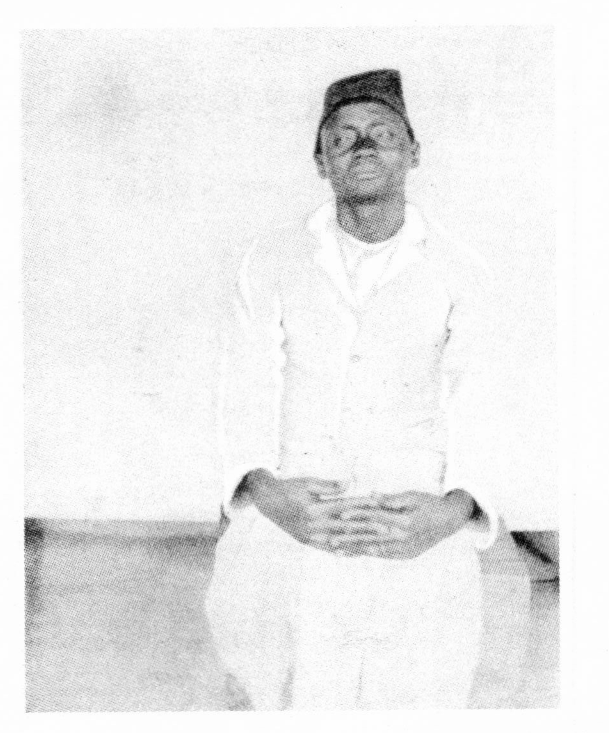

Type of Agricultural artisan

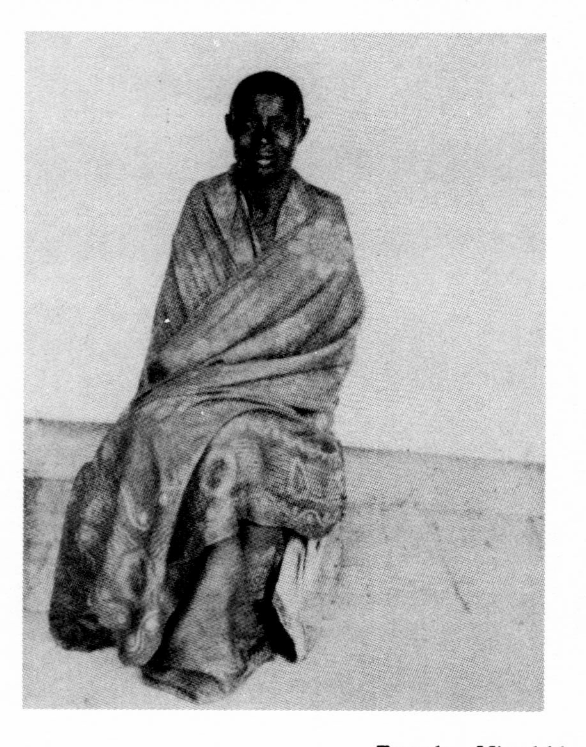

Female. Mixed blood, Muhuma and Negro

tied to a tree, and it was said that buffaloes struggled so fiercely that, if the hunter did not come and spear them soon, they would even break a leg in their efforts to escape.

For antelopes, pit-traps were often used, and they were so cleverly concealed that men have been known to fall into them. They were often made long enough for three animals to fall in one behind the other, and they narrowed at the foot so that the animals' legs were pressed together and they could not move.

Nets were also used for trapping smaller game. The hunters encircled large areas with nets from three to four feet high, and men stood here and there hidden behind screens of shrubs so that they could spear the animals as they were caught in the net. Beaters went out with dogs and drove in the game. Should a dog catch and bring down an animal, the owner of the dog claimed it and distributed the meat as if he had speared it, but the dog received a larger share of the offal. When nets were used, the owner of the net took the head and skin, the owner of the land the right shoulder, and the man who first saw and drove the animal the back. When small game was trapped the priest could not claim a portion, but the men often gave him some of the meat.

Various kinds of birds were snared, especially by young people, who set snares in the runs which were used by the birds. A few men also made a business of it and had large numbers of snares to attend to. Partridges were snared by the leg, by a noose attached to a bent stick. The bird when running put its foot into the noose; this released the spring, the stick flew up and the bird was jerked into the air. Kites were snared and their heads put on nets and traps, for it was said that they were magical and made the trap or net sure to catch.

When monkeys were troublesome, they were netted and the men had to stay very near to kill them as soon as they got into the net, for they were quick to escape. Another method of trapping them was to put some food in an empty house and leave the door open. A cord was attached to the door and carried to the place where a man sat concealed and watched. When one or two monkeys had ventured in to take the food, the door was jerked to, and men who were in waiting ran up to secure and kill the monkeys.

Fishing was done with basket-traps, draw-nets, and lines and hooks, but the last is the only method used now. Fish were eaten fresh, or cut open and dried in the sun. The fishers of Kibero did a brisk trade with the Barega on the opposite side of the Nile.

CHAPTER XIV

TRADITION AND FOLKLORE

Tradition—the visit of king Isaza to king Death—the story of Nyinamweru and Ndaula—Wamala—the story of Mukaikuru, who taught Mpugu the royal customs—the royal bow of Mpugu—the story of the royal band of flutes—Kamrasi and the cows—folklore —why the hare is the friend of the cow—the hare and the leopard— the children of Ruhanga—why the dead do not come back

TRADITIONS OF THE KINGS AND ROYAL CUSTOMS

The Visit of King Isaza to King Death

A MESSENGER from Nyamionga (Death) was once sent to King Isaza asking him to make brotherhood with him, because he wished to be on friendly terms. Isaza said to his people, "This is impossible; he is a ghost." Nyamionga, however, sent a wooden pot of milk in which he said was half a bean with his blood on it, and asked Isaza to smear the other half bean with his blood, put it in a pot of milk and return it to Nyamionga. Isaza would not drink the milk, but gave it to his servant Kwezi to drink and to make brotherhood with Death. The messenger returned and told Death all that had happened, how Isaza was deceiving him and making a common person his blood-brother.

When King Death heard this he was annoyed and determined to trap Isaza, so he sent his daughter, who was a most beautiful girl, to go and make love to King Isaza. When she arrived, she entered the queen's throne-room, *Muchwa*, and sat down. As she was sitting there, some of the servants saw her and reported to the king that there was the most beautiful girl sitting in the *Muchwa* house. Isaza's curiosity was aroused, and he sent for the girl and was astonished at her beauty. He sent her to one of his wives to be prepared for marriage. After ten days' preparation she was brought to the king and he married her.

The young wife watched Isaza daily to see how he acted. One day one of his favourite cows fell ill, and he watched over it and even by night he ran to help it, whenever he heard it sigh or move. The young wife, whose name was Nyamata, said to herself, "He likes this cow even more than me," and this decided her how to act.

Before her child was born she escaped and returned home to tell her father how fond Isaza was of cattle, even preferring them to women. Isaza looked everywhere for his wife and had the whole country searched, but no trace of her could be found.

Some months passed and one night, when the *Nkorogi* cows were being milked, a man approached the king and asked if he had seen the young bull and heifer which were standing outside the gate. They were, he said, superior to any he had seen. The king rose at once to go and look at them and was overjoyed to see such beautiful animals. He had them kept near where he might daily see them and pat them. In time they mated, and the king watched with anxious delight to see the calf that would be born. He tried hard to get the bull to mate with other cows, but all in vain: it would not go near them. When the heifer was about to calve, Isaza would not go to bed but remained up until early morning, when he lay down and fell asleep; but, before doing so, he told the men to wake him at once if anything happened.

He had been resting only a short time when he was awakened by the men, who came to tell him that the cow and the bull had jumped over the fence and were running away. Isaza rushed after them until they came to a crater-lake, when both of the animals ran into the water. Isaza followed. On and on they went, deeper and deeper, until they were out of sight under water, and still Isaza ran after them. To his surprise he came to land again, and there were the cow and the bull going on before him to an enclosure like his own, but somehow different. He followed them into the enclosure and there he saw a man sitting in state like a king. Death at once said, "So you have come now. Why would you not make brotherhood with me when I sent to you, but have now come invading my country?" Isaza replied that he had only come for his cattle. King Death answered, "They are here, and there is your wife, and that is your child, so you may as well sit down."

After resting a time, Isaza wanted to go home, but Death would not allow him and he had to stay. From time to time he tried to get away and return home, and whenever he did so his struggles caused an earthquake.

On earth the servants followed the king to the crater-lake, but were unable to trace him further. So they returned, and Bukuku became king.

Mukonko, the gate-keeper of Isaza, tried to keep his disappearance secret for a time in order to gain power and make himself king; but Bukuku, Isaza's prime minister, discovered the plan, killed Mukonko, and became king.

Bukuku had only one child, a daughter, whose story, with some account of Bukuku's successors, is here quoted from *The Northern Bantu*, pp. 6–9:

The Story of Nyinamweru. King Bukuku had one child, a daughter. While she was still a girl, a medicine-man came to the king and warned him against allowing his daughter to marry, saying that, should she marry and have a son, the king would die. King Bukuku accordingly guarded his daughter and, when she was old enough to marry, he built a house for her and surrounded it with a strong, high fence, with no gate or outlet, setting a man with his wife to guard the road leading to the house and thus prevent the girl from holding intercourse with the world. Inside the enclosure king Bukuku placed his daughter, whose name was Nyinamweru, with her maid, Mugezi, and warned them against holding any communications with men. Food, that is to say milk, was brought daily by the guardian Lumbumbi, who climbed the fence and handed it down to the maid inside. For several years all went well, until one day a man belonging to the priestly clan, called Bacwezi, arrived. The man was a stranger in the place and wandered to the enclosure, seeking someone to tell him the way. He had his dog with him and, as he could find no entrance to the enclosure, he walked round, calling to the two women inside and enquiring for the entrance. They explained to him their situation and told him how they were secluded to avoid men. This, however, only increased the man's curiosity, and being struck by the beauty of the princess, he made love to her. Gathering some wild flowers he presented them to her and finally gained the women's permission to climb into the enclosure. Simbu was the name of this man; he became the husband of the princess Nyinamweru and remained with her several months in concealment. He then left the place secretly. In due time the princess gave birth to a son and named him Ndaula. Nyinamweru nursed her child for two years without the infant being discovered. At the end of that time her maid became afraid that the child would be seen playing in the enclosure, and that its presence would endanger their lives, should king Bukuku learn of its existence. She therefore persuaded Nyinamweru to give the child to the guard, Lumbumbi, who was bidden to take and cast it into a stream and drown it. The mother most reluctantly yielded to this advice, and little Ndaula was taken by the guard and cast into the river. Fortunately the child's umbilical cord was tied to his wrist and, when Lumbumbi cast him into the river, the string by which the cord was tied to the wrist caught on the branch of a tree and saved the child from drowning. Later in the day Lumbumbi passed the place and heard the child crying, and went to see how it could still be alive. When he saw what had happened, he regarded the child's preservation as an intervention of the gods, took it home to his wife and told her to nurse it. When Nyinamweru was told how her son had been preserved from death, she was delighted and gave Lumbumbi a milch-cow to supply milk for the child. (Another version says that Lumbumbi was a potter and the princess sent him cows for the child under pretence of buying pots.) The boy Ndaula grew up to be a man and was commonly known as Lumbumbi's son. He herded the cattle and was a dauntless youth, full of mischief, delighting above all things to tease the king's herdsmen, who were haughty and expected everybody to give way to them and their cattle at the watering places. It chanced one day that the king had ordered his cow-men to give his cattle salt to eat at a certain place, saying that he would be present to examine the cattle. At the appointed time Ndaula also appeared with his cows and drove them to the spot to eat salt. The king's herdsmen tried to keep the cows away, and a struggle ensued between them and Ndaula, in which the king was fatally speared. At the trial which followed Ndaula explained who he was. He then sent for his mother Nyinamweru who confirmed his story, and the people not only pardoned his offence but also crowned him king. From the time of king Ndaula it has been the custom for a mother to make her child an amulet and put it on his neck in remembrance of the string which saved Ndaula's life. King Ndaula reigned a short time and then sent for his father and brought him and his relatives into Bunyoro. Ndaula married and had a son whom he named Wamala. When Wamala grew up, his father abdicated in favour of his son, in order that he might be free from the responsibilities of government and able to make war upon the surrounding tribes. Ndaula was constantly victorious in the wars he undertook, enlarged the boundaries of his country, and enriched the people. In his old age he is said to have disappeared, because it was not customary for kings to die. (Another version states that Ndaula was caught or killed in the west by one Luyonga we Nyamata, and Wamala came to the throne.)

King Wamala continued to reign until he became an old man when, like his predecessor, he disappeared, and his son Kyomya succeeded him on the throne. Kyomya also increased the size of the kingdom by conquering many of the surrounding tribes. Wamala appointed three men, named Mugarara, Ibona, and Mugenyi, to be priests, and two women, Nakalanda and Nabibungo, to be priestesses to the chief gods. These men were the first of the class of people afterwards known as the Bachwezi, who are the priests of the country.

Nothing else is known of Kyomya except that, in his old age, he too disappeared as his forefathers had done, and that his son Kagoro succeeded him on the throne.

Kagoro warned by ghosts to leave his country. When Kagoro had reigned some years, he was warned by the ghosts of his ancestors that they were displeased with his people, because they robbed each other and lied to one another. The king called the people together and told them that, unless they ceased from these bad habits, he must leave them. They, however, took no heed of the warning, and accordingly king Kagoro called together his near relations and departed with them secretly, carrying with him two baskets containing truth and love, and leaving behind him two baskets containing lying and hatred. One young woman who refused to go with the party was left in a house with certain sacred drums named Kajwimbe, Nyalebe, and Kyamukumbwiri, which are still retained as royal drums. For some years the people hoped to find one of the princes whom they could induce to become king, but after a prolonged search it became evident that they must find some other person to rule over them. Accordingly the prime minister, Nakolo, was sent to the Bukedi country to seek a prince who would come to reign in Bunyoro. Nakolo found a prince named Nakoko and returned with him to Bunyoro, where he became king.

King Mpugu. When prince Nakoko was crowned he was named Mpugu by the people, because one side of his body was dark and the other light. He came with three brothers, who with himself formed the Babito dynasty. It is said that when the Babito family first arrived in Bunyoro, they did not understand cow-keeping. They had to learn the art from the Banyoro, and also how to live on a milk diet.

In the information I have more recently obtained there was no mention of the kings Kyomya and Kagoro, and it was Wamala who was said to have left the country because it had grown utterly bad. He left behind him baskets of evil, containing lying, adultery and murder, and a drum, and with him went all the princes who knew anything of the customs of the country. It was also said that the woman Mukaikuru, whose story follows, was Wamala's wife.

The Story of Mukaikuru, who taught Mpugu the royal customs

Mpugu, the first of the present line of kings, came from the eastern side of the Nile and knew nothing of the cow-customs, the use of the royal drums, and other ceremonies. All the princes who knew anything about the customs had left the country, and there was no one to instruct Mpugu. Mukaikuru, the wife of one of the princes, had seen them go off on their way out of the country and had followed them at a distance. When they sat down to rest she stole behind a tree and listened as they talked. As she listened, she overheard one ask another who would tell the people all the customs of the sacred herd, when to drink the milk and how the cows had to be herded apart to keep them sacred, and who would instruct them in the daily ceremonies of the king's sacred food, in the new moon ceremonies, in the use of the drums, and so forth. The woman listened eagerly while they discussed and described all the customs, and when they rose to go on she left them and returned to her home.

When Mpugu, then, became king and asked for help and information as to the royal customs, there was no man left who knew anything. One, however, had heard Mukaikuru speak of what she had overheard, and he informed the king, who ordered that she should be brought to him. She stood by him and instructed him in all he had to do.

He was so pleased that he built her a house *Kasenda* in the royal enclosure, and princesses had to wait on her. In the house there was a pit in which millet was stored, and it was also used to throw men into, if any dared to go in to see Mukaikuru. She would have no grass or carpet on the floor, but only cow-dung, which was smeared upon it by princesses. No princess who was unwell might enter her house and, when the king moved his enclosure, the pit was filled up before the house was burned down.

The office thus created by Mpugu was continued, and in succeeding generations a woman of the same clan, the Mukwonga, always held it. She was always an old woman and stood beside the king through all the ceremonies of his coronation to prompt him if necessary.

The Royal Bow of Mpugu

The royal bow of the kings of Bunyoro is said to be the weapon which Mpugu brought with him to Bunyoro when he became king. Mpugu was a noted hunter, and in this capacity was known under several names, among them being *Lukidi* and *Nyabongo*, and his bow was named *Nyapogo*. As king of Bunyoro, however, he found that he was so occupied with his daily duties that he had to deny himself the pleasures of sport, and he decided to decorate his bow and place it with the quiver among his treasures near the throne.

He gave a bull to be killed in order that the bow might be re-strung with the sinews from its back. The bull was handed over to Muhinda ba Mpona, who killed it and extracted the sinews. When he had done so, he laid them down and left them, going away to do something else before cleaning them. In his absence a dog came in, seized the sinews, and carried them away. Muhinda returned, found that the sinews had vanished, and, on making enquiries, found that the dog had eaten them. He had to confess the loss to the king, who was so angry that he had him killed and his sinews taken out and used, with those of another bull, in place of those he had lost.

From that time whenever a new king came to the throne, the tribe of this man, the *Bahinda*, gave a man to supply new sinews for the bow, and they were cut from him while he was still alive. It became an honourable office to supply the sinews and for two days before the operation the man had to wear charms and dress in two white bark-cloths; he had to keep apart from women and eat special food. After this purification he himself directed the operation of removing the sinews from his right side, and these were used along with those of a bull, which had to be a white yearling. The man invariably died after the operation.

The Story of the Royal Band of Flutes

Mpugu was succeeded by Nyimba, who was followed by King Chwa I, who was a great warrior, and used to go out regularly at the head of punitive and marauding expeditions.

On one occasion he was returning from an expedition into Ankole, where he had been victorious, having cut up the royal drums and taken much spoil, when he was told that there was a herd of cattle hidden away in a forest through which they were passing. With a few of his warriors he wandered into the depths of the forest, and by some accident became separated from his men and was lost. They searched until darkness came and again the next day but could not find him, so they returned to the capital and informed his sister, the queen, of what had happened.

Chwa, though he was married to a wife called Arapenyi, had no child, and the chiefs could find no one they considered suitable to govern the country. At last they agreed that the queen, the late king's sister, should reign, and for a time things went fairly well. Then the queen became enamoured of a man of the cow people and asked the chiefs to agree to his taking his place as her consort to assist and advise her. pointing out that, being a woman, she could not lead her armies and that a consort could go for her. The chiefs were not favourable to the idea, for the man was not a prince, and they asked for time to consider the matter.

While they were still in perplexity news arrived concerning the woman Arapenyi, who had been found in Ankole by two men who had gone there to sell salt. They recognised her and asked her how she came to be there. In reply she told them that she had been captured when her husband, King Chwa, was lost, and that she had a child who was with her. The men saw the child, whose likeness to the late king was striking, and brought their story back to Bamuroga, who at once sent two chiefs, a *Muhuma* and a *Munyoro*, to visit the woman secretly and, if the story was correct, to bring her and her child back. The chiefs recognised Arapenyi and saw that the likeness of the child to King Chwa was unquestionable, so they helped the woman and child to escape by night and brought them to Bamuroga.

For a time the matter was kept secret and the woman and her child lived in hiding, but at last the queen demanded an answer to her proposal and Bamuroga said they would bring the answer the next day. The chiefs then took the boy prince with them to visit the queen, who recognised him as the son of her brother, greeted him with affection, and listened to the story of how his mother had been captured and then brought back from slavery. The boy had to sit on her lap and she showed him every mark of affection.

Later, the queen asked Bamuroga if the child might not come to stay with her, for she was so pleased to see him. He, however, was suspicious of her intentions and said it was impossible. The queen then held a council in secret with her immediate attendants, and decided that the boy would have to be killed. Among her attendants, however, was the flute-player, Musegu, who went to Bamuroga and told him the whole plot: how the queen was going to ask for another interview with the little prince, and had arranged to have him speared while in her presence. It was arranged that Musegu, who would be present at the interview, should warn the followers of Bamuroga when the deed was to be done by blowing his flute.

In a short time the queen asked Bamuroga to allow the child to come and see her again. Bamuroga consented, and the queen made her preparations by placing her men with concealed weapons in suitable positions ready to attack. Bamuroga, however, also took with him an armed party with their weapons concealed. The prince sat on a rug in front of the queen who talked in a friendly manner with him, but, as she gave her signal for him to be speared, Musegu set up a strange, shrill piping and the prince, who had been told to rush back to his protectors when he heard the sound of the flute, sprang back among Bamuroga's men, some of whom surrounded him, while others rushed in and slew the would-be assassins, among them the queen's paramour, and made the queen prisoner.

The prince, who was then called Ruguruki, was at once declared king and he proclaimed that Musegu should become a member of his own clan, the *Babito*, and appointed him and his sons to be the royal flute-players who had to be in the king's presence on all ceremonial occasions. Their persons were to be sacrosanct, and they had free access to the king at all times.

Kamrasi and the Cows

There was a time when the king used to have cows sleeping by his throne-room door, but for some years this has been abandoned. It is said that King Kamrasi had some favourite cows which he used to have near so that he might go to see them during the night. In his day, and in that of his forefathers, it was believed that the kings who had passed away used to come to see their sons and watch over them. The cows of Kamrasi were called *Ndambike* and lay round the door. It so happened that one night, when the dead kings came to look on the living king, they stood outside and Kamrasi heard one of them say he would not go in because he did not wish to soil his clothing and the cows had made such a mess that it was impossible to pass. The other kings remonstrated and begged him to come, and at length he did so. Kamrasi, however, feared that he would not in future get the kings to come and see him if he kept the cows there, so he had them moved away, and they have never been brought back.

These ghosts finally ceased to visit the king when Kabarega introduced guns, and it was said they were afraid of them because of the noise they made.

Folklore

Why the Hare is the Friend of the Cow

At one time a lioness and a cow lived together on the most friendly terms. They had in common a well of excellent water, which was always clear even when the rains were heaviest. In the course of time each had a child, and the calf and the cub played about together.

One day, as the cow and the lioness stood together at the well, the cow said, "If your child muddies the water we have to drink, I will gore it to death," and the cow had fine long horns tapering to a sharp point. The lioness said, "If your calf spoils the water, I will tear it to pieces," and she showed her large teeth, white, long, and sharp.

Some days later the two children were playing after breakfast near the well when the calf knocked some dirt into it and made the water muddy. The cow, when she discovered what had happened, said, "We had better run away before the lioness comes home and discovers what you have done, for she will kill you."

They started off at once, going as quickly as the calf could run, and in the evening they met a herd of elephants. They asked the cow, "Where are you going in such a hurry?" The cow said, "We are running away from the lioness because my child has fouled the water of the well, and we had agreed that, if either of our children dirtied the water, the parent of the other would put it to death. As my child has done the wrong, we are running away to save his life." The elephants replied, "Stay with us, we will protect you against the lioness. What can she do against our tusks?" The cow looked at the great tusks and body of a huge male elephant and said, "This animal can indeed protect me. I will stay." In the night the lioness was heard roaring in the distance, and in the morning the elephants said, "Go, for we cannot protect you against such an angry lioness."

The cow set off again with her calf and ran many weary miles, when she met a herd of buffaloes, who asked her, "Cow, cow, where are you going and why do you run?" The cow told her sad story and was going on when the herd said, "Stay with us, what can one lioness do against such a number of us?" The cow and her calf were tired and gladly consented to stay. Again during the night the roar of the lioness was heard as she hunted the cow and her calf, and the buffaloes were afraid. In the morning they said to the cow, "Go, that lioness is too much for us. We fear we cannot save you." The poor cow with her calf had to start off again and ran many weary miles.

Towards evening she was passing some rocks where a hare sat enjoying herself, and by her side was a lion-skin. The hare asked, "Cow, why are you running like this? Where are you going?" The cow told her tale, but thought, "This little animal can't help me, when the other large animals have failed." The hare, however, said, "Come into my house and I will save you." The cow was very tired and it was getting dark, so she accepted the invitation, though she did not expect much help. The hare took the cow and calf into an inner chamber in her rocky house, which was a large cave, and shut the door.

She called and asked the cow, "Have you any milk?" The cow replied, "Yes," and the hare went in and milked a pot and put it aside by the outer door. She next asked for some of the cow's blood and drew off a pot of it from a vein and placed the pot with the other near the door. She then said, "Give me some of your dung," and the cow did so, not knowing what the hare was going to do with all these preparations. The hare wrapped the dung in leaves and placed it by the pots and again took her seat on the rock.

She had only just done so when up came the lioness, running along. The hare asked "Where are you going, running so fast?" The lioness said, "I want to catch a cow and her calf. Have you seen them? I want to kill the calf for spoiling my well of water." The hare said, "No, I have not seen them." The lioness asked, "Then what are these foot-marks?" and she followed them into the cave. The hare followed and asked, "Why do you walk into my house? How dare you take so great a liberty? Don't you know I can kill you?" and she snatched up the pot of blood and threw it with all her might against the lioness's side, where it broke, letting a stream of blood run on the floor. "Look at your blood," said the hare, and the lioness trembled as she saw it and felt the blow on her side. The hare then took the pot of milk and dashed it on the lioness's head, saying, "Look at your brains," and the milk ran down on to the floor as the hare said, "I have knocked them out." The lioness began to cry and try to get out of the house, whereupon the hare threw the bundle of dung against her side, saying, "Look, I have pulled out your intestines." The lioness was so frightened that all her strength left her. The hare then threw down the lion-skin, saying, "Look at that skin which I took from a lion I killed three days ago," and as the lioness turned about, she threw the skin first in one place and then in another in front of her, until at length the lioness bolted out of the door and ran back home, leaving the cow and calf.

In this way the hare saved the cow and her calf, but from that time lions have been embittered against cows, and always try to kill them. The hare lives among the cows and does not fear them and has milk from them when she wants it.

The Hare and the Leopard

Once, many years ago, a hare and a leopard lived together. The hare was nurse to the leopard's two children and also had charge of the house. One day the leopard went out hunting and the hare was nursing the children in her lap. She let one child fall, and it injured its back so that it died at once. The hare was very frightened, and put the two children to bed side by side and covered them up as though they were sleeping.

In due time the mother leopard came home carrying the meat, which was a goat she had killed. She threw down the meat and asked for the children to nurse them. The hare brought the living baby, saying, "Nurse this one first. The other is fast asleep." After a time the leopard said, "Bring the other," so the hare took away the first baby and put it in bed and, after pretending to cover it and lift the other, she brought back the same living baby. The leopard said, "This is the same baby," but the hare denied it, saying, "No, that is the other." After a few moments the leopard got up to go and look for herself in the bed, and as she did so the hare ran out of the house and down to the river. The leopard uncovered the other baby and saw that it was dead. She raised a cry and rushed out after the hare.

When the hare reached the river she rolled in the mud and then swam to the other side and sat on a hillock to await the leopard. After a few minutes the leopard came panting along and did not recognise the hare as her nurse. She asked, "Have you seen a hare pass here?" The hare said, "No. We have been hunting leopards for the king. We have killed nine and want one more to complete the number he asked for. You had better run away; the hunters are coming and may catch you." As the hare said this, there was a noise in the grass near and the leopard, fearing that it was the hunters, ran away back again, leaving the hare in safety.

The Children of Ruhanga

Ruhanga had three grandsons who were without titles; so one day Nkya, their father, an elder son of Ruhanga, said, "These children have no titles to distinguish their places of honour, and we make mistakes. Will you not give them titles?" Ruhanga said, "Wait and we will settle it in the evening."

In the evening he called, "Children, children, children!" and all three came, not knowing which was wanted. He said, "Go and bring my things, which are three, in such and such places." He had killed an ox and put the head in a basket in one place, a milk-pot with a leg-rope in another place, and a basket with an axe, a head-pad to put the basket on to carry it, potatoes, and millet in another.

The children went and the eldest took the basket with the potatoes, the millet and the axe and used the head-pad for carrying it. As he went along he ate some of the potatoes. The second son took the milk-pot and the leg-rope, leaving the youngest son the basket with the head. They all delivered their burdens to Ruhanga, saying, "Here are the goods."

Agricultural class. Potter

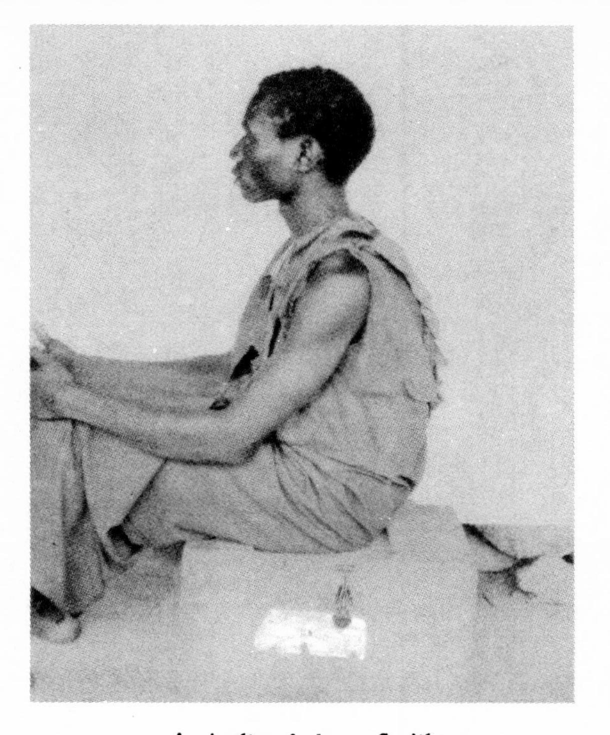

Agricultural class. Smith

Ruhanga looked and asked, "Who has been eating my potatoes?" The others accused the eldest son and he had to admit that he was the culprit. Ruhanga said, "Never mind."

Another evening Ruhanga gave each child a pot of milk and told them to hold them and not to put them down. After a time they got drowsy, and the youngest son spilled some of his milk. He said to the next brother, "I have spilt some of my milk and grandfather will be angry," and the second son gave him some of his. He then fell asleep but did not spill any as his pot was not full. The eldest son slept and his pot slipped, and he spilled all his milk. When he waked he begged his brother to give him some, but the second said he could not do so, as he had already helped the youngest.

In the morning when Ruhanga came to them, the youngest son (whose name was Machuli) had a full pot, the second son (Mugati) had not so much, but the eldest son (Musiganjo) had none. Ruhanga said, "Machuli is the best. He shall be over all and rule you all. He is *Kakama* or King. His brother Mugati who has helped him shall look after his milk. He is *Kahuma.* The eldest brother, Musiganjo, will be *Kaihiro,* the slave of all, to build and carry and eat potatoes."

Why the dead do not come back

At one time men rose again from the dead and came back to earth to their friends. Only animals never returned. There was a man who lived with his sister, and she had a dog of which she was very fond, and the dog died.

When people rose again, it was the rule for all the living to adorn themselves in their best to go and meet their risen friends. The man and his friends said to his sister, "Put on your good clothing and come to meet the risen." She replied, "No. Why should I go when my dog is dead and gone?" Ruhanga heard her and was angry and said, "So people don't care what becomes of the dead. They shall not rise again, for death will end their careers." Now when a man dies he does not come back.

The people still believe that the dead come to see them in the eventide, and they dress up in their best clothes and sit by the door with a pot of milk and other food and remain silent lest they should disturb the dead who come to partake.

Widows say that their husbands will wear the clothing that they offer them, and they leave things about in the house for them.

VOCABULARY

All, byona
Arm, mukono
Arrow, engobe

Bad, kibi
Be, kiraba
Beast, enyama iswa
Beautiful, kisinga, ekinula
Believe, kukiriza
Bird, ekinyonya
Bitter, kisila
Black, kilagula (mbogo = *black, of cows;* emiyumbu = *black and white, or grey, of cows*)
Blood, esagama
Boat, obwato
Body, mubiri
Bone, gufwa, magufwa
Born, kuzala
Bow, obuta
Breath, emwika
Bright, kirukwera
Brother, mugenzi, mwene
Burn, kuwokya

Carry, iweka
Chief, munyoro
Child, mwana
Cloud, ekichura
Club, omingo
Come, ija
Command, kulagira
Cut, kusala

Dance, zina
Dark, omuruima
Daughter, muhala, mwana mwisiki
Day, musana
Death, kugwa (*king of death*, Nyamionga)
Die, kufwa
Do, kola
Dream, kulota
Drink, kunywa

Ear, okuta
Earth, etaka
Enemy, munyanzigwa
Eye, eriso

False, bisuba
Father, ise
Fear, kuitiri
Few, ekikoito
Fight, kulwana
Fire, omubiro
Fish, enchu
Food, ebyokulya
Foolish, mudomo
Foot, kigere
Forest, ekibira
Friend, nkanyanyi

Ghost, muzimu
Give, kuire
Go, genda
God, Ruhanga; *the Creator*, Ruhanga, Nkya ya Enkya, Namuhanga, Eyehangira, Ensozi ne migongo
Good, kirungi
Green, kikola

Hair, omuviri
Hand, engalo
Hard, kyumire
Hate, kunoba
Head, omutwe
Hear, wurura
Heart, mutima
Heavy, kilemera
High, ruhaihirira
House, enju

I, nyowe
It, ekyo

Kill, kuita
King, Mukama
Know, kwatagereza

Large, ekikoto
Leg, kugulu
Lie, byama
Light, kyanghirira
Lightning, emihabya ya engula
Live, muomezi
Liver, obuna
Long, ekiraikira
Loud, iraka bye nangu

Love, kugonza
Low, kigufu

Make, kola
Man, musaiju
Many, kingi
Marry, kuswera
Moon, okwezi
Mother, nyina
Mountain, olusoki
Mouth, omumwe

Neck, ebikya
New, kichaka
Night, ekiro
No, nangwa
Nose, nyindo

Old, mukulu

Part, kitchweka
Priest, embandwa *or* mandwa

Quick, yanguwa

Rain, enjula
Red, ikitukula (mikaju =*red, of cows;* mikuru =*brick red or terracotta, of cows*)
River, kisalo
Run, iruka

Sea, enyanja
See, dola
Shadow, ekituru
She, gwe mukazi
Shield, ngabo
Short, ekigufu
Shoulder, ebega
Sing, zina
Sister, munyanya
Sit, ibala
Skin, oluhu *or* kikolo
Sky, haiguru
Sleep, kubiama
Slow, mugala
Small, ekike
Smell, kunuka
Soft, kyoroba
Son, mwana mwojo, mutabani
Sorcerer, mulogo; *or if he works by night*, musezi
Soul, omutima
Speak, gamba
Spear, ichumu
Spirit, kiroro (*of inanimate things*)
Stand, emara
Star, enyunyuzi
Stone, ibare
Strike, kutera
Sun, ezobo
Sweet, ekinula

Take, tola
Taste, komba
Tell, kugamba
That, ekyo
They, abo
Thing, kantu
Think, kutagereza
This, kino
Thou, iwe
Thunder, kuhinda
Tongue, oluhimi
Tooth, erino amanyo
Touch, taha ingala
Tree, omuti
True, mazima

Ugly, kibi

Walk, genda
War, okulemaga
Water, amaizi
We, itwe
Which, kintuki
White, kirukwera (mokotu *or* kibono *or* kitara =*white, of cows*)
Who, noha
Whole; ekihikirira
Wind, omuyaga
Wise, yetegereza
Wish, gonza, kukola
Woman, mukaizi
Word, kagambo

Yellow, kyenju
Yes, nukwo *or* ego
You, mwe
Young, muto

COUNTING

1 = emu.	*Index finger extended.*
2 = ibiri.	*Index and second finger extended, the others bent.*
3 = isatu.	*Index finger held down by thumb, the other three extended.*
4 = ina.	*Index finger sprung up from thumb to strike the under side of second finger, the others extended.*
5 = itano.	*Closed fist.*
6 = mukaga.	*The little finger held down by the thumb, the others extended and waved slightly.*
7 = musanju.	*The second finger bent in and held by the thumb, the others extended.*
8 = munana.	*The first finger placed under the second and all extended.*
9 = mwenda.	*The four fingers and thumb extended.*
10 = ikumi.	*The fingers and thumb extended, but the hand held palm downwards.*

20 = amakumi abiri.	80 = kinana.
30 = „ asatu.	90 = ikyenda.
40 = „ ana.	100 = igana *or* kikumi.
50 = „ atano.	200 = magana abiri *or* bikumi bibiri.
60 = enkaga.	1000 = mutwali gumi lukumi.
70 = ensanju.	10,000 = kakumi.

THE SEASONS

Dry season, kasambura.
Rains, great, ekyanda kifire.
„ *small*, mujumbi, enswa (*when the flying ants come out*).
Month, okwezi = *twenty-eight days + two dark days.*

THE DAY

Cock-crow, enkoko ekokere.	*10 a.m.*, Manyaganyana, nyamzitaba.
Sunrise, akinyango.	*12 noon*, kulanulwa, kuinuke, eyangwe.
Morning, nkya.	*1 p.m.*, ente nitaba, mwombyankola.
5 *a.m.*, aluobuere bukaire; nkya.	2 „ ninywa.
6 „ zilagire, nturuka.	3 „ nalwebagyo, zakuka.
7 „ kwesera kukire, kwesere.	4 „ nyana zitaha.
9 „ esetule ente, esetuka.	6 „ kisonbagwe.

INDEX

UGANDA PROTECTORATE

Boundary of Protectorate — — — —

Railways ++++++++ Main Roads . . . .

Scale: Miles

0 20 40 60 80 100 120

ANGLO-EGYPTIAN SUDAN

BELGIAN CONGO

KENYA COLONY

TANGANYIKA TERRITORY

LAKE VICTORIA

30°
32°
34°
36°
4°
2°
0°
Equator 0°

Gondokoro
Rejaf
Bahr el Jebel
Dufile
Nimule
Arua
Kitgum
CHUA
GULU
Wadelai
Gulu
LOBOR
R. Assua
Victoria Nile
Port Atura
DABOSSA
TURKANA
Mt Lubur
L. Stefanie
Lake Rudolf
R. Swam or Turkwel
KARAMOJO
Langatelio Mts
L. Sugoto
L. Kirkpatrick
Kamolinga
Debasien Mt
LANGO
TESO
Soroti
L. Salisbury
Kum
BUNYORO
Butiaba
Lake Albert
Kibero
Hoima
Masindi
Port Masindi
L. Kioga
R. Kafu
MENGO
R. Mayanja
R. Sezibwa
R. Nile
BUKEDI
R. Mpologoma
Mbale
Mt Elgon
L. Baringo
R. Semliki
TORO
Ft Portal
MUBENDI
BUGANDA
Mubendi
Mitiyana
Bombolo
Namasagali
Kamuli
BUSOGA
Iganga
Jinja
Mjanji
R. Sio
R. Nzoya
Mumias
Sio
L. Wamala
Kampala
R. Katonga
Ruwenzori
L. George
Katwe
MASAKA
Entebbe
Buvuma I.
Kisumu
Kavirondo Gulf
L. Nakuru
L. Elmentita
L. Naivasha
L. Edward
ANKOLE
Bukakata
Sese Is.
Masaka
Mbarara
KIGEZI
R. Kagera
L. Mutanda
Kabale
Mt Sabinio
Bukoba
Nairobi
L. Magadi
Ukerewe I.
L. Kivu